KARAOKE
CAPITALISM

FT Prentice Hall
FINANCIAL TIMES

In an increasingly competitive world, we believe it's quality of thinking that will give you the edge – an idea that opens new doors, a technique that solves a problem, or an insight that simply makes sense of it all. The more you know, the smarter and faster you can go.

That's why we work with the best minds in business and finance to bring cutting-edge thinking and best learning practice to a global market.

Under a range of leading imprints, including *Financial Times Prentice Hall*, we create world-class print publications and electronic products bringing our readers knowledge, skills and understanding which can be applied whether studying or at work.

To find out more about Pearson Education publications, or tell us about the books you'd like to find, you can visit us at **www.pearsoned.co.uk**

KARAOKE CAPITALISM
MANAGEMENT FOR MANKIND

JONAS RIDDERSTRÅLE
KJELL A NORDSTRÖM

FT Prentice Hall
FINANCIAL TIMES

An imprint of **Pearson Education**
Harlow, England • London • New York • Boston • San Francisco • Toronto
Sydney • Tokyo • Singapore • Hong Kong • Seoul • Taipei • New Delhi
Cape Town • Madrid • Mexico City • Amsterdam • Munich • Paris • Milan

PEARSON EDUCATION LIMITED
Head Office:
Edinburgh Gate
Harlow CM20 2JE
Tel: +44 (0)1279 623623
Fax: +44 (0)1279 431059

First published in Great Britain in 2004

© Bookhouse Publishing Ltd
Grevgatan 20
114 53 Stockholm
Sweden
www.bookhouse.se
jan@bookhouse.se

The rights of Jonas Ridderstråle and Kjell A. Nordström to be identified as authors
of this Work has been asserted by them in accordance
with the Copyright, Designs and Patents Act 1988

ISBN 0 273 68747 6

British Library Cataloguing in Publication Data
A CIP catalogue record for this book can be obtained from the British Library

10 9 8 7 6 5 4 3 2

Typeset by Bookhouse Publishing Ltd (Sweden)
Printed and bound in Great Britain by
Henry Ling Limited, at the Dorset Press, Dorchester, DT1 1HD

The Publisher's policy is to use paper manufactured from sustainable forests.

Contents

Preface

Turn around. Look around. What do you see? Markets rule but protestors are marching against global capitalism. The NASDAQ composite index has gone down the drain. Disasters have cast their daunting shadows. Perils are lurking at every corporate corner. Teargas has hung in the air of Seattle, Gothenburg and Genoa. Stock markets have evaporated. Docu-soaps have invaded our living rooms. Corporations like ABB and Enron have been turned upside down and inside out.

In brief: bricks and bullets, bubbles, bin Laden, big brother, and bosses bad to the bone.

No Logo
No Logic
No Method
No Moral
No Fun
No Funk

This is the backing track to *Karaoke Capitalism*.

Our aim is simple: to take you on a trip around the gutters of commerce and society as well as the galaxies of commercial inspiration. This journey is based on the realization that, whether we like it or not, we are all citizens of a world dominated by markets. We are surrounded by the mania of markets and live in a society where money is meaning; where freedom does not always equal happiness; and where technological opportunity does not necessarily lead to profits.

Karaoke Capitalism was forged in times during which celebrating was often the last thing on anyone's mind. Even so, *Karaoke Capitalism* – through the darkness – shines a torch into some of the more obscure recesses of capitalism in search of inspirational gold.

A few years ago, the not so democratic leader of a former USSR republic proudly announced: "Yesterday my country was teetering on the abyss. Now we have taken a giant leap forward." How right he was.

Despite such dangers, we are going to ask you all to jump into the future. By all means keep your eyes open. This is no small step for man. Quantum leaps are required when we are moving from one world to another.

"Hard times give you the courage to think the unthinkable," says Intel chairman Andy Grove.[1] Now, the unthinkable is on the verge of becoming probable. Just consider the following signs of our times:[2]

- The best rapper is white
- The best golfer is black
- France accuses the US of arrogance
- Denmark sends a mini-submarine to a desert war.

In such weird, wonderful and worrying times, where everything is possible, the only thing to really fear is fear itself.

Karaoke Capitalism is a book of ideas, different perspectives, soundings in the darkness. It is a book about people – management for mankind – the individuals prepared to grasp the microphone and make their voices heard. The book shows that experiencing and expressing your individuality, being different, lies at the heart of the modern enterprise and modern life. We are all individuals now. The choices are ours. But so are the responsibilities – for our own life and the life of others. Liberty comes with duty.

The book brings back reports from the front. We write about what we see, read and hear – not about the world as we would like it to be. Before prescription there must be description. We're not arguing that what is happening right now is necessarily good or bad, right or wrong. We're merely suggesting that it is indeed happening now. Does this mean that we like all the things that we bear witness to? No. Do we dislike it all? No again. There is a difference between the message and the messenger. "Nothing is good or bad but thinking makes it so," noted William Shakespeare. The important point is that people must form their own opinion about the changes that we are experiencing and what kind of future they would like to create. The truth may set you free, but first of all it could well piss you off.

Traditional business books usually excel at making vertical analyses. You find a well-defined problem and then start drilling. Sooner or later you hit intellectual oil and attempt to siphon it into your tank. In contrast, our approach is more environmentally and intellectually friendly (and unlikely to leave you with inflammable material on your shoes). *Karaoke Capitalism* is an attempt at making a horizontal analysis – linking changes in many different areas and walks of life together so that they form a tapestry of our topsy times.

In music you talk about composing and sampling. We used 5000 post-it notes in creating this puzzle. New ideas = old thinking put together in novel ways. Such a horizontal perspective was important to us because in a world of rapid change and information overload, it is easy to lose track of the big picture. Three questions guided our search. What has happened since we wrote our last book *Funky Business*? Why did it happen? And what are the implications for societies, organizations and individuals around the world?

Our first objective with *Karaoke Capitalism* is to invite people to think, rather than telling them what to think. Great questions open up doors – answers usually close them. Our second goal is to arm people with the most potent competitive weapon of our times: knowledge. If we have succeeded, the book is part survival kit, part hitchhiker's guide to the galaxies of business. It is a self-help book, but a different one in that we have tried to build a bridge between the outer and inner contexts. In order to figure out how to create a good life for yourself, succeed at work and create competitive corporations you need a hypothesis about how the world works.

The Clash once advised us "know your rights". In the age of the individual we must not only know our rights, we must all live our rights.

Of course, creating *Karaoke Capitalism* was not a glorious act of individualism. We had a real backing band rather than a tape.

Stuart Crainer of Suntop Media once again helped us hone our literary style. We are most grateful for all his help. Couldn't have done it without you. Jan Lapidoth, Richard Stagg and all our other publishers across the world have provided valuable input to the book. Thanx! Britt-Marie Hesselbäck, Karoline Gustavsson, Sara Gazelius at SpeakersNet plus a global tribe of fantastic people at other speaker's bureaus do a great job of helping us and our clients every day. We very much appreciate all your help. Our colleagues and friends from CASL, IIB and Executive Education at the Stockholm School of Economics always provide a lot of inspiration. Jonas Åkerlund and Robin Siwe are the artists behind the cover photo of the book – great job – our pleasure. Jaqueline Asker makes marvelous slides for our gigs. Christer Jansson and Katarina Lapidoth are responsible for the design of *Karaoke Capitalism*. They are most certainly true professionals.

Last but not least, we are much obliged to all managers, journalists, architects, researchers, artists and other interesting individuals who have listened and talked to us, sent us e-mails and letters during the last few years. If it hadn't been for you, this book would not have seen the light of day.

Enjoy the ride.

Jonas Ridderstråle & Kjell Nordström
Stockholm October 2003

ENDLESS SOLOS

In the world of karaoke capitalism there is endless individual choice. But this costs. You can pay either in cash or competence. Inside the karaoke club regions, companies and single human beings face the ultimate choice: copy the others or create your own future. Benchmarking and best practice will merely get you to the middle. Don't imitate – innovate.

The music of choice

Brothers and Sisters:
You have the right to remain silent. You may refuse to answer the questions.

Do you understand?

Anything you say or don't say, everything you do or don't do, may be used against you under the new laws of commerce.

Do you understand?

You have the right to consult someone before speaking or acting. If you cannot afford an adviser, you, alone, must answer the charges.

Do you understand?

Knowing and understanding your rights as we have explained them to you, are you still prepared to do business as usual or are you willing to re-think the questions and answers?

The times are a-changing. For better or for worse, our rights may be used or abused. We may all be on our own, but we are certainly not alone.

At this very moment, an Indian IT entrepreneur is packing up his luggage to move back home after a lucrative sojourn in Silicon Valley; a Spanish woman is telling her husband she doesn't want to have any children; a graffiti-artist is spraying the words rap and hip-hop on a 19th century building in the center of St Petersburg; a British teenager, unwilling to pay an extra £300 for a flight that includes a sandwich and a beer, is booking a £10 airline ticket with EasyJet; an elderly Norwegian couple are buying a summer house in Thailand.

All over the world, people are beginning to exercise their right to express themselves.

Stop and listen to the variety of voices. The baroque clarity of church song has been relegated to history. Forget the choirs. The grand march of governmental brass bands is muffled. Corporate songs with their facile professions of loyalty are silenced. Man and markets dominate the scene. We are all soloists now.

I am. You are. In fact, you have never ever been more than right now. He is and she is, but we are no more. The riff of our times is the gloriously eclectic sound of individualism. Our world has moved from

the Madonna of the Bible to *"Lady Madonna"* of the Beatles to *Madonna* the iconic chameleon; from *we* to *I*. Express yourself!

The new riff pulls us in improbable directions – Bollywood via the Buena Vista Social Club to Britney Spears. It is as individual as we are. As unique as DNA. Fingerprinting males and females.

Whether they are Harry Potter creator J.K. Rowling, golfer Annika Sörenstam, Nelson Mandela, super-architects Frank Gehry and Toyo Ito, or even our old

All over the world, people are beginning to exercise their right to express themselves.

friend Bill Gates, individuals are shaping and re-shaping the world. After the collapse of communism, the rise and fall of dot-communism, and the sometimes violent questioning of capitalism, the dominant *ism* left on earth is individualism.

Individualism knows no limitations. Even death. As we write Frank Sinatra is planning an unexpected comeback. Five years after the hunk of Hoboken passed away he is back on the road with ten shows at the Radio City Music Hall in New York. Old Blue Eyes will be displayed on a big screen with a 40-man live-band backing him. People are expecting the New York gigs to be followed by an international tour. As the British press recently noted, these days "being dead is a lame excuse for not touring".[3] It turns out that Frankie boy was absolutely, totally, 100% right. Now, we can all do it our way.

This point was brought home to us recently. We were in a nightclub. The club conformed to our stereotype of what we thought a nightclub should look like: dingy darkness, an obscure decorative theme, pumping music shaking the floor and expensive drinks.

Being dead is a lame excuse for not touring.

We danced. Joining us was a friend who had also come along. After a while we noticed that our rhythmic movements bore little relation to hers. We may bear little if any resemblance to John Travolta in *Saturday Night Fever* – our dance moves being epileptic rather than eclectic – but in this case it was obvious that she was dancing enthusiastically and happily to another beat.

Then we registered that instead of listening to the music provided by the nightclub, she was wearing her own personal MP3-player from which her favorite songs were being pumped out at maximum volume.

Welcome to the age of the individual

On October 31, 1517 individualism as we know it was born. Martin Luther nailed his ninety-five theses to the door of the Wittenberg Palace All Saints' Church. The event signaled the beginning of the Protestant Reformation that was so fundamental to the development of capitalism.[4] Rather than relying on the Church to interpret the Bible, Luther gave this right to single human beings. He re-invented Christianity. Some 500 years later, capitalism is re-inventing itself. People are now free to interpret just about any piece of information as they see fit. The arrival of such illuminated individuals will mean to our societies and organizations what Protestantism once meant to the Catholic Church. "Homo Faber" – man as his own maker – is here to stay.[5] Get ready for the second reformation.

Not that long ago, the Scandinavian subsidiary of a large US multinational corporation received an e-mail from headquarters. Despite the harsh winter, one of the company's top people was to honor them with a short visit. Attached was a list of requirements. The visiting American wanted a hotel room with white wallpaper. She also required white roses, lilies, tablecloths, curtains, candles and sofas. In the white room she expected to have a CD player with a collection of Latin and r'n'b artists as well as a VCR. To drink, she requested mineral water (Evian exclusively) and Snapples (lemon, raspberry and ice-tea). In addition, she needed a make-up table, plenty of fruit – but only mango, papaya, green grapes (without seeds), honey-melon and watermelon. Finally, she would just love to have some chocolate-chip cookies, brownies and vanilla ice cream.

The visitor did not anticipate a Formula 1 hotel room. But who could request such things? The demanding hotel guest was none other than J.Lo – Jennifer Lopez, latino-r'n'b pop diva/movie starlet extraordinaire.[6]

Now, free your mind of Ms. Lopez's fondness for ice cream in winter and consider this: what would you do if the head of R&D, the best sales person, the top designer, or someone else with an absolutely unique talent at your company sent a similar list? Perhaps, they already do. In the future, some of them most certainly will. If not, there is a clear risk that you have recruited the wrong people. Individualism *über alles*.

Companies are getting the message. The new top-of-the-line Volks-wagen Phaeton comes with individualized climate zones. The driver may be in the desert, while the passengers are in Patagonia. You decide. Unit-linked savings enable us to be our own personal investment managers. Soon, we may have "personalized medicine" where each patient will receive individualized treatment based on genetically determined drug responses.[7] At Spanish conglomerate Mondragon individual employees have a say in everything from how work is conducted to the selection of the CEO.[8] Today, everything is individualized. An open world requires open systems and an open architecture. Pick up a piece of paper and write down the words *open* and *transparent*. Put it right next to your bed and look at these words every evening and each morning. Engrave them in your mind. Work against openness at your own peril.

The game of chance is over.

You choose

Quirky tales perhaps, but they have a serious point. Whether dancing to your own beat or having people dance to your beat like J.Lo, individualism represents the triumph of choice over control and the victory of careful selection over chance.

We have come a long way in a short time. Not that long ago, our lives were largely shaped by chance. It was chance you were born and raised in East Germany. Chance that you lost all your hair before turning 30. Chance you never developed big breasts. Chance that you ended up working in the mine, the field, the forest, on the sea or wherever. And then there was nothing much that you could do about it. Lack of choice simplified things. But it killed opportunity and hope stone dead.

Now, the game of chance is over. We have been liberated. For more and more people throughout the Western world, and increasingly elsewhere, lives are instead shaped by choice. In fact, this process can begin before you are born. There used to be one way of getting pregnant.

Today, there are almost 20.[9] Later in life, you can choose to move to London, Laos or LA. You can choose to have a hair-transplant. You can be red and curly this week, and have garlands of dreadlocks next. You can choose the way you look through a myriad of different nips and tucks.[10] You can choose to work for Sun, Siebel, Siemens or which ever company you prefer. And while you are at it, you might like to choose a different gender.

You have the freedom to know, go, do, and be whoever you want to be.[11] You have the power of choice – with an eternal cooling off week.

Choice rules. The mayors of both Paris and Berlin have come out and are now living openly as homosexuals.[12] Gay-bating rap-star Eminem and gloriously gay Elton John sing a duet. The Prime Minister of Japan is a middle-aged heavy metal fan with a slight resemblance to Ludwig van Beethoven (or is it Keith Richards?).

Individualism picks up speed like a rolling stone. Consider the case of Jerry Hall. After leaving Mick Jagger, she immediately found herself a new boyfriend. His name was Paul Allen – one of the two original co-founders of Microsoft – a man who people claim lived with his mother until the age of 40. It may only have been a small step for Miss Hall, but when we move from Stones to Bits, from a guy who wrote *Sympathy for the Devil* to the best friend of William Henry Gates III, it is relevant to talk about a giant leap for mankind. Jerry is no longer under anybody's thumb. Satisfaction is based on choice.

Satisfaction is based on choice.

There is no stopping us now. It's up to me, myself and I.

Hand us microphones and we can instantly turn ourselves into entertainment superheroes. The opportunity to create new identities is a fact of contemporary life. The choice is ours. Reinvention happens. We are living in a cosmopolitan karaoke club with choice as never before – 1,958 songs and 1,966 different life-styles. And we can exercise our new won power and express ourselves as never before. We can be whatever and whoever we want to be. Pop-up personalities. Reality TV for real.

So, ladies and gentlemen – make up your minds. What would you like to change this week – your spouse, shirt, self or socks? In this world of karaoke capitalism, choice overwhelms.

Individual choice is the Holy Grail of market forces. Think about it. Demand is merely a reflection of millions and millions of individual decisions. And market forces are the most powerful faith of our times. Consumption has become an act of confession. "I shop therefore I am," says American artist Barbara Kruger. Choices that once converged in the age of collectivism are now diverging. Preferences are also increasingly personal. The compromise is on the verge of extinction. Average customers or normal colleagues are now on the list of endangered species. From freedom follows fragmentation.

Skills, thrills and greenbacks

And now the bad news. The karaoke club isn't open to all. Only shining stars are guaranteed entry. Elvis has not left the building. The owners reserve the right to refuse admission. Even in a world of choice money talks, indeed money shouts more loudly than ever. In reality, cash still shapes our lives. The freedom available to super-capitalist George Soros, CNN-founder Ted Turner or pop-stars Justin Timberlake and Robbie Williams is a whole lot greater than the freedom available to a poor, single, immigrant mother with six kids living in the decaying suburbs of one of our great metropolises.

Greenbacks lubricate the wheels (and sometimes own them). Michael Bloomberg spent $92 per vote out of his own pocket to become the new mayor of New York.[13] All it took was $69 million to become mayor of the greatest city in the proudest "democracy" on planet Earth. The Italian Prime Minister, Silvio Berlusconi, owns a media empire. In Italy, at least, he knows the press is likely to be on his side.

Inside the karaoke club, celebrities rule and capital reigns. Or as

Money talks

another New Yorker, Woody Allen, once put it: "Money is better than poverty, if only for financial reasons."

We have rid money from the physical fetters of the past. Before you have finished reading this sentence, enormous sums will have traveled the world from one country to another. In the boardrooms of Big Business Inc. or the investment banks of the City of London and Wall Street there is little room for sentimentality over the death of distance. Capitalists do not make pilgrimages to the grave of geography. Instead, they cheerfully dance around its tomb.

Choice can be bought either by old-fashioned cash or through the possession of the right skills. Our lives are increasingly shaped by competence, or by the absence of competence. Competence takes many forms – being a great athlete, singer, dancer, artist, or chef. Don't get us wrong. An investment in knowledge pays the safest and often the highest interest. But joining the tribe of talent is not all about having a degree from the right university – though that helps. The gap between the median weekly earnings of high school and college graduates has increased from 28% to 43% in the last 20 years.[14]

To understand the power of competent individuals, consider Microsoft. The company went public in 1986. During the first day, the stock started

A unique talent grants you a global passport.

trading at $21 and closed at $28. If you had held on to that original share for some fifteen years, adjusted for splits, it would have been worth $10,000.[15] It would be a bit like buying a mountain bike and later trading it in for a BMW Z4 sports car. Henry Ford once shared some of his wealth by instituting the $5 per day salary. Bill Gates used stock options.[16] So far, Microsoft has created more than 20,000 in-house millionaires.

Having no education can be an economic death sentence, while a unique talent grants you a global passport. Knowledge nomads are definitely free to know, go, do and be exactly whoever they want to be.[17] As the renowned sociologist Manuel Castells puts it: "Elites are cosmopolitan – people are local."[18] We used to have aristocrats, then bureaucrats. Now we have *cosmocrats* – the new elite possessing either cash, competence or both.[19]

Today, more than ever, human beings are brands. My life is my piece of art, said Oscar Wilde. This was given a new meaning when Bill Clinton signed the contract for his memoirs. *The New York Times* estimated Clinton received more than $8 million which compares with the advance of $8.5 million received by Pope John Paul II.[20] (The pontiff obviously found this insufficient as, soon after, he moved into the more lucrative music business with his first rap CD – *Abbà Pater*. We joke not.)

You don't have to be a big name celebrity to cash in on your life. On our travels we came across a young British entrepreneur called Chris Downs. At the end of 2002, Chris launched an unusual auction on eBay. What was on offer was over 800 pages of personal information, including Chris' bank statements, mobile phone bills, supermarket receipts and his credit reference data.[21] And how much did Chris sell off his personal data for? £150. How much will you get?

Capitalism karaoke style

Collectivism in all its many forms and manifestations – political communism, homogeneous national cultures, and monolithic organizations – is being challenged. It was challenged in the Eastern Block and the Wall came down. It was challenged at IBM and the company almost went bust before it changed. It is challenged in Japan, causing deflation and a recession. In one week in August 1998, the Japanese stock market lost more market value than the Russian economy produces in a year.[22] People and organizations in the industrialized world simply have far greater choice than ever before. They know their rights.

Both our own lives and corporate destinies are shaped by the choices we make rather than through the vicissitudes of chance. Capital and competences may be the entry requirements, but not even access to these resources guarantees success. There is a final choice.

Position yourself in a karaoke bar. What do you see? People enter the stage and sing a Sinatra tune. In all likelihood it sounds terrible. Then they have a beer and their next performance is somewhat better. After five or six beers, not only do they think that their voices have improved dramatically – they also feel as if they are actually in the process of becoming Frankie. Formally speaking, a karaoke club is a place for institutionalized imitation – you go there to be someone else. Here's the problem. Imitation only gets you so far – and may be bad for your liver. You can consume all the alcohol in the world or be extremely talented but this does not alter the fact that imitating someone else will never make you truly successful.

The choice is clear. We can settle for singing someone else's lyrics to someone else's tempo and tune, or we can try to break free from the sameness of songs already sung – copy or create.

And it is by no means only individuals who are living in a karaoke club. Our world is full of karaoke companies. In business there are even names for this imitation frenzy: benchmarking and best practice – as if these fancy labels would make a difference. Let's face it. No matter what the pundits say, benchmarking will never get you to the top – merely to the middle.[23]

As individuals, organizations and regions we can blindly copy someone else - and we do. Minimalist architects are all studying Mies Van der Rohe. General Motors watches Toyota. Europe and Asia are looking toward the US. Now, many of us can be whoever or whatever we want to be whenever. The problem is that far too many try to be the same someone else, rather than themselves. Innovators don't imitate. They know that there is no point in trying to become a "mini-me" GE.

People, companies and nations can continue to reduce uncertainty and become a me-too version of an original or they can embrace risk and create the future classics. Make a mental note of the fact that according to author Herman Melville: "It is better to fail in originality than to succeed in imitation." Then remember that not even originals are always the real McCoy – not even Frank Sinatra. His great comeback is merely a karaoke copy of the concept that Elvis, or more correctly Elvis' surviving relatives, launched a few years ago.

For some people, imitation is enough. A woman was telling us of a recent trip to Las Vegas. To celebrate their 40th wedding anniversary, she

For some people, imitation is enough.

and her husband had gambled small amounts of money and wallowed in the ersatz splendor of karaoke capitalism's spiritual home. They had taken a trip on a gondola, complete with fake Venetian gondolier and fake Venice. The lady loved it. She had, of course, visited Venice, but Las Vegas' version of Venice – a kind of Las Venice – was much better. The water was clean. There were no unpleasant scents. The gondoliers spoke English. Fakery was preferable to reality. Dutch architect and thinker Rem Koolhaas refers to this as a world of controlled environments versus junkspace. Controlled environments are safe, secure and sound. Junkspace is for those without the hard currencies of our karaoke times.

Certain individuals might of course claim that markets are always right. If fakery is what people want, let's give them fakery. We beg to differ. Short term, imitators may beat true innovators, but in the long-term, creators thrive at the expense of copycats. This is true for countries, corporations and individuals. In fact, in a world where cover versions rule true originality is worth more than ever. As poet Robert Frost put it: "The best way out is always through."

This is a call to arms. To succeed, as individuals and in business, we need to dare to be different. Cash and competence gain us entry to the club. Then you must make up your mind: either to accept the backing tracks or to express your own individuality. In the world of karaoke capitalism, success is not about getting a back-stage pass. Following the rules is merely an imitation of life. Only imagination and authenticity places us front-stage. And the future, as always, belongs to those at the frontier. The time has come to fall in love with yourself and your rights. Who knows, the world may just love you for it. Or as Marshall Mathers, a.k.a. Eminem, puts it: "Will the real Slim Shady please stand up"!

2

FREED BY ROBOTS

Technology creates opportunities and opens up possibilities for longer and richer lives. Technology frees us to be ourselves – if we have the capital or competence. The democratization of information should not be mistaken for the democratization of power. Information makes real sense only when you are capable of understanding it. Power is transferred from those who control information to those who control knowledge.

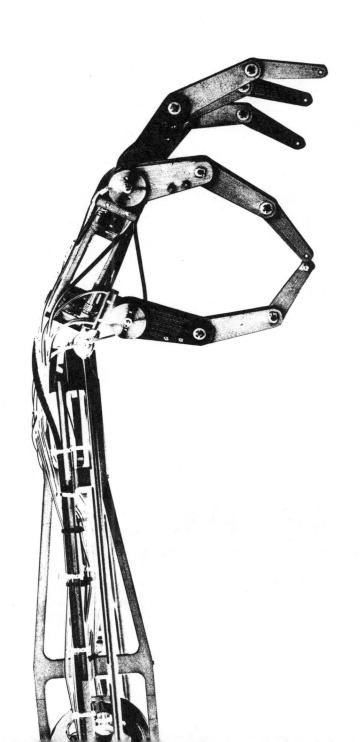

The individual and the machine

Let's consider the broader picture. How did we get to this world of individualization?

Change is – and has always been – driven by the three forces of technology, institutions and values – the tools, the rules and the norms. For better or worse, if we do not shape these forces of change, they shape us.

Technological development can be thought of as emancipation from the basic conditions handed to us by God or evolution, depending on your perspective. Today, most people in the (post-) industrialized world are free to live their lives regardless of wind, sun, rain, temperature, etc. Competence has conquered climate. Engineering helps us to control the environment. Now, man rather than the Man is in charge.[24]

Technological development never stops. One bright idea leads inevitably to another. Technology is pushing us through Maslow's hierarchy of needs. It never asks for permission. Like market capitalism, technology does not say please. It moves on and on and on. After information technology come biotechnology and nanotechnology. We are playing atomic Lego. More leads to even more.

The progress of technology is usually seen in mechanistic terms. It can appear as if the robots are winning – think of the IBM chess computer beating Gary Kasparov. This misses the point. The relentless progress of technology is pushing us forward to better understand ourselves as people, as unique individuals. Paradoxically and miraculously, it individualizes.

U= ATCG

On October 12, 1492 Columbus discovered America. A little more than 500 years later the secrets of the human genome were revealed.[25] We have a new map and we are embarking on a journey of internal discovery. "Our bodies, or more precisely the bodies of our children, which have always seemed to us more or less a given, are on the verge of becoming true clay. And not just our children's bodies, but their minds as well. We are starting to catalogue which genes control intelligence, and starting to figure out how to manipulate them," writes Bill McKibben in *Enough: Genetic Engineering and the End of Human Nature.*[26] While the digital revolution changed what we do, the genetic revolution changes who we are, says the futurist Patrick Dixon.[27]

If you listen to the experts, there is a great likelihood that the early 21st century will be written not in the 0s and 1s of computers but in ATCGs, the four letters that determine our DNA – deoxyribonucleic acid (A for adenine, T for thymine, C for cytosine and G for guanine).[28] The genetic code is made up of three billion letters, replicated twice within each of our 50 trillion cells. A paper copy of the genome that we carry within each of our cells would make up 248 Manhattan phone directories.[29]

The difference between the genetic code of one person and another is less than 0.0003% – hard to believe when looking at Arnold Schwarzenegger alongside British comedian Rowan Atkinson.[30] In a world dominated by individuals and market forces such differences are amplified. IQ may only account for less than one tenth of the variance in most studies on what determines the success of people, but it still separates.[31]

The genes also determine your predisposition to longevity and life quality. What will cause your natural death and when? Genetic differences affect anything from susceptibility to disease and resistance to infection, to response to drug treatment.[32] When Al Pacino's John Milton character in the *Devil's Advocate* movie is revealed as Satan, he claims that God is the ultimate prankster. The same can be said about genes – though the humor is occasionally quite perverse.

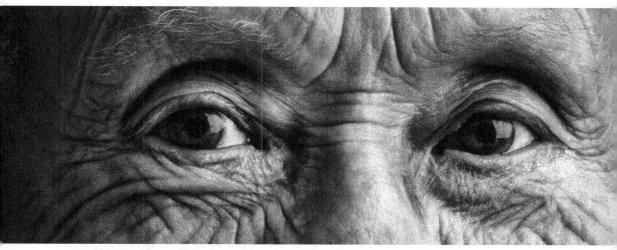

What if you found out tomorrow that you are likely to live to be 100 rather than 75-years old? How would you change your life?

The cost of sequencing a single gene has dropped dramatically.[33] Scientific discovery and the financial resources that are consumed have had an instant impact on genetic patent requests. Such requests jumped by more than 2,000% in one year during the 1990s.[34]

Technology rolls on. It is now possible to replace defective DNA before a baby is born. In vitro fertilization is now reckoned by fertility clinics to be a more reliable, though less pleasurable, method of becoming pregnant than sexual intercourse – we guess this depends on who you are sleeping with. Designer sperm is a reality. A sperm bank where donors are Nobel Prize laureates is up and running. There is something bizarre about a world in which people first accept an award from the hand of a king and then go to the clinic to use their own hand for an entirely different purpose. Artificial wombs are only a few years away. Soon we will be able to build our kids cafeteria style.

New tools trigger new questions. What if you found out tomorrow that you are likely to live to be 100 rather than 75-years old? How would you change your life? Would you? What if you were told that the extra 25 years came with a price tag of $100,000? What about the implications for insurance companies? Or just consider the issue of pension funds for companies and governments that are already under a lot of pressure!

Later you find out that your child to be will suffer from Attention Deficit Disorder – ADD. For a small sum, the "defective" DNA can be replaced, and while they are at it they can also prevent the hair-loss that he (they already know) would otherwise suffer from at the age of 27. Fix one or both problems? Who will pay for it? What reads like science fiction today, could very well be reality tomorrow.

"Ultimately, the dream of biologists is to have the sequence of DNA, the programming code of life, and to be able to edit it the way you can a document on a word processor," says Michael West CEO of Advanced Cell Technology.[35] Sooner or later, cut and paste people could be walking the streets of our cut and paste world - hyphenated individuals in a hyphenated society. What still prevents the dream (or nightmare) from becoming a reality is that most human traits and diseases are dependent on the extremely complex interplay of numerous different genes.[36]

There are also issues to confront on a macro-level. Should scientific progress be the privilege of a select few - the destined and gene-doped elite - while the others remain destitute and clean? The debate on large pharmaceutical companies not making drugs for the treatment of HIV and AIDS available to those countries needing them the most is a small diversion compared to what may come.

The debates will continue to rage. The ethics of science and technology is the debate of our times. In the nineteenth century the discussion centered on how best to manage the human side of industrialization. In the twentieth century the debate focused on the distribution of the wealth created by mass production. In the twenty-first century the nature of being is up for grabs. "As society gets more complex, perhaps it must select individuals more capable of coping with its complex problems," ponders Daniel Koshland, ex-editor of *Science* (while Dr. Strangelove is lurking in the shadows).[37]

The important thing is to stop blaming technology. Technology does not make decisions. People do. Technology does not divide. People do. Technology is for mankind. The more pertinent question is whether man is for or against mankind.

New Net U

The debate of the future cannot cloud the reality that currently the main impact of technological progress in the post-industrialized world lies within the fields of information and communications technology.

Over the past three decades, the cost of computing processing power has fallen not by 99% but by 99.999%.[38] At Singapore Airlines, where the average customer spends half a day on an airplane, there is more computing power in the in-flight entertainment system than in the cockpit.[39] The world is online, hanging on the end of a mobile phone or a PC.

The information society is no longer solely an American phenomenon.[43] Millions of people worldwide are joining the digerati. In 2001 Europe passed the US in terms of numbers of Internet users.[44] Over 50 million Chinese now use the Web.[45] More than one third of all Beijingers aged 18-29 say that they have been online.[46] For many young Chinese, rock-star Marilyn Manson is as much of an icon as Chairman Mao. The Web gives them access to a new world and new world-views.

One day of international phone calls in the year 2001 equaled all global calls made in 1981.[40]

In 2003 there were more than 600 million people on-line.[41]

In 2003 there were some 1.2 billion mobile phone users. Nokia estimates that by 2008 there will be more than 2 billion.[42]

Inevitably, usage is combined with abusage. A few years ago, there was a lot of talk about how IT in general and the Internet in particular could be used to educate and integrate large numbers of people in the third world. Now, the Web is dominated by porn, music and games. Grand notions of changing and improving the world have been buried in a tide of spam and delusions of enlarged genitalia. As we write, the most searched for man and woman on the Web are Osama Bin Laden and Pamela Anderson!

The Internet may not be changing the world in the ways once imagined but it, and IT in general, affects our personal lives as well as our institutions in surprising ways. Not that long ago, *The Economist* noted that whereas the German stock market once experienced trading passes on Jewish holidays, volume now slumps during student holidays and, in Japan, the airwaves clog up at 10 p.m. when teenagers send goodnight messages to one another.[47]

The impact of IT is personal. IT is individual technology. It is, after all, in our homes. The Net is a karaoke medium. It gives us the freedom to know, go, do and be. In the Internet-world we can be boys or girls. We can choose to be Europeans or Africans. We can be young or old. We're in control.

The Internet individualizes. Some 18% of those who surf chat sites in the United States are transvestites.[48] They are transvestites in that they appear on the Web with a different gender than the one that they happen to have. In reality John in the chat room may be a balding middle-aged man from the Midwest with an expanding waistline. But when he goes on-line, John may choose to be 19-year old Laura who has recently gone through some major plastic surgery. John may continue to be Mr. Average when he goes downtown to grab a beer with the boys, but with a mouse in his hand he is reinvented. He is treated differently. He feels better about himself. He is interesting, stimulating, respected and admired.

Trivial perhaps, but we are witnessing large numbers of people questioning one of the basic pillars of Western society, the concept of the self. The self is not something that we are supposed to play around or toy with. It is meant to be stable. The self is given and eternal. No more. Once again, technology is enabling us to explore our own personas.

Alexander Bard and Jan Söderqvist, authors of *The Global Empire*, go as far as to argue that the traditional concept of an individual will eventually be replaced by the more attentionalist *dividual*.[49] This is someone who is actually pleased with harboring a number of different

John may continue to be Mr. Average when he goes downtown, but with a mouse in his hand he is reinvented.

personalities. The dividual can be a functional and valuable member of many tribal networks – gay and straight, punk and classical, Harley-Davidson and Piaggio – at the same time. Ultimately, the authors claim, this development will mean the death of psychotherapy as we know it. Yesterday, we went to the shrink to treat schizophrenia. Tomorrow, we will go for advice on how to become more multi-personal. We are moving from one to many, or perhaps too many. The ultimate in individualism may well be that we possess the ability to be more than one individual.

Transparency triggers talent

Technology is also bringing about more mundane – though equally profound – changes. Thanks to the Internet and other media, more and more people at more and more places are now getting access to more and more information about more and more things.[50]

And just what do people with access to relevant information do? Think about kids. What do children with access to relevant information do? Simple. They begin to question things. They say: "Mother told me that you can actually do it. And Grandma, she told me that when you were young, you were never allowed to do that."

Grown ups act exactly the same. It doesn't matter whether they are citizens, capitalists, customers or colleagues. Arm people with information and they will begin to ask questions. This is why dictatorships always seek to control the sources of information. Think of Adolf Hitler and Joseph Goebbels controlling German radio. Dictators of corporate bureaucracies used a similar recipe when sending out directives and information on a need-to-know basis. One-way technologies enabled them to rule the ignorant. With interactive and open systems all this changes. Now, technology works against autocrats.

One of us has a younger brother who is a medical doctor. He is in deep, deep, deep trouble. More and more of his patients claim that they know exactly what they suffer from and precisely what drugs would remedy their problems. Prior to visiting a doctor, the patients consult the Internet for advice. After a couple of hours in front of the computer, they have all the information in the world – but limited knowledge.

People with access to the relevant information are now challenging those whose historical dominance relied on a monopoly over information. Huge communications networks make our world and its leaders more transparent. And since an information advantage is one prerequisite for legitimacy, many authorities are in for some hard times as these advantages now evaporate. The emperor is naked. And in the karaoke nudie-bar no one is immune from scrutiny – think of former GE CEO Jack Welch's recent divorce where all the secret perks from his ex-employer were revealed; lifestyle guru Martha Stewart's alleged move from interior decorating to insider trading; or Tony Blair justifying his Iraqi actions in front of a judge.

After a couple of hours in front of the computer, patients have all the information in the world – but limited knowledge.

But Transparency Avenue is a two-way street. Not only celebrities but we, too, are becoming more transparent. In cyberspace you can shop naked while whistling the national anthem, but it could be dangerous to shop for the naked. We may be biographically anonymous on the Net in that we can appear under any name, gender or age, but we certainly cannot be *buyographically* anonymous. There is always someone watching us. Transparency is double-edged. Imagine the local Wal-Mart, H&M or Carrefour salesperson knowing as much about the customer as American Express, MasterCard or Visa. Nice or nightmare? What used to be private is now made increasingly public. Order something over the Web, changing your name slightly – Joan and Kelly – and see how many e-mails or snail-mails you receive addressing this other you.

Even more scary perhaps, at least for those who do not necessarily shop for the naked on the Net, is the fact that once companies have targeted customers, they can divide them into A, B, C, D, etc. members. Will they serve unprofitable customers? Unlikely. So while for some, digitization opens up the possibility to develop multiple identites, the ability to separate people with more or less surgical precision into niches will also increase the divide between those with the money and the skills and those without. Cash and competence are always at work. Information technology indeed opens up opportunities to develop new personalities, but it may also reinforce existing identities.

Increased transparency and the rapid growth of information transfer

infrastructure could easily be interpreted as the ultimate democratization of information – though pre-processed information in the form of access to databases and news agencies often comes at a hefty cost. But the increasing availability of information should not be confused with the democratization of knowledge. And it should certainly not be mistaken for the democratization of power. In reality, the more widespread and diffused the information the more knowledge becomes a factor to take into account. This is true even when neglecting the fact that the knowledgeable may have better access to information via the Internet etc. When this happens the locus of power shifts.

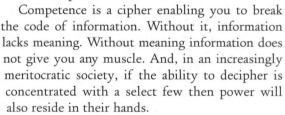

Competence is a cipher enabling you to break the code of information. Without it, information lacks meaning. Without meaning information does not give you any muscle. And, in an increasingly meritocratic society, if the ability to decipher is concentrated with a select few then power will also reside in their hands.

Take the case of the Enigma code machine that helped the Allies to interpret German messages during World War II. Without such a machine the information contained in the messages made no sense. From a practical point of view, the difference between not being able to intercept the messages and not being able to decipher them would be minimal. Similarly, if you had the Enigma but could not pick up the messages the machine was of little practical use – probably worth just a few pounds if you reassembled it and sold the parts.

We now all – or nearly all – potentially have access to all the data we could ever want. The key is our ability to do something with it. In an age of access, competence is a powerful lever. Yesterday, those with an information access monopoly could hold "ordinary" people at bay. Today, increased diffusion of information enables those with the capabilities to understand the meaning of the information to join people with financial resources in creating the new elite. Power is transferred from those who used to control information to individuals who control knowledge. The others continue to fall behind.

And there are many who are already lagging behind. Despite what we said earlier, for most people the prospect of a digital economy is not even a distant dream. Only 6% of the world has ever logged on to the Internet.[51] In Brazil, only one tenth of all people have access to a fixed phone line.[52] In fact, more fixed phone lines exist on Manhattan than in all sub-Saharan Africa.[53] For many, the concept of a digital divide is still more real than the digital dreams that we are routinely told about. If we really want to get rid of this divide we must understand that access is not enough. People also need education and continuous training to gain the critical knowledge.

3

CHANGING THE RULES

The institutions of the past are being reshaped. We live and work in a Welfare Society that looks as if it has been designed by IKEA. More opportunities come with an increasing number of responsibilities. Fragmentation and disappearing social capital require that we all become individual institutional innovators. Power is shifting from the rule-takers to the rule-breakers and rule-makers.

Who to turn to?

He heard it before he could feel it. Like the sound of his father's rifle they had used to shoot quail years ago. As he looked down, the crack opened up, widened. The surface beneath his feet gave way. He plunged through the ice – one last glimpse of the world above the surface. Then, all hell broke loose.

The cold was stunning. As he hit the bottom a rock almost cracked his skull. The fisherman could taste the blood in his mouth. Struggling to get to the small, sunlit opening above him, one of his legs got caught in a net. The more he twisted and turned the more he got stuck. No time to reflect. The man was fighting frantically to stay alive. After a while, the icy-cold water unexpectedly began to feel warm against his body. The fisherman's mind started to drift away.

He could see things so clearly now – the summers spent with his family; his mother laughing loudly; two of the boys playing near the shore; in a few moments his entire life passed before his eyes. Then, all of a sudden, he broke loose. He was free. He could see the light again. The future, so bright.

Two days later they found him. People had to use an axe and a saw to free him from the ice. He was deep-frozen. His face was all blue – almost purple, some of the islanders said. One of his limbs had to be cut off before they could fit him into the coffin. The man left a wife and seven young children. He was 37-years old.

Now, what should they do? Who would support them? Where could they live? They were left with all the questions. His mourning family turned to God for guidance. They became refugees of the temple.

A few years later, one of his sons moved west. He left their church and community behind. He had married a local woman. They had two sons. Fishing was no longer a viable means of supporting a family. They sought refuge in the Welfare State – the new cathedral of modernity.[54] He got a job as a construction worker. They were building the new world. Life was good. The state provided and protected. The kids were doing fine at school. His wife started working. They enjoyed employment security. There was a safety net to support them. They were refugees of the tower – once the home of kings and queens, now the residence of democratically elected leaders. The family prayed that the Prime Minister would continue to help them.

But out of the blue something happened. Once again the solid surface gave way. Interest rates, oil price, taxes and budget deficits went up. Markets went down. The new cathedral collapsed. He lost his job. Where was the safety net? The family almost lost its faith. Now, what should they do? Who would support them? Where could they live? They were left with the very same questions. Think now.

Emptying the temple

The old faiths have failed us. The next driver of change is the dismantling of the institutions that dominated the past. In the post-industrialized world and increasingly elsewhere, we are leaving many of the arrangements of yesterday behind us. Traditional institutions are becoming history.

We recently spent a day in conversation with a group of protestant bishops. The bishops were surprisingly normal. Ordinary people with a faith in the extraordinary. They were dressed in middle-aged casual wear as if they were just off the golf course. They wanted to understand our view of the world. This, they knew, was different than their own. And so, we told them how things looked to us.

The world we described was the one we all encounter every day with lots of opportunities and possibilities, but also responsibilities, uncertainty, dissatisfaction, and fear.

We told them that a lot of people were disillusioned and felt they had no place to turn. Religion offered little in the way of tempting solace. People felt as if they had tried the temple but, somehow, it had failed them. They also felt abandoned by the state which had promised generous pension provisions and support through uncertain times but which was now backtracking. We told them there is a great risk that average European kids will grow up to live lives marked by increasing poverty, loneliness and meaninglessness.

There was a silence as the bishops thought about the abandoned and lonely generations of the future. Then one of the bishops spoke. "That is our market," he said. "That is our opportunity."

The bishop is right– and the bishop is also right to embrace market forces so readily. The loneliness that is symptomatic of an individual-centered world should represent a great opportunity.

The trouble for the temples of the world is that we have already tried that particular route to happiness. Religious beliefs once created meaning. They made sense of the madness. In 1900, two-thirds of all English people attended church every week. Today, only 5% do so. In dedicatedly Catholic Spain numbers are also falling. In 1975, more than half of all Spaniards said that they attended church regularly. Now, the figure is less than one fifth. Over the last half century the number of priests in Spain has fallen from 77,800 to the current 18,500.[55] The safest job on God's earth is now one of the most insecure. People in the West are leaving the temple behind.

But there are exceptions. A few years ago, parts of Alabama and Oklahoma started pasting labels on biology textbooks warning that Darwin's ideas about evolution is merely a

That is our market, said the bishop.

theory.[56] In the US, 95% of the population claims that it believes in God.[57] Nine out of ten Americans pray regularly, 75% of them on a daily basis.[58] According to a recent Gallup 89% of all Americans want their children to receive some form of religious instruction.[59] This is one of the reasons Europeans struggle to understand Americans who retain a stronger sense of "meaning" – national and religious – than most Europeans.

Tearing down the tower

As the temples emptied we sought solace in the warming embrace of the state. One dominant institution was replaced by another – the nanny state. The state would provide, no matter what. The state was regarded as a bulwark against despair. It, too, failed.

The modern project has been dismantled and driven-off to the dump. Governments are in retreat as people (are forced to) make more and more choices for themselves and their own lives. In 1996, Bill Clinton declared that the era of big government was over in his State of the Union address. He has been proved right.

Government is rolling back. In 1900 government spending in now post-industrialized countries amounted to less than one tenth of national income.[60] Spending then rocketed. Things peaked in 1980 when, as a percentage of GDP, Sweden spent 60% on government. It is now down to 54%. During the same period, the Dutch moved from 56% to 40%, the US from 31% to 29%, and those on the toughest diet, the Irish, cut almost half of their spending from 49% to 26%.[61] The overall tendency is clear.

Brits and teeth usually make up a sensitive combo – just look at the international man of mystery, movie star, Austin Powers. There is even an episode of The Simpsons where Bart refuses to open his mouth when he is at the dentist's. In response, the dentist shows him The Great Book of British Smiles. Bart, scared stiff, immediately opens his mouth.[62] Dentists in the socialized British medical system now earn more than half of their income from private dental work, and more than one quarter of all Brits pay for private dental work.[63]

People in Europe and parts of Asia and the Americas live and work in a Do It Yourself (DIY) Welfare Society that looks as if it has been designed by IKEA. It comes in self-assembly flat packs. And as you may have noticed, there are no assembly instructions.

On the back, in small letters, you will read a warning – 99% responsibility. The neo-liberal DIY society was falsely marketed. While it brings more opportunities for certain people, it most certainly results in more responsibilities for us all. We have moved from a world of dependability into one of individual accountability.

As British management thinker Charles Handy has observed, the market – the dominant force of our times – is merely a mechanism for sorting the efficient from the inefficient. It is not a substitute for responsibility.[64] Remember that market capitalism does not say please. The machine just moves on. Markets conquer, but above all they divide. Capitalism elevates the power of the elite.

So, the new reality is that the temple is marginalized. Bishops and other religious leaders realize where the need is, but what they offer no longer strikes a chord in most parts of the Western world. The apparatus of government is similarly out of step. Look at how few people now vote for our governments or how few people are active in mainstream political parties.

Less government is accompanied by less faith in those who govern. The political process simply does not connect with huge swathes of people. Mona Sahlin, the former Vice Prime Minister of Sweden, has noted that if nothing changes, in less than ten years time her Social Democrat party will have zero members. Current members are dying more quickly than they are capable of recruiting new ones. In the UK, more people voted before the last episode of the TV-show *Survivor* than in the elections to the European parliament.[65]

Turning to the Town Square

But we are still left with all the questions. In fact, we have more questions than ever before. Don't despair. A growing number of questions is just one of the many side effects of increased individual freedom. Try asking the old authorities for the answers. Ask His Holiness the Pope or the Dalai Lama: Where should I live? Should I have any kids? Which contraceptive should I use or should I not bother? What about the millions of people dying from AIDS in Africa? Jesus, Muhammad or Siddhartha, help me.

And if the temple does not work, let's try the tower. Please, Mr. or Mrs. Prime Minister: What should I study? With what should I work? Why do only four Western countries reach the UN target of giving 0.7%

Help me to find meaning in moneymaking.

of their GDP in foreign aid?[66] What about the beggar on my own doorstep? Blair, Bush and Putin, what is the good life really about?

The temple and the tower no longer automatically provide the answers. And so we have turned to market forces. The market – the town-square – is the most important institution of our times. Even the People's Daily, the organ of China's Communist Party, now carries a weekly financial supplement.[67]

Let's forget about values for a while and become victims of value. Get down on your hands and knees and ask the market; what should I do with my life? NYSE, NASDAQ and FTSE, help me to find meaning in moneymaking.

The weird thing is that in this age of mammon mania the very institution of property rights, so central to the development of capitalism, is under attack. Capitalism without ownership is a bit like a sea without water. In a world where knowledge is the most critical resource and just about anything can be digitized, things are different. Information wants to be free. Consider Napster where you could download MP3 files with your favorite music without charge. It was possible to shut down Napster, but can you stop people from file sharing? As we write, the record industry is suing 261 people for allegedly sharing music files on the Net. "Record companies suing 12-year-olds for file sharing is kind of like horse and buggy operators suing Henry Ford," comments popular music artist Moby.[68] Whether it is Napster, Gnutela or whatever, people will continue to swap stuff. My hard disk is suddenly your hard disk and vice versa. The Internet was built on stealing so perhaps we shouldn't expect anything else. We are all shoplifters now.

Bowling alone

It is not only the church and the state that we have abandoned. Other institutions are crumbling. We are leaving trade unions behind us. We are leaving our neighbors behind us. We are leaving the nuclear family behind us.

In some parts of the world, the changing size of family units have already caused food and dairy companies to introduce smaller boxes and bottles that fit the new socio-economic landscape. Due to the large numbers of divorces and break-ups many people find themselves in the tricky situation of having less money but still wanting to look and feel more attractive when they re-enter the relationship market. This constitutes a true challenge for all contemporary business entrepreneurs.

Families, like other organizations, are experiencing changes in all three dimensions of time, space, and mass. A lot of kids now grow up with two dads, three mothers (whereof one lives in another part of the world), two half-sisters and a brother to whom they are not really related. And then we expect them to work for one company and one boss for the rest of their lives.

The reality is that a lot of these kids don't have a clue what life-long loyalty means. Whether we are talking about loyalty to a country, a company, a brand, a rock-band, a husband or a wife does not really matter – it's gone. Loyalty used to be given. Now it has to be earned, in our personal lives and in business.

For many people the traditional family no longer works as a useful unit of analysis. Paradoxically, it appears that those most keen on the institution of marriage are homosexuals who have historically lived together in ways that others are now adopting. The demise of the old way of doing things is still not fully understood by governments who appear increasingly desperate to re-assert the pre-eminence of the traditional family unit. They encourage conventional family life at every turn. The French have recently introduced an 800-euro "birth bonus". After all, the family is enshrined in the 1804 Napoleonic Code. "Our attachment to the family surpasses economic logic," the French Prime Minister Jean-Pierre Raffarin observed.[74]

Conclusion? The traditional social capital that it took the West more

More than half of all the households in Stockholm consists of singles. Over 60% of all marriages end in divorce.[69]

In America, less than one quarter of all households consist of married couples with kids.[70]

One-third of all babies are born to unmarried women – sixty years earlier it was 3.8%.[71]

Unmarried cohabitation between homo- or heterosexuals is up 72% over the last decade.[72]

In 1998, 17% of all same sex female households had children, up 20% in less than ten years.[73]

We go to the bowling alley and we bowl alone.

than two centuries to build is now in the process of being erased - in one generation. Fragmentation, individualization and isolation are the new reality. We all know a lot of people, but still feel lonely. People are alone in a crowded room. Or, as Peter Katz, author of *The New Urbanism*, puts it: "We're a society awash in networks, yet starved for community."[75]

In the US this development is manifest in the bowling alone phenomena examined by Harvard's Robert D. Putnam.[76] He found that from 1980 to 1993 the number of people who went bowling in the United States increased by 10%. At the same time, the number of people playing league bowling decreased by more than 40%. We go to the bowling alley and we bowl alone. Phil is there, but he is reading the *Financial Times*. Loula is also there, but she is listening to her Walkman, while Juan is watching CNN.

This trend is just one sign of increasing fragmentation. Consider nations. In 1950 the United Nations had 58 members. Half a century later it had 191.[77] Czechoslovakia used to be one country, now it's two. Yugoslavia was one nation – today it's five.

Think of entertainment. In music the 1950s belonged to Elvis. The 60s to the Beatles. The 70s... maybe ABBA (some bias here). The 80s –difficult – Jacko, the King of Pop? The 90s – forget it. Now – Uhh!

Look at television. In 1983, 106 million Americans watched the last episode of *MASH*. A decade later, 80.5 million watched the final episode of *Cheers*. Five years after that a mere 76.3 million Americans watched Seinfeld sign off. At the same time the number of households with TV sets had increased by almost 20%.[78]

Togetherness is not what it used to be. Many of us grew up in countries with state-controlled TV channels. Back then, at work, people gathered at lunchtime to discuss the latest episode of *Upstairs Downstairs*, or *Dallas*. People got together to talk about the same things. In today's fragmented media landscape with 40+ channels and 400 million+ Internet-sites, we have little in common to talk about. What you have listened to I haven't heard. What you have seen has not passed by my eyes. Your world is not mine and my universe is not yours. Reality and our lives are increasingly split.

A gay bohemian rhapsody

The dramatic decline of social capital appears on the surface to be a bad thing. But depreciating social capital may not necessarily be so disastrous, especially not from an economic point of view. Like most stories, there are two sides to be told.

Geographical areas with low levels of innovation tend to score high on social capital.[79] Perhaps people are so busy playing in bowling leagues and engaging with the community that they don't have the will or time to innovate. Over time, relationships in a particular area can become so rigid that it ends up complacent and conforms, isolated from the outside.

On the other hand, places where innovation flourishes, such as Seattle and the Bay area in California, generally have below-average levels of social capital. Weak social ties appear to promote innovation and economic growth. So, if we want to create the next fantastically successful high-tech cluster, among other things we should ban bowling leagues and fraternization with the neighbors.

There is another interesting element to this story. The best proxy of weak social capital and thus also a high level of innovation is a region's openness to diversity and cultural activity. The more gay couples, designers, architects, musicians, dancers, photographers, artists and actors we find at a particular geographical spot the greater the self-renewing capabilities of that region. They may not be bowling together, but they definitely appear to have the capabilities to create competitive products and services.

To succeed, we need more, not fewer nonconformists.

The conclusion from this is that gays and bohemians drive economic growth. Take them away and the economy comes to a grinding halt. To succeed, we need more, not fewer nonconformists.

Perhaps this phenomenon explains why, especially (and ironically) among conservative parties around the world, there is a growing concern that individualism perhaps has gone too far. There is much talk about the need for some kind of "communitarianism" – another word for going back to the core of traditional (family) values.

Outlaws in a world without laws

Old habits die hard. Many of them make up an intricate web of institutions that is self-reinforcing and effectively blocks change. Consider the nation state and its links to international law. Imagine if the mayor of New York City had a bad day at work and suddenly decided to use nerve gas to get rid of everyone living in the Bronx or Brooklyn.[80] Within hours, or perhaps even minutes, the National Guard would step in and remove him. No one would object. In fact, we would all praise the swift actions taken. Then ponder this. Saddam Hussein actually did use nerve gas to kill parts of the Kurdish population living in Iraq. Since he was the ruler of a nation state, international law (which apparently operates under the principle that the institution of democracy is upheld within all countries) protected him. Fortunately nothing lasts forever.

Crumbling institutions and a realigned society make for emotional and institutional chaos and confusion. Deregulation is all encompassing. The old certainties have gone. When institutions are no longer given but up for grabs, success boils down to being an active shaper of tomorrow rather than settling for being shaped by yesterday.

We agree with Paul Evans from the French business school Insead who argues that people do not dislike change, but being changed. Yet, the reality is that not all people easily deal with a metamorphosis of the magnitude that we are now going through. Uncertainty gives birth to unrest – always has and always will.

People do not dislike change, but being changed.

Those who lack the capacity and willingness to make sense of fragmentation – to operate in an institutional vacuum of increased individualism – will have a tough time. They simply will not possess the adaptive capacity so vital for success in a fast-changing world. Both attitude and ability are central.

People lacking such 'protean' capabilities, as sociologist Robert Jay Lifton calls them (referring to the Greek sea god Proteus who could take any shape at any time) will be at a huge disadvantage.[81] They will suffer from what Lifton labels "psycho-social dislocation". Rather than "proactionary" or protean, their behavior will often be reactionary. And the faster and more fundamental the changes at a particular geographical spot, the more likely are we to find such people. Saudi Arabia went from shepherds to sheiks in almost no time. Japan developed from feudalism to post-industrialism during the same period. Osama Bin-Laden and Shoko Asahara, the leader behind the Aum-cult that launched the nerve-gas attack in Tokyo's subway system, are also bi-products of a world that has been and still is going through changes of seismic proportions.

Some people will seek to protect or even recreate what no longer is – a world with closed geographical borders, traditional family values for all, mandatory visits to the temple, lifetime employment, etc. What they fail to understand, however, is that no matter what they do, the future belongs to individual institutional innovators rather than fanatic fundamentalists. Power is being transferred from the rule-takers to the rule-breakers and the rule-makers.

4

MATERIAL GIRLS AND BOYS

Meaning is no longer given – by church or state. Materialism rules! To move beyond the meaning of lite and rising loneliness individuals have to create their own communities by finding biographical buddies wherever they may be. We are witnessing a changing of guards from local citizens to global tribesmen and women.

The meaning of lite

Technology and institutions are not the only things changing. The third and final force for change is our values – or perhaps some would say our lack of values. Our age is one in which daily lives have been stripped of meaning. The modern self, says author Salman Rushdie is "a shaky edifice we build out of scraps, dogmas, childhood injuries, newspaper articles, chance remarks, old films, small victories, people hated, people loved".[82] So no wonder that the search for meaning is on.

Our forefathers took the meaning of their lives and work for granted. Thanks to religions and governments, meaning was automatic for the people. A generation or two ago, religion wasn't simply a one-day a week commitment. It permeated lives. In fact, Christianity may well be the ultimate in karaoke. God even sent down his son to provide a best-practice example that we could all benchmark against and learn from. The objective was crystal clear – become more like Jesus.

When Protestantism came along our working lives became inextricably entwined with religion. The Protestant work ethic associated hard work with godliness. Work was good – even if it was dispiriting, soul destroying, back breaking and terribly paid. Not only in the Western world but also in places such as Japan, many people sought to prove their worth through work. It created meaning. Status in our employment organization meant something. It gave us a place, a neat,

clearly prescribed place, in the organization and in society. Work was about a sense of belonging as much as the work that people actually did. We belonged – physically as well as figuratively in some cases – to the organization. We were company men (and women).

The meaning offered by the temple and the tower has now been subsumed by the meaning of mammon. But if the Protestant work ethic was pivotal to the birth and growth of capitalism, as the German thinker Max Weber once claimed, perhaps we should also ask ourselves what happens to capitalism when we take it away.

In the karaoke world, identity is no longer linked to production, but to consumption. You shop, therefore you are. The right to be, the right to choose and the right to consume are central to our very being. We have the opportunity to invent meaning for ourselves.

Societies are measured by the buildings they create. The Egyptians built the pyramids. The Greeks left the Acropolis behind. The Romans gave us the Coliseum. Modern times bring us the shopping mall.

In this new world, individualism, choice and markets are relentlessly – sometimes confusingly – interwoven. This is the new reality. The churches are empty. The malls are full. Most large cities in Europe now have more gas stations providing 24-hour service than churches (or mosques and synagogues for that matter) that are open all night long.

The meaning of life has given way to the meaning of lite.

Let there be lite. Look around and we see institutions stripped of content. We may call it a material world, but the strange thing is that materials are always cheaper whereas the soft stuff is increasingly expensive. Lite rules.

Look at newspapers. Instead of being attached to a particular place or viewpoint the most popular new arrivals in the newspaper industry are like the European daily free newspaper *Metro*. Media lite – information instead of ideas and ideals.

Values have changed. In 1968, when asked about the goals of their lives, 41% of college freshmen said that their aim was to be well off financially, whereas three quarters of them wanted to develop a meaningful philosophy of life. Thirty years later, 78% wanted to be financially well off and only 41% were interested in developing a meaningful philosophy of life.[83] Perhaps time has proven the author F. Scott Fitzgerald right when he pointed out that the problem with the American dream is that it does not have a second act. What awaits beyond wealth?

"I have all the characteristics of a human being – flesh, blood, skin, hair – but not a single, clear, identifiable emotion, except for greed and disgust," says the character Patrick Bateman in Brett Easton Ellis' novel *American Psycho*. Meaning is elusive. The new elite can take its pick and make its choice. But what do they choose? What do they want? What do they really aspire to? What is their notion of a good life?

More than ever people seek self-expression and self-identity through their purchases.

The answer appears to lie in the market place. People express their individuality through the conspicuous consumption that economist Thorstein Veblen wrote about. They shop to be. More than ever they seek self-expression and self-identity through their purchases.

While general consumption has grown by some 29%, adventure travel is up 46%, gourmet chocolate 51%, pearls 73%, luxury cars 74% and yachts 143%.[84] Time has proven actress and femme fatale Mae West right. Too much of a good thing really can be wonderful.

The next frontier in our quest for meaning is space. The Zero Gravity Corporation plans to take people up in a modified plane so that we can experience zero gravity. Apparently companies are expressing an interest. A full day's astronaut training may cost $4,000 and include two hours flying with several dives providing 30 seconds of zero gravity each time.[85]

Nothing succeeds like excess, claimed Oscar Wilde, so hail to the great global cocktail party – a fragmented world where solidarity is an endangered species. We can still hear the ring of Bud Fox's words at the beginning of the movie *Wall Street*: "There is no nobility in poverty today." Greed may not be good, but greed appears to work. The more important concern is whether abundance will ever push us past greed.

Tribes 'r us

Uncertain, unsure, sometimes fearful, people seek out others who share their values. Human beings loathe loneliness. And so, young people without meaning in their lives make the trek from industrial Birmingham in the middle of the UK to Al Queda training camps in the Himalayan foothills. The young join cults or extremist movements rather than traditional carriers of values for the same basic reasons that they join entrepreneurial start-ups rather than traditional business organizations. These tribes offer something fresh and less predictable for men and women with otherwise unsurprising lives.

Some people don't recognize themselves in the lite life of the karaoke world. The mirror leaves no reflection. "I'm just an American boy raised on MTV. And I've seen all those kids in soda pop ads. But none of them looked like me," sings country-rocker Steve Earle in *John Walker's Blues*, a song in which he tries to understand what drove John Walker Lindh to become an American Taliban. Reactions against the lyrics forced Earle to move his family to a guarded hotel.

We all want to belong. Mankind has always been and will continue to be tribal, but in new and different ways. Proximity is no longer enough. *Where* does not equal *who* anymore. The reality is that geography, culture and religion no longer automatically overlap. For instance, there are now 15 million Muslims living in Europe.[86] Instead, many of the new tribes are biographically structured: specialized academic communities, Hare Krishna, fan clubs, Amnesty International or computer gamers. Here's a daring hypothesis. In 2042, soccer's world cup final could be between Homosexual's United and Hell's Angels FC – rather than between nation states such as Brazil and Italy!

Consider the People's Republic of Britney Spears. This tribe has more supporters than many European nation states have inhabitants – despite

Maybe the new tribes are just different.

the dubious qualities of her latest album. To most business organizations, the People's Republic of Miss Spears is more important than a country such as Belgium. The People's Republic of Britney Spears has greater purchasing power. It is young and has more meaning for many than an old fashioned nation state.

The new tribes are global communities made up of people who actually perceive that they have something in common – no matter where they were born. These biographical tribesmen and women already know each other. They just haven't been properly introduced. "We're all listening to the same music, watching the same movies, drinking the same vodka at exactly the same time," comments Gucci's Tom Ford.[87]

Perhaps Professor Putnam was looking at the wrong things when concluding that social capital is declining. Maybe the new tribes are just different. Instead of bowling (alone), they may actually be doing something slightly more interesting together with people from more distant parts of the world.

Again the three forces interact. Technology provides tools for tribes to link up and join hands – internationally. IT enables the locally marginal to become globally significant. But there is a darker story to be told. For the sake of argument, let us suppose that in each and every village there is one pedophile or neo-Nazi. These individuals are locally marginal but when they hook up on the Net and become a group, a tribe of let us say 250,000, they move from the margins to significance. Again, blaming technology misses the point. It is individuals who are good or bad.

As an effect of biographication, value systems change not only in terms of space, but also in two other dimensions. Once upon a time they were eternal. We died with the same set of values that we were brought up with. Today, values are temporary. Norms used to be like our skin, now they are increasingly like shirts – some of us can and do change by choice. In addition, most people used to have only one set of values. In the world of karaoke capitalism we can profess to many different beliefs at the same time. It is me and my tribes rather than *the* tribe. We can be members of the academic tribe, parent tribe, the art tribe, or the Finnish tribe. Geography still matters of course – such as when it's the Olympics. It's biography in addition to geography not at the total expense of space. The important thing to grasp is that while not that long ago we all used to live our lives in mono, now at least some people can live in stereo. Values are more ephemeral.

Look at football. Some 50 million people across the world follow Manchester United. But for some citizens of the Man U tribe the attachment to the club is so weak that they don't even know that Manchester is a city in England. Connections are no longer as dense. Attachment is more fleeting. "We used to say that the chances of changing your team [were] less than [those] of changing your partner or even your sex," says Jose Angel Sanches, marketing manager of Real

Madrid, the club that recently bought superstar David Beckham from Man U.[88] "But the way people enter football in Asia is different: they enter through the stars." People are beginning to follow individuals instead of institutions – even in (formerly?) collectivist Asia. When the stars move on so does the tribe of followers.

Tracking the tribe

Companies already target global biographical tribes. Corporations go after different communities with single-minded intent. Whether these are shopping-based, interest-based, fantasy-based or relationship-based does not really matter. In fact, this development is reflected in the ways in which many multinational companies are organized. Once upon a time they were structured country by country or region by region – reflecting the power of geography. Now, many of them are globally organized product by product or segment by segment – reflecting the importance of biography.

Or look at the array of gay Internet sites. Gay.com and planetout.com have millions of visitors every month. Compare this to the typical magazines for the gay population, the *Advocate* with an 88,000 circulation or *Out* with a 115,000 circulation. In essence, new technology allows you to reach much more than a paltry 1% of the gay population.[89]

The message of all this is that people will find meaning – even if that meaning is repugnant to others in society – and that men and women will choose to communicate and congregate with others who share their perspectives. Young and capable people who see few physical borders drive this development. Business has been the first traditional institution forced to adopt, or at least adapt to, changing values. Unlike most other historical establishments, corporations are under constant pressure to perform. Capitalism triggers change. Whether they like it or not, market forces drive organizations to move on and then move again. In such a world, power shifts from those stuck in a rut of local logic to global tribesmen and women.

5

THE AGE OF ABNORMALITY

Abnormal is the new normal. We have given up the idea of building a society based on the principle of nurture. Instead, we are applying the laws of nature. The bubble economy has given way to the double economy of graft and grief, misery and opportunity. The gap between haves and have nots is increasing between as well as within countries. As a single human being, it is increasingly difficult to have a life while also making a living.

The double economy

Once upon a time the Western world was normal. It used to be so normal that even the economy was normally distributed. This was the world of a flourishing middle-class, mass-markets, standardization, security and stability. Normality was reflected in TV-programming, music, fashion, etc. – it was omnipresent. For companies, success was a question of appealing to the local average where the bulk of business was. The average was the world of the Volkswagen, the white wicker fence and a steady salary – the world of monochrome normality.

In the industrialized West, the project of modernity largely revolved around the creation of this magnificent middle. The flabby belly of post-war capitalism was made up of large numbers of people, who were supposed to eat, sleep, work and consume in a rather predictable manner. Your life = my life = all our lives. Political parties needed the middle. Local companies, in their pursuit of economies of scale, needed the middle. Even capitalists needed the middle. The growing public sector inflated the under and upper class world into a shapely Bell-curve.

That was then. This is now. Forget about normal. Think abnormal. In practice it appears as if the idea of creating a society based on the principle of nurture has been abandoned. Instead, the laws of nature rule again. Changes are pushing us into a fundamentally different world of economic Darwinism, one in which abnormality is the norm. The Bell-curve dream has gone pear shaped.

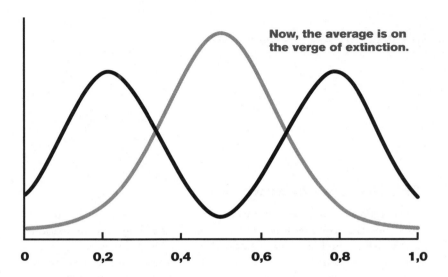

This development is not as strange as it sounds. Indeed, in retrospect, the "normal" world that most of us grew up in could turn out to be nothing but a historical parenthesis in time – an exception that lasted for less than 100 years. Now things are back to (ab)normal. It's just natural.

Take away ideological ambitions and economic incentives and the middle begins to give way. Remember that markets are machines that merely divide things based on whether they are efficient or not. Markets do not mind too much about the middle. The flabby belly of the Western world has had a hard time of it. Since the early 1980s the number of middle-class bankruptcies in the US has increased by some 400%. Of these bankruptcies 40% were related to medical problems and 20% to divorce. Around two thirds of the people affected found it impossible to catch up.[90] In 2003, it is estimated that some 1.5 million Americans will file for bankruptcy.[91]

In the future, when our kids look back at the last decade there is a great likelihood that they will not think about the bubble economy though that was what got the headlines at the time. Instead, they will talk about the transition into a double economy, a binomial society, a polarized world of wealth and poverty, opportunity and misery, luxury and low-cost. Changes in technologies, institutions and values are pushing us into a world of karaoke capitalism where virtuous and vicious realities are the alternatives on offer – capital and competence versus chance; opportunities versus responsibilities; liberty versus duty; individual splendor versus loneliness.

Washington DC's infant mortality rate of 16.2 children out of every 1,000 equals that of Sri Lanka.[93] For Europe, the equivalent figure is 9.4.[94] The number of babies born underweight in the US capital equals or even tops that of Zambia.[95]

So far, most of our modern thinking on politics, sports, business, self-development, architecture, democracy or design has been driven by what is average – normal and mainstream. Now, the average is on the verge of extinction. When success is a question of exploring the extremes instead of appealing to the average, we must rethink how to organize corporations and our own lives. From a business point of view, a world of markets requires that we go back to nature – in a Charles Darwin rather than French philosopher Jean-Jacques Rousseau sense. The double economy will bring greater emphasis on the survival of the fittest. But another type of strategy may also be pursued by companies and individuals: survival of the sexiest.[92] Those staying in the middle-of-the-road will be run over by modern monopolists.

Some 16% of the population of Europe live on less than 60% of the average income. Without social protection transfers, this figure would rise to 24%.[96]

The enlargement of the EU in May 2004 with ten Central and Eastern European countries will further increase the gap between the rich and the poor: the least prosperous regions will have only 31% of the average GDP per capita. The most prosperous parts will be ten times richer.[97]

Split vision

The world used to be simple. We had industrialized and developing regions. Some nations were rich and others were poor. No more. In the double economy it's increasingly hard to talk about rich and poor countries. Most places tend to be both.

While it is increasingly difficult to talk about rich and poor countries and regions, it is also true that the developing part of the world is not really catching up. On the contrary, most people living there continue to fall behind.

Half of all inhabitants on planet Earth have never made a phone call.[98] Agrarianism, industrialism, and post-industrialism co-exist across planet earth – even within countries. Two thirds of the world's labor force still works in the agricultural sector.[99] What is the source of air pollution that kills most people in the world? Cars? Factories? No. It is cooking fires. More than 1 billion people still cook in huts with no ventilation.[100]

Since the dawn of industrialization, the differences in productivity between the center and periphery of the world economy have grown by more that 5,000%. This has accelerated over the last decade.[101] If we take a closer look at economic growth during the last two decades, we can see that the "richest" countries have grown by an average of 1.9% per year. Countries placed in the middle have grown by 0.7% per year, while the poorest third have hardly grown at all.[102]

The combined assets of the world's three leading billionaires exceed the combined GDP of all the least developed countries in the world, including 600 million people. And the top 20% still consume 86% of all goods and services.[103]

The World Bank estimates that people in low-income countries account for less than 4% of global private consumption.[104]

In Africa, 174 children out of 1,000 still fail to reach the age of five.[105]

The end result is that there are some 3.5 billion poverty-stricken people waiting in line outside the karaoke club.[106] "There are (still) people in the world so hungry, that God cannot appear to them except in the form of bread," noted Mahatma Gandhi. "Here is the great irony of 21st century public health: while many hundreds of millions of people lack adequate food as a result of economic inequalities, political corruption, or warfare, many hundreds of millions more are overweight to the point of increased risk for diet-related chronic diseases," wrote Professor Marion Nestle (a somewhat ironic surname) in a recent *Science* editorial.[107]

But not all is grim. Infant mortality rates, educational opportunities and poverty rates, for instance, have improved during the past decade.[108] In fact, the GDP of poorer countries has grown about as fast as that of richer nations over the last 50 years. The trouble is their populations have grown so much faster.[109] Studies also show that the share of the world's population living on less than $2 a day has decreased by some 20% during the last three decades.[110] We may interpret the statistics in many different ways, but anyone who has spent as much as an hour in a poor Asian, African, European or South American country knows that a lot remains to be done. Please don't blame globalization for this imbalance. Instead, blame people – whether dictators, warlords, corrupt government officials or incompetent administrators.[111]

This may surprise you. Until recently the "richest" country in the world was the Soviet Union – at least in terms of natural resources.[112] Or consider some other "rich" countries. Nigeria has oil and Indonesia precious woods. South Africa is "rich" in terms of diamonds and gold, whereas Brazil has jungles and minerals. Mexico has a lot of silver and oil. Venezuela is almost drowning in the latter. Yet, in our knowledge-based economy few people would claim that any of these countries are "rich".

Countries with flourishing economies keep on growing because, among a host of other factors, they control and create knowledge – the hardest currency of karaoke capitalism.[113] For instance, the University of California spends 21% more on R&D than Mexico and produces six times as many US patents.[114] No wonder that only 3 out of the 50 top Latin American companies are considered high-tech.[115] The rest sell commodities. And the average commodity is now worth one fifth of what it used to be worth 150 years ago.[116]

Top Five Competence Creators

Country	Japan	South Korea	United States	Sweden	Germany
Patents granted to residents per million people	994	779	289	271	235

Source: nationmaster.com – World Intellectual Property Organization 2001

Crime and punishment

There's more. Within the so-called "rich" world borders are being redrawn.[117] The double economy is a society with gated communities and ghettos, reservations for the rich and sealed off places for the poor. Recall the controlled environments and junkspace that architect Rem Koolhaas talks about. Combine technical change, favoring more skilled workers, with global competition that puts a lot of new pressure on the unskilled. And then, think of all the institutional changes, including the break-up of families, which are splitting our societies.

This Twin-Peaks-world is a true paradise for security companies – one of the fastest growing industries in the Western world. The greater the gap, the more protection is needed. Here again, it appears as if markets rather than governments provide the solution. In the 1970s there were more public police officers than private security guards in the US. Today, there are three times as many private security guards as policemen. In California there are four times as many.[118] If you're a TV producer, forget about *Hill Street Blues. Securitas Group Swing* is the future.[119]

The brave and well-protected new world is inhabited by capitalists, *competents* and *commoditents*, people who have or can and people who simply have to; people with choice and people with little chance; masters and servants. In addition to an uneven distribution of capital, our world is being torn apart by three other strong forces: talent, training and ties.[120] To succeed you need the right skills, the proper schools and strategic friends in the right positions. These factors determine whether people are free to choose or simply free to lose.

While talent is nurtured, the losers in the double economy are simply and clinically disposed of. The United States has 1.8 million prison inmates guarded by 300,000 correctional officers – plus some 4.5 million people on parole or probation.[121] Include the police and private security guards, and almost 9 million people are involved and occupied in the human control and containment industry.[122] It is estimated that as many as 30% of all African American men between 20 and 29 have some contact with the penal system.[123] Compare this with Japan, a country

Top Five Crime Creators

Country	United States	Russia	Belarus	Dominica	Montserrat
Prisoners per 1000 people	6.41	6.37	5.77	5.73	5.57

Source: nationmaster.com

with about half the population, where there are less than 100,000 people in jail.[124]

These numbers worsen the already pitiful levels of involvement in the political process. During the 2000 US Presidential election, some four million Americans were deprived of their right to vote. That's almost the entire population of Finland. In nearly all American states, prisoners are not allowed to vote and, in a growing number of states, they lose their future right to vote. Forever.[125]

The division into *haves* and *have-nots* is merely the logical consequence of relying more or less solely on a market mechanism. Markets sort the efficient from the inefficient. That is their essence. Markets recognize efficiency, but it is also just about the only thing they understand. A society based on the laws of nature rather than the principle of nurture is bound to be a tough place to survive. Apply the logic meticulously and we end up with two piles – the destined and the doomed. Indeed, the more assiduously you apply the principle the clearer and higher the piles become. Efficiency and empathy don't necessarily make a happy couple.

> **Efficiency and empathy don't necessarily make a happy couple.**

Division of labor

At a national and societal level, market forces are dominant in the karaoke version of capitalism. The double economy is also at work in the business world. In 1999, Jack Welch, former CEO of General Electric and until recently the most admired manager in the world, made more money than the combined salaries of the 15,000 so called *maquiladora* workers who assemble products for GE in Mexico.[126] Fifteen years ago, the highest paid CEO in the US was Chrysler's legendary Lee Iacocca with some $20 million. In 2001, Larry Ellison of Oracle made $706 million.[127] Talented individuals call the shots whether they are, J.Lo, Jack or Larry.

Twenty years ago, the salary difference between a US CEO and a factory worker was a factor of 40:1. A few years ago it was more than 400:1.[128] (You may also remember that in The Republic, Greek philosopher Plato argues that no person in the community should earn more than five times the pay of the average worker.[129]) The phenomenon of extreme wage inequality is actually relatively recent. CEOs of large US firms were paid one third less for every dollar of earning they produced for shareholder in 1980 compared to 1960.[130]

Between 1988 and 2001 European CEOs increased the gap with typical industrial workers by 92% in the UK, 62% in Germany, 46% in Spain and 33% in France.[132]

During the 1990s executive pay in the US rose by 570% while the average worker got 37% more in their pay packet (just beating the inflation rate of 32%).[133] And in 1998 the top earning 1% Americans earned as much as the 100 million lowest earning.[134]

William Gates III has not only created some 20,000 in-house millionaires, he is also pretty well off on his own. Bill is as wealthy as the least wealthy 110 million Americans. When Mr. Gates "retired" at the age of 44 his personal fortune was greater than the US gold reserve in Fort Knox, and twice as big as all the dollar bills in circulation.[135]

The bull market of the 1990s and the rise of stock options changed things. The dot-com meltdown made little difference. According to *Business Week's* executive compensation scoreboard, CEO compensation fell by 16% in 2001 and by 33% in 2002. But, while average pay fell, median CEO compensation actually increased by 7% in 2001 and by 6% in 2002. Typical CEO pay still continues to grow faster than most other salaries and there are few reasons why we should expect things to even out. No matter what people in general and shareholders in particular may say and think, competitive companies compete with capabilities, competencies and knowledge. And ideas belong to talented people.

The double or nothing society is most visible in the United States, but not exclusively. In fact, it is spreading like poison ivy to other parts of the world. During the last 20 years the salary difference between your average Swedish factory worker and CEO has increased from a factor of 1:9 to one of 1:46. And this is happening in a country renowned for its focus on equality.[131] The same trend is visible throughout the rest of the world.

Graft and grief

So, how do we seek to join the new elite? Simple. We work harder and harder. In the karaoke world you have to sing for your supper and you have to sing louder and longer.

As an individual citizen of our abnormal world, you are either on or off – 0 or 1 – double or nothing. Belgian psychotherapist and leadership guru Manfred Kets De Vries provides a scary summary of our times by suggesting, "Either you make an input or you become an output."[136] In the karaoke world, some people work themselves to death, taking on double jobs, just to scrape a living. After all, as author Richard Sennett points out, "Time is the only resource freely available to those at the bottom of the pyramid."[137] It used to be high risk-high return. Now, for the typical contemporary worker in the West it is high risk-low return. No job security. No big pay check. "If there is nothing very special about your work, no matter how hard you apply yourself, you won't get noticed, and that increasingly means that you won't get paid much, either," says Michael Goldhaber, the author and thinker who first coined the phrase *the attention economy*.[138]

We appear able to spend money quicker and quicker, but generating cash takes us longer and longer. The typical US citizen works almost 2,000 hours per year – that's a full two weeks extra compared to two decades ago.[139] In 1999, the average married couple worked almost 4,000 hours – seven weeks more than ten years ago. The typical European works 350 hours less per year than the average American.[140] When you ask people how many of them would work fewer hours for less pay you get the following response: the US 8%, Germany 38%, the UK and Japan 30%.[141]

Now, we are all under pressure.

While the US ranks among the leaders of the world economy in terms of GDP per capita, the situation looks very different when you compare GDP per hour of work. Belgium moves from number 10 to lead position, the US drops from number one to nine, and for Japan the decline is even more spectacular, from number three to 20.[142] Values matter. Europeans definitely appear to value leisure more than people in most other parts of the world. But obviously, we are also paying a price for it – lower economic growth, less wealth, etc.

Whereas some people are forced to take on double jobs just to stay alive, others put in double time – 90-hour weeks – at the office because they realize that they compete on competence. And knowledge is perishable. They need to exploit their skills right now – otherwise they risk becoming obsolete, commercially worthless. Today, there is a best-before-date on people and their skills. Our world used to be inhabited by the quick and the dead. Now, some of us are quick and dead-tired. According to Aaron Fisher, author of *Is Your Career Killing You?*, in the US alone, the costs of job stress are in the area of $200-300 billion per year.[143]

We have moved from dependability to accountability. Now, we are all under pressure. Yet, these demands always feel personal. People can no longer afford to get off the treadmill. If they do there is a risk that they will suffer – financially, spiritually and physically. Taking a break may indeed break you. For many, calling time-out is no longer an option. As the distance between the rungs on the income ladder has increased, so have the costs of slowing down. Income disparities lead to hard work.[144] If 20 years ago in the US a family decided to drop from the middle upper 5% to the middle upper 20%, they would lose 29% of their income. Today, the figure is 44%.[145] The principle is valid in other parts of the world, but the consequences are not as great – yet.

As former Clinton cabinet member Robert Reich has noted, more and more of us will find it increasingly difficult to strike that delicate balance between making a living and having a life.[146] It's going to take blood, sweat and tears.

Burn!

"Work is entertainment", claimed German philosopher Friedrich Nietzsche. Many knowledge workers would buy into that hypothesis. But having fun at work also comes with risks. European management thinker Leif Edvinsson, has spent the last decade championing the importance of intellectual capital in organizations. Now he is concentrating his efforts on countering the effects of the way we work.[147] "Every 15 minutes someone succumbs to burn-out in Sweden alone. This is incredibly costly as companies lose human and structural capital. At the level of society wealth creation is consequently slowing down at a huge social cost," says Edvinsson.

How do we design working life as well as we do our cities?

"While it takes weeks to chemically treat cancer, burn-out takes much longer to treat. We spend about one tenth of what we spend on medical treatment on the context of knowledge workers. Yet the context has a much bigger impact."

This is a global problem. In Japan, for instance, people talk about *karoshi* – death by overwork. "In order that people may be happy in their work, these three things are needed," claimed British social reformer John Ruskin back in 1851, "they must be fit for it; they must not do too much of it; and they must have a sense of success in it."[148] Everything changes, yet most things remain the same. According to Leif Edvinsson, the questions we should be asking now are: How can the brains of people operate to their best? How do we design working life as well as we do our cities? And leaders should focus on creating the context to give people the confidence as well as mind satisfaction.

In Europe the discussion has largely revolved around whether employers or unions should take on a greater responsibility. The role of individuals seldom figures prominently in the current debate. Yet, we know that whether we like it or not, in the karaoke world responsibilities rest with single human beings. Former US president Ronald Reagan, a person who certainly can't be accused of down-playing the role of the individual, knew that in order to produce results you also need to rest.

During an after dinner speech he wryly observed: "It's true that hard work never really killed anybody, but I figure why take the chance."[149] Perhaps, in the future saying yes to life will mean saying no to other things. Taking a break may indeed bring you back to life.

Of course, the effects of working harder and harder go beyond the exhausted individual. More work creates more stress that, in turn, impacts on the institution of the family – or whatever we prefer to call it. The new reality is that while we used to work shifts at the factory, now we work shifts at home. An increasing number of people who we know fit the DINS acronym used by sociologists – double income no sex. Dual careers have become duel careers. They are the winners, but still find it difficult to cope. "The trouble with the rat race," says actress and comedian Lily Tomlin, "is that even if you win, you're still a rat."

And those of us who do have children may experience the Ray Romano syndrome. Romano, the guy behind the hugely popular TV show *Everybody Loves Raymond*, was recently interviewed by *Newsweek*.[150] "After kids everything changes," he said. "We're having sex about every three months. If I have sex I know my quarterly estimated taxes are due. And if it's oral sex I know it's time to renew my driver's license."

> **Modern cosmocrats outsource the family to have more time to work.**

In response, many people with a family now outsource parts of it. They have someone taking care of the kids; they have a person doing the gardening; they have someone doing the cleaning; they have people taking care of each and every activity related to their home and family. We even heard a story of an executive with a wider span of control at home than at work. At home there was the nanny, the chef, the gardener, etc.

There is nothing new in this. Scottish economist Adam Smith said that the separation of home and labor was the most important of all modern divisions of labor. Historically, the wealthy outsourced domestic mundanities. But they did so to be able to relax. They had drinks and cocktails. They went on picnics and boat-trips. Today it is different. Modern cosmocrats outsource the family to have more time to work.

Stress has always been around, but now it has hit the elite and is therefore deemed a decent disease.

The new elite must constantly defend its position. These peop le are who they are because of what is inherent in their minds, not inherited money – working intellectual capital rather than cash in the bank. Talent is usually sold in units of time. And since some knowledge loses value really fast they must work around the clock.

Hangovers, jet-lag and insomnia

Time pressure is on. In a 24/7/52 world you can be jetlagged without leaving your home. At a single location many time zones may exist simultaneously. A growing number of restaurants serve breakfast and drinks at the same time. The time available is shrinking. In the 1990s more than 50% of all holiday trips were weekend trips.[151] In the future, the ultimate status symbol could very well be eight hours of uninterrupted sleep every night. And each and every little second or minute that we can save seems to be valuable. Even nanoseconds count. In 1997 spending on takeaway meals and restaurants exceeded spending on groceries in the United States.[152] Sales of prepared food are booming. Speed and convenience are of the essence. Flavor is secondary.[153]

Impatient investors of capital and competence are pushing us into an age of anxiety, the stress society, an endeavor economy. The average length of time stocks have been held on the British and American stock exchanges, for instance, has fallen by some 60% in the last 15 years.[154] The National Mental Health Association estimates that 75-90% of all visits to physicians are now stress related.[155] In Sweden, people have access to some 4,000 drugs. More than 100 of these are meant to relieve anxiety and stress. No real pals – but lots of pills. While the *Viagra* and *Prozac* families both make the list of the top selling drugs so does Astra's *Losec*, the No. 1 cure for ulcers. Sex, sadness and stress seem to be the new trinity.

Stress has always been around, but now it has hit the elite and is therefore deemed a decent disease – something to be taken seriously. The doyen of leadership Warren Bennis talks of young leaders being smothered in possibilities – "The world's their oyster and they can choose what they do. They have so many options and possibilities. I think this causes a certain anxiety".[156] The world is their oyster; the future a clam. Or as Danish philosopher Sören Kierkegaard once put it – anxiety is the dizziness of freedom. Freedom is intoxicating – responsibility the hangover.

We deal with stress in different ways. But we all have to deal with it. The late Coca-Cola CEO Roberto Goizueta was interviewed by the magazine *Fortune*.[157] The reporter reflected that Mr. Goizueta was under a lot of pressure and asked him how he slept at night. "I sleep like a baby", Roberto responded. That's wonderful said the reporter. "No, no" replied Goizueta, "I wake up every two hours and cry!" More of us than ever before know exactly what he meant.

6

TALENT TAKES OVER

Talented individuals are mobile monopolies with global passports. They control the key to competitiveness, the scarcest resource: competence. Managers and politicians will have to learn how to deal with people who are free to know, go, do and be.

Street smarts rule

Steven Spielberg's sci-fi movie *Minority Report* featuring Tom Cruise in the leading role is set in the not too distant future. With the help of three precognitive individuals, the police can arrest murderers before they commit their crimes.[158] The film was a huge success grossing an estimated $410 million. From this the movie company 20th Century Fox, will make some $21 million. Meanwhile Steven and Tom get to share $74 million.[159] So, who is in charge in the movie industry, in the entertainment industry, in any industry?

Economics and business is the science of scarce resources.[160] There is only one Steven Spielberg. Combine deregulated capital markets with globalization and digitization making also other markets more efficient. The result is that access to financial resources is no longer the constraint it used to be. There is an abundance of capital – though this might not be apparent to most people. Abundance leads to lower prices. The price of capital is called interest rates. And during the last few years, interest rates have come down dramatically in most parts of the world.

Today, the scarcest resource is not investment but imagination. Consider this. In 1998, CBS, Fox and ABC paid $12.8 billion to broadcast National Football League (NFL) games until 2005. The very same year the Minnesota Vikings franchise was sold for $250 million. In fact, the three networks could have bought all 30 NFL teams and had free broadcast rights.[161] They didn't.

As a citizen of the karaoke society you have a choice. Either you try to join the new elite by chance – playing the lottery – or you develop the skills you were born with. Do whatever you want, but make sure that you are really good at it – world-class. Competence will buy you choice. It increases your power in relation to politicians, employers and capitalists. For single individuals the only viable strategy is to become scarce.

Held hostage by talent

Not that long ago James Bond was the great hero, he fought communists, he made love to beautiful women and topped it all off with a dry martini, shaken not stirred. Every once in a while he popped by to see Q, the nerdy scientist who provided him with weird cars and high-tech spy gadgets. On the cinema screen 007 is still the hero but, in the real world of competence-based competition, the true champion is Q. The nerds really have won.

Skeptics may say that talent power was a phenomenon of the new economy and that the war for talent has now become the war of the talented. These days, aren't people happy just to have a job? In the very short run, they may be right, but there are solid reasons why what we are now witnessing is merely the end of the beginning.

Regardless of industry, success is a question of brains rather than brawn. Of course, matter still matters, but less so. Intellectual capital is the scarce resource. Remember that the average commodity is now worth one fifth of what it was 150 years ago. Wealth is created with wisdom.

This development, of course, is not reflected in the conventional balance sheet – probably the only 500 year-old super-model still capable of arousing a few people. The balance sheet, despite its long-lasting allure, often captures less than a quarter of the real value of many modern companies. Research by the economist Jonathan Kendrick shows that the overall ratio of intangible to tangible resources has shifted from 30/70 to 63/37 during the last 70 years.[162] No longer can the most critical resources of a firm be touched (at least not without risking a lawsuit for sexual harassment).

In the real world of competence-based competition, the true champion is Q.

The good news is that you can never be too smart. We have yet to find a company that went bankrupt because it had too much talent. Indeed, a recent research report shows that only 7% of all managers strongly agree with the statement "our company has enough talented managers to pursue all or most of its promising opportunities".[163] Research even indicates that three-quarters of executives worldwide rank human performance ahead of productivity and technology in terms of strategic importance.[164] The same study also reveals that 80% of all executives claim that by 2010 attracting and retaining people will be the number one strategic issue.

The twist to this development is the demographic fact that, at least in the post-industrialized world, the pool of talent will start shrinking. Over the next decade, the number of 35 to 44-year olds will fall by 15%

as a proportion of the total population, in Europe as well as North America.[165] Collapsing birth rates and an aging population are the main ingredients of this ticking gray bomb.

Conclusion? Most organizations will be held hostage by a small number of people. We call such stars core competents. These are the few people who really make things happen. They know how to use their strengths and manage around their weaknesses. And we find these knowledge nomads all over the map. Steven and Tom are not alone. We find them in sports – imagine English football team Arsenal with or without the French player Thierry Henry. We find them in business. At Microsoft people even talk about "Bill Capital". BC is the currency used to capture time spent with Mr. Gates in technology and business reviews.[167] When computer viruses "Melissa" and "Love letter" created worldwide chaos, did the FBI use its own experts to capture the perpetrator? No, the Bureau was forced to contact a seventeen-year old Scandinavian hacker. Talent has many different faces. It comes in a variety of shapes and forms.

In the US, 11,000 people a day turn 50.

By 2020, 50% of Europe's population will be over 50.

If nothing changes, Japan's population will fall from today's 126 million to less than 100 million in the next 50 years.[166]

Competents are mobile monopolies. They stay only as long as they are offered something that they desire. When that is no longer the case, capable human beings will leave to work for someone else, somewhere else or set up one-person companies – Me Incs. In the US, the so-called "Free Agent Nation" consists of 16 million soloists, 3 million temps and 13 million micro-entrepreneurs – more people than employed in the public sector.[168]

The talent market does not operate like markets for raw materials. Competent individuals are unique and different. Economists would even describe the talent market as imperfect. Power is now in the process of being transferred from the owners of financial capital to those in control of intellectual capital. In the gold-collar niche of the labor-market, firms may end up as price-takers – being forced to accept whatever fees or salaries talented men and women suggest. Organizations are at the mercy of those who control the most critical and scarcest resource.

The FBI was forced to contact a seventeen-year old hacker.

The side effects are obvious. For the more unfortunate souls – commoditents or common knowledge workers – the new reality is a world of cut-throat competition. These individuals are selling a non-differentiated service, which there is an abundance of, on a global market, in competition with millions or perhaps even billions of others, to companies with international reach. And more and more people are affected by this. An Indian or Chinese engineer is just as good as one from Spain or Germany. They are free to work for domestic or foreign firms at home and in the case of Indians also abroad. These engineers will do so for less than $20,000 per year. The first wave of low-cost labor and competition that once caused a major structural revolution in the industrial West, including mass unemployment in textiles, shipping, mining, car manufacturing, will now start hitting not only blue-collar workers but also people with a university diploma.

A few years ago, Trieu Nguyen taught architecture to students in Ho Chi Minh City, Vietnam. Now, he works in an office building close to the city's airport where he checks technical drawings for a student accommodation block in the south of London.[169] In July 2003, news service Reuters announced that it would move some 600 jobs from the US, the UK and Singapore to India.[170] This is the beginning of the second wave. Result? The architect, engineer, accountant or just about any knowledge-worker who lacks real talent is no longer safe. Our advice is simple: move up the labor food chain or get out of the way.

To those who have shall be given

The list of organizations realizing that power now belongs to (some of) their people is getting longer and longer. According to Charles Handy, a few years back some 30% of the equity in American companies were tied up in promised stock options.[171] At Microsoft, Bill Gates owns 25% of the company and the employees approximately 15%. If the stock price increases by 10% per year, the employee shareholders' stock would increase by around $7 billion. If remunerated like that the profits of Microsoft would disappear.[172] So the relationship between employer and employee is changing radically.

At more and more organizations, talented men and women demand an ownership stake. Of course, the stockholders start twisting and turning, whining and screaming. Occasionally they do succeed in stopping such compensation schemes or at least they minimize "the damage" by handing over a smaller part of the company. But, in five or six years' time, the star employees are likely to demand even more. What will the stockholders say then? What can they do?

Robin Hood is not dead. This time though, he's not stealing from the rich to give to the poor. Now, money flows directly from the capital investors into the pockets of the holders of intellectual capital. (Alternatively, money goes straight from the customers, via the capitalists to the competents by-passing traditional workers.)[173]

Executive greed is also partly the consequence of increasingly faceless corporate governance structures.

Remember that we are looking at a very small group of highly skilled people. In the rest of the labor market competition is increasing by the minute. It is also vital to underscore that we are talking about talent, not titles. Core competents are not necessarily senior executives. Lavish salary bonuses and stock option plans for the top executives are not the ultimate evidence that competence makes capital dance.

Do not mistake the glorification of greed for the triumph of talent. Too often, these compensation schemes are designed along the lines of a

Contrary to popular belief, historical revolutions were driven by the middle class and intellectuals.

traditional hierarchical logic – rewarding bosses instead of brains. Title and talent do not necessarily overlap. Neither is there a well-functioning market for executives. Too few people are continuously evaluated and often they are assessed by people they already know.

So called executive greed is also partly the consequence of increasingly faceless corporate governance structures that are incapable of balancing the system. There are now hundreds of millions of anonymous capitalists, shareholders who never show up at annual meetings, who never use their voice, financial institutions that do not (or are not allowed to) take an active part in the boards of the companies in which they have invested our pension funds and savings.

The revolting elite

Contrary to popular belief, historical revolutions such as the French, Russian and Chinese, were not driven by workers but rather by the middle class and intellectuals. In the case of China, farmers supported these two groups. This time though, the cosmocrats of the world are leading the way. Armed with cash and competence, in the karaoke economy, cosmocrats can know, go, do, and be whoever they want. People in general cannot. Although we are looking at barbarians with brains charging forward, the new elite is also beginning to flex its muscles. Foreign experts get tax cuts in Denmark and other countries. In the US there is a visa program for top-notch scholars. If you are not attractive, talent won't invite you to dance.

Consider Singapore, one of the world's freest economies, but also a place that has maintained very tight social control. Yet, when we move into a transparent and open world, where skilled people have more or less endless choice, Singapore is being forced to change. In an effort to attract top talent it is liberalizing its policies so that people can, for example, watch *Sex and the City* on cable TV. Now, you can dance on bar-tables again. The Singaporean government has even started hiring self-declared homosexuals. Shock! Horror! In fact officials cite the study about gays and bohemians we mentioned earlier – who said that business research didn't make a difference?[174]

Stan Davis and Christopher Meyer, the authors of *futureWEALTH*, point out the logical implications of our move into a world where those who control the most critical resources have a global passport: "When land was the productive resource, nations battled over it, the same is happening now for talented people."[175] Whether we like it or not, the success of all regions, and all organizations depends on their ability to attract people who make a difference.

The Left demanded that Barnevik should hand back the money not to the workers, but to the shareholders!

This leaves politicians with an entirely new agenda. When people with cash and competence are in charge, power is concentrated, yet not centralized. Those at the helm are not easily overthrown or even influenced. Questions abound. How do you create loyalty in a group of people who are free to know, go, do, and be? It is extremely difficult to order Kylie Minogue, Sir Richard Branson or Anna Kornikova to do things. To what extent can the mobile and the potentially mobile be taxed? The answer is simple: with great difficulty.

Meanwhile, others find themselves stuck in one location, lacking the resources necessary for playing the global game of locomotion. And increasingly governments, for reasons of practical necessity rather than ideological conviction, will find it tempting to tax what is stuck. So what is glued to the face of planet earth? Property and the poor are two prime candidates.

As a result, the entire political landscape may be redrawn. Left-leaning politicians once backed workers. Now, they are as likely to support their arch enemies – capitalists. When it finally became known (in an open world sooner or later just about anything becomes transparent – there is nowhere to hide) that former ABB CEO Percy Barnevik had received a pension package worth some $100 million, the most critical voices came from the left. They more or less demanded that Barnevik should hand back the money not to the workers, but to the shareholders! The owners of ABB include the Wallenbergs – one of the most influential and wealthiest industrial dynasties in Europe.

The battle of labor versus capital is increasingly consigned to history. The new battle is between traditional workers and capitalists on one hand and (insatiable) talent workers on the other. Socialists are backing capitalists for a number of very practical reasons. Historically, the left has always preferred to deal with a concentrated group of capitalists because this made it easier to gather a group of fifteen people or so and sit down in a room to draw up the grand master plan for continued social engineering. Centralized political and economic powers usually make a happy couple.

What is new is that the future pensions of workers and the expected profits of companies are increasingly interlinked.[176] Managers of pension funds invest in the stock market. The future well being of traditional workers is heavily reliant on how well these companies do. If competence is (too) handsomely compensated, profits may erode. As long as this behavior is limited to a small group of executives the situation may not be too dangerous (economically if not ethically). But over time, these people will provide a benchmark for less visible competents. When star MBAs, designers and engineers start karaoke copying – asking for more and more – things could get really out of hand for the capital owners. Such an enlargement of the talent group could have an extremely negative impact on profits and share prices. Over time, this development could also diminish the possibility of the pensions of traditional workers actually growing.

So, in response to executive greed, (socialist) governments across the world have started to set up committees to investigate how to get top-management teams to stop asking for more. Oddly enough, these groups often include people representing ownership interests. The logically zany but rhetorically brilliant argument they produce is that top managers should show restraint. Otherwise there will be little money left for the workers to share. The assumption is that the capital owners would use the money to increase the salaries of workers who are virtually interchangeable with millions of others across the world. Unlikely, we think. As business scholars we were under the impression that it was the responsibility of the capital owners to prevent executives from being paid more money than they really deserve by bargaining and using market forces to their advantage, but apparently we misunderstood and still misunderstand Economics 101.

Look beyond extravagant executive behavior and you begin to realize that the transfer of power equates to an organic quasi-socialization of our societies. Power is transferred from the capitalist rulers of the industrial world to a few (knowledge) workers. But rather than clapping hands, the left starts crying. Welcome to the real revolution. The next question of how to get this new ruling class to share some of its wealth with others remains unanswered. Hypothesis: try a carrot, not a stick.

There are also soft arguments behind this unholy alliance of socialists and capitalists. Many regard intelligence-based inequalities as one of the most unjust forms of apartheid. It is OK to admit that someone else is faster or stronger, but to say the same thing about smartness is still not politically correct. IQ is not PC. Perhaps this is why study after study (especially of males) show that more than 50% of all individuals rate themselves as above average when it comes to quality of work and skills. Too often competence is also mixed up with character and contribution to society. Level of intelligence says absolutely nothing about the value of a human being but it may well say something economically.

If the left does not get its act together, sooner or later one or more of the right wing parties will seize the opportunity to become the voice and choice of knowledge workers rather than capitalists. There is a golden opportunity for someone to start a new political movement – after capitalism come *competalism*. The Karaoke Party may soon have another meaning.

Self-selection and self-deception

The repercussions from the new opportunities facing the mobile cream of the crop will be many and widespread. First, there is mobility. We expect a major redistribution of gifted people. Despite the death of distance, we are all shareholders of a state – but now some of us can choose. The wealthy and able can select themselves in and out.

In 2003, Sweden had a referendum about whether or not to join the European Monetary Union (EMU). An overwhelming majority of the people said no. Case closed? By no means. Swedish citizens with talent and money are free to join EMU tomorrow. All they have to do is move to Germany, Spain or France. The concept of democracy, as we know it, is based on an underlying assumption of a closed geographical room. No more.

The shift is underway. In certain areas where centrifugal forces are already at work, we can observe the consequences. In 1970, 4.7% of the US population was foreign born, 30 years later, it was 10.4%.[177] The karaoke cosmocrats are on their way. Percentage-wise, the number of men and women with a Masters degree in either business or science who leave Sweden has reached the same level as the percentage of the total population that left the country a century ago when hundreds of thousands migrated to America.[178]

The US is not the only magnet. Some countries use the magnetic power of gold. In 1998, the leaders of Iran offered former Soviet scientists doing research in labs related to germ warfare a $5,000 monthly salary (more than they would make a year in Russia).[182] Or have you ever heard of Saif Saaeed Shaheen? In August 2003 he won Qatar's first ever gold medal at the world athletics championships in the 3000 meters steeplechase. The weird thing is that two months prior to that his name was Stephen Cherono and he was competing for his native country Kenya. Even weirder is the fact that in the finals he was racing

In 1990, the percentage of Silicon Valley high-tech entrepreneurs with a Ph.D. or Masters Degree varied significantly between people with different backgrounds. 55% of all Indians had such a degree, 40% of the Chinese, but merely 18% of the whites. Eight years later, one third, or 2,775, of all Silicon Valley CEOs were Indian or Chinese.[179]

Some 60% of the best American physics papers and almost 30% of life science papers are written by people born outside the country.[180]

In 1999, approximately 25% of all Ph.D. exams in the US were taken by foreigners.[181]

against his brother who was still running for Kenya. Weirdest of it all is the fact that Saif/Stephen did not move (in fact we don't think he has moved) to Qatar out of love or fear. He simply changed nationality to make money. His new country promised him a monthly salary of a little more than $1,000 – for life. There are rumors that Qatar also paid a transfer fee to the Kenyan Athletics Federation.

How should we react? What do we do when countries behave as companies and sports teams like Barcelona or the LA Lakers have been behaving for decades – buying whatever and whoever they want? Should we be surprised? Probably not! Will we see more of it? You bet.

The new reality is that some places are talent havens. But, for every talent hotspot there is an Arctic tundra where no one wants to go. The winners will import knowledge producers and export knowledge products. The losers will do the opposite – if they can afford. Clearly, these processes could have a major impact on economic growth around the world. There will not be a mass exodus of capable individuals from most nations but governments and experts claiming that the fears of a brain drain are exaggerated, deceive themselves.

Their argument is based on the assumption that all people are created equal. In a double economy this is patently not the case. Small numbers make big differences – remember the genes. This is particularly true in an economy where the winner increasingly takes all. Just imagine the Russian or Czech ice-hockey teams having to enter the Olympic tournament without the stars who regularly play in the American National Hockey League (NHL).

Our colleague at the Stockholm School of Economics, Professor Udo Zander, goes as far as to argue that ultimately a totally connected world will lead *not* to increased homogeneity, but more heterogeneity across space.[183] In responding to the conditions in a particular country, the people living there have three basic options. They can remain loyal and stay put; or they can voice their concerns in order to change things but decide to still remain; or they can leave.[184] There are no options in between, no neat compromises.

A few years back, for many people in the world the final option was not viable – at least not without facing the risk of being shot in the back. Now, more and more of us can move. But, then there is the second hurdle: the freedom to go generally costs. The absence of critical resources not only deters many individuals from trying to exit, but also triggers the doorman at the receiving end to stop you. At the end of the day, says Professor Zander, what drives people to move is the "perceived gap between life aspiration and expectations, and the means to fulfill them in the home country within reasonable time".

Imagine the Czech ice hockey team having to enter the Olympic tournament without the stars who regularly play in the NHL.

In other words, the prime candidates for exit are the most ambitious people living in the most abominable places. This is the Catch-22, which particularly faces leaders of developing countries. If they go for equality and openness there is a clear risk that the most ambitious citizens will move rather than remain to carry the burden of the others. On the other hand, if these leaders opt for a system with greater income disparity, the ambitious may stay, but the rest of the people will suffer. Talented women and men "will look for societies that to the best of their knowledge promise a way of life that they have been dreaming of," says Udo Zander. People who share a dream will assemble at places putting that dream into practice. Money is not everything. Ideas and ideals still matter.

The US has a head start on most other parts of the world in this attraction game since it is based on a genuine idea. There is a story to be told and American citizens are believers. People believe in the idea called the United States of America (and in God). If we buy into the idea we can all be Americans. It takes generations to become Japanese, French or German – countries based on geography rather than biography.[185] It takes but years, or perhaps only months, to become American, even if you are nineteen years old and currently live in Seoul in South Korea. But, since the US is based on a clearly identifiable idea, it is bound to attract enemies as well as friends. You can be against the idea of America. Large groups of people dislike the American way. It is more difficult to find individuals having similarly strong opinions about let's say Switzerland, Spain or Slovenia.

Long term, the result of this redistribution of talented people across space could well be increased polarization – local homogeneity and international heterogeneity. A worrying thought, adds our friend Udo, "is that World War I followed a period of cosmopolitan capitalism and the first great wave of migration".

(R)evolution takes time

We will not experience the dominion of talent tomorrow. What still impedes this development is the lack of internal transparency at many organizations. This makes it difficult to measure individual performance and contribution. In certain industries the track record of single human beings is easier to quantify. In the financial industry, for example, the results of each broker can be closely monitored and the shift toward core competent power has already happened. Look at the pay checks some of these brokers receive.

What also delays the takeover of talent is the inability of prima donnas to act collectively. Even stars are more powerful in constellations. Capitalists will not simply hand over control and cash to a group of nerds and in the political left owners of companies may actually find unlikely allies to keep talent at bay.

Those with competence must also start to act. At the moment, only a limited number of people move around – though 17% of all Americans change residence and 3% move to another state every year.[186] Generally, there is no history or tradition of individuals playing the international labor market. A meager 1.5% of the worldwide labor force works outside its home country. In the European Union, the equivalent number is 2%.[187] Eventually, however, the humble, silent and loyal gold-collar employee will become dusty history.

7

CUSTOMERS IN CHARGE

Friction-free commerce is a shopper's paradise. A profusion of markets, surplus supply, continuous commoditization plus inexpensive information = perfect competition. Today, customers call the shots.

The iron-laws of information

The Vatican and Sony Music recently announced that the much-awaited follow-up album to John Paul II's first platinum-selling rap record, *Abbà Pater*, would soon be released.[188] The new album will feature the Pope's prayers as interpreted by 'N Sync and Britney Spears – 'Oops he did it again' or 'Hit me papa one more time'...?

Now, we don't know about you, but when we think of the Vatican, we tend to think of it as a – let us say – *moderately* conservative organization. When the leader of the Catholic Church has to go pop, something has happened. Why this divine version of customer delight – Vatican Voodoo? Could it be an effort to capture the attention of the young catholic tribe currently losing its interest in a historical institution?

In the supply-driven and normal world of yesterday, customers were scorned. Despite all the catchy slogans saying "The Customer Is King", they were often treated as the lepers of the business world. Buyers had to settle for one-size-fits-all solutions. Fifteen years ago, the Stockholm School of Economics did not even have a marketing department. The closest thing to such a place was called the Institute of Distribution Economics. The mindset focused on logistics rather than on getting consumers to fall in love with products and services. Those days are gone. Powered by new technology, contemporary customers want it all – and they want it now. The overload economy is here. Repulsion has to be replaced by attraction. Successful companies know this. Indeed, it seems that even His Holiness the Pope is beginning to understand it.

IT may not distribute power evenly across our world, but it certainly empowers the consumer. To understand the makeup of the engine behind this seismic shift toward customer control, we must look at the combined impact of three "ancient" laws – in Internet time at least.

First, there is *Moore's Law*, a prediction by Intel founder Gordon Moore, that every 18 months chip density (and thus also computing power) will double while at the same time costs remain unchanged. Then add *Metcalfe's Law*, an observation by 3Com founder Robert Metcalfe suggesting that the value of a network is proportional to the square of the number of people using it. Having a telephone, for instance, makes sense only if at least one more phone exists. Or apply this principle to tribes. Compared to being alone, having a partner is worth not twice but four times as much (and accordingly a *ménage a trois* is nine times more fun than solitude).

The result is that IT-driven change is not only amplified by decreasing costs vis-à-vis performance. Growth is also self-reinforcing in that these networks display elements of increasing rather than decreasing returns – the more who join, the more sense it makes for you and us to get on the bandwagon.[189] This is the exception to the rule of scarcity that otherwise guides economics and business. As a consequence of the two laws, computing power and the number of people active on these networks have expanded beyond our wildest fantasies.

Repulsion has to be replaced by attraction. Even the Pope is beginning to understand it.

To really grasp the impact of advances within the field of information technology on business, we need to add a third and somewhat more theoretical statute: *Coase's Law*. In 1937, a lawyer turned economist, Ronald Coase, wrote his highly influential article *The Nature of the Firm* which later won him a Nobel Prize.[190] Coase argued that firms exist only under conditions when they outperform markets in terms of minimizing transaction costs. This may sound like rocket-science but in reality economics is more similar to meteorology. Indeed, when it comes to predicting the future, economists and meteorologists have much in common.

Think about climate. Temperature determines what people wear. If it's really cold outside, few people walk around in shorts. You could, but it wouldn't make sense. Information is to economics and business what temperature and climate are to meteorology. Temperature can be high or low. Information can be plentiful or scarce. Temperature determines what is efficient to wear. Information determines the most efficient way to organize trade and other economic activities.

When information is abundant and equally distributed, we get market places – a bazaar.

By and large, transaction costs are caused by either a lack of information – we don't know – or asymmetrically distributed information – we know either more or less than they know.[191] When information is abundant and equally distributed, we get market places – a bazaar. Likewise, when information is sparse and unequally distributed we end up with companies – or hierarchies, as the economists prefer to call them.[192] Efficiency guides effort. We don't get these archetypical organizational forms automatically, however. Some people will continue to wear a fur coat in the sun and others will walk around in shorts in the snow. Nevertheless, over time forms that do not fit in a particular information landscape will become extinct – out-competed by rivals with more efficient organizational models, in the same way as dinosaurs once disappeared.

From this perspective, the impact of IT in general, and the Internet in particular, on our economy resembles the way in which global warming influences our climate. In the information jungle created by the combined effects of Moore's and Metcalfe's law, markets begin to conquer hierarchies, because markets feed and breed on information. Eventually, global warming may make us all hot, but the current IT development should definitely make all managers of hierarchical and vertically integrated companies drip with nervous sweat right now.

Imperfect world; perfect markets.

Globalization, deregulation and digitization have propelled us into a world of market mania. There are now more markets for more things covering a larger geographical area than ever before. The development has been mind-boggling. One day of international trade in 2001 equaled all international trade back in 1949. One day of foreign exchange in 2000 equaled all foreign exchange in 1979.[193] Materials and money roam the world.

But these markets are not restricted to physical assets or capital. An Internet site, such as Yet2.com, allows companies to acquire, sell and license intellectual property.[194] There's more. A McKinsey study suggests that some 20% of world output is open to global competition.[195] In 30 years, the study predicts that the equivalent figure will be 80%. We ain't seen nothing yet.

The number of business and investing titles on Amazon.com in the summer of 2002 included more than 150,000 different books.[197]

The number of telecom carriers worldwide 1989: 200. The number of telecom carriers in the United States 1999: 3,000.[198]

www.live365.com allows you to listen to more than 40,000 different radio stations.[199]

There are 40,000 distinct items available in the average American supermarket. The typical family needs 150 to fill 80% of their needs.[200]

The United States has more than 3,000 specialty mass magazines with circulations between 50,000 and 1,000,000.[201]

Everything is up for sale. While there is nothing new about abundance – in 1900, Paris had 70 daily newspapers – the excess economy is picking up speed – at the double.[196]

As markets become more efficient, entry barriers facing new-comers that were once the size of the Great Wall of China are beginning to experience the same fate as the walls in Jericho and Berlin. A similar argument is largely true for mobility barriers. With less costs sunk in, say, manufacturing facilities or large sales-forces, changes in strategic positioning are no longer as costly. Combine this effect (enabling new firms to enter industries without the resource commitments of the past and the old-timers to expand capacity) with the internationalization of business (meaning more competitors) and the daunting result is that, at least in the post-industrialized world, supply often exceeds demand. IT improves productivity. But, as the godfather of

The result is over-capacity.

re-engineering Mike Hammer has pointed out, what is good for a single company is not necessarily that great for an industry. Productivity gains are desirable for individual firms, but when all organizations push to get to the productivity frontier, the result is over-capacity.[202]

Today, over-capacity is the norm in most businesses. The worldwide automobile industry, for example, has the capacity to produce approximately 20 million vehicles a year more than the world market demands.[203] But, while there are certainly more products and services available, more does not necessarily imply greater variety or wider choice. On the contrary, services and products are often becoming more and more similar. The intriguing result is an age of abundance with a surplus of 'similars'. Karaoke copying reigns. Commoditization days are here.

An age of abundance with a surplus of similars.

With markets functioning better through more or less total transparency, the search costs for finding the best deal are also plummeting. Say you are in the market for a home-theater system. Using an intelligent search engine on the Web, you can probably shave $500 off the price that your local dealer offers you. And it takes two minutes to do the search. The Net, mobile or fixed, becomes for the shopping generation what the pill was to the love generation of the 1960s. It allows us to shop, rather than sleep around. This time, we can all be more promiscuous without the risk of any physical side effects - except for square eyes and a mouse-arm.

Let's add things up: Market mania + Surplus supply + Continuous commoditization + Inexpensive information = Perfect competition. Our friends, the economists, define perfect competition as: "A market structure that is characterized by a large number of small firms, a homogeneous product, access to information by all buyers and sellers, and freedom of entry and exit".[204] Under such conditions, firms risk ending up as price-takers – the customers tell companies what they are willing to pay. Marginal revenues will just about cover marginal costs – proceeds from the last product sold will only cover the variable costs incurred for manufacturing and selling that particular product but not leave any profit.

In the karaoke world companies are forced to do business in a genuine bazaar. And we all know how a bazaar works. There are 379 vendors trying to sell you tomatoes. And all the tomatoes look the same. All the tomatoes taste the same. So, you shop around. You bargain. The price is 5, 4, 3, 2, 1, 0. They are giving away tomatoes, hoping to make it all up on oranges. Wacky? Just look at what has happened to mobile phones, where many operators let you have one for free as long as you sign up for two years.

You are in control. In the world of perfect competition the price is up to you. Today, the fashion industry looks like this. The ball bearing, personal computer, chemical, concrete and coffee industries are all moving closer to this state of total global competition. In fact, you have to look really hard to find one single industry that has not been "bazaared". No wonder that in the US alone, during a single year corporations spend some $233 billion on advertising (that is six times the US educational budget.)[205]

The worldwide conquest of market capitalism has resulted in a cosmopolitan shoppers-paradise. Forget about kings and queens – the new consumer is a demanding dictator. And right now, these customers may very well be on the Web, trying to link up with others to use their collective bargaining power – Dictators United. Unlike the despots of the real world, these autocrats cannot be overthrown or threatened to resign by brute force. In effect, power is now being transferred from producers to consumers.

My way

Customers are in charge. Yet, it seems few companies have realized the full consequences of this paradigm shift. They do not have accurate customer profiles or interaction-transaction histories with their key customers. Many corporations do not have a clue how much it costs to acquire a customer. Some of them know zilch about customer retention rates, average customer revenues or profits per customer. Few organizations have a senior executive responsible for the total customer experience. Even fewer understand exactly why customers prefer to buy their products and services. Inside the karaoke club, all customers are unique individuals. So we can't afford to treat them as Jane and John Does.

Spending time with customers is the essence of management.

Do consumers really care about what most managers spend their time doing? Do managers really think about customers when they are carrying out most of their activities? We suspect the answer to both questions is no.

They should. Spending time with customers is the essence of management. John Chambers of Cisco Systems spends 80% of his time in conversation with customers, and requires every executive to spend at least 50% of their time face-to-face with customers.[206] This is probably the cheapest course you can ever take on customer relationship management.

And don't expect dumb acquiescence when you talk to your customers. They know what they want. The new digital consumer will pose fundamentally different and much tougher requirements on any executive and all organizations. Management writer and *Economist* journalist Frances Cairncross even argues that: "Internet technologies make the task of dealing with customers much more difficult – by making the customer's life easier."[207]

Take music as an example. Do you want to listen to the songs before buying the album? Have you ever wanted to buy a couple of songs by an artist rather than an entire CD? Would you like to put together your own compilations? Have you ever wanted to re-mix a song, or perhaps just beef up the bass? Ever felt like giving away your "own" music to friends – or have you even thought of selling them to other consumers? If you answered yes to any of the questions above, you constitute a challenge to most companies in the music industry. On top of everything else, these organizations also have file-sharing customers to worry about. To some this development is a threat – Universal Music recently slashed 30% off CD prices in the US. To others the new situation constitutes an opportunity – Apple's Steven Jobs has launched iTunes where you can download songs for 99 cents apiece. True entrepreneurs don't try to escape change – they embrace it. Whether traditional companies like it or not, many consumers will want to: [208]

Checkout what you can offer them before actually committing to buying it.
Componentize your offer and buy it bit by bit, piece by piece.
Combine and re-combine the offer in any way they see fit.
Change the offer into something that they like even better.
Copy and share the offer with their friends.
Communicate the offer to others.
Co-brand your offer with their personal alterations or re-combinations.

But, how many corporations are really ready to do business in this way? "When you put up a website, you're not erecting a billboard, you're opening up a door," says IT-guru Esther Dyson.[209] The doors are opening. Remember that an open world requires open systems and an open architecture. You can try to swim up the Mississippi, but it's probably not a very good idea. Go with the flow.

Under siege by customers

Certain pundits would claim that the idea of the empowered consumer sounds great in theory, but that examples of it are rare in reality. They're right. The rational and calculating consumer may still be a contradiction in terms. The technology part of the equation is a small thing compared to changing human conduct. Altering human behavior takes time. Change is about learning and learning is slow. Even if you are extremely gifted, it takes years and years to become a great opera singer.

Several things impede the growth of customer control. People need to act more like the rational *homo economicus* so familiar to economists – comparing prices, displaying no signs of loyalty, constantly shifting to other suppliers, and so on. A large percentage of customers also need to have access to the Web and be IT literate. Consumers must be aware, or alternatively be made aware, of the potential power in their hands.

This last point constitutes a great opportunity for the unions and central banks of the world. Rather than focusing on increasing salaries, the former could take on the challenge of uniting the working consumers of the world to lower prices (the negative consequence is of course that this would make it even more difficult to raise salaries). Meanwhile the latter could fight inflation by providing a platform for customer power rather than by raising the interest rates.

Despite the initial inertia, long-term, our prediction is that the uninformed, humble and loyal customer, who was often bullied by companies in a world where demand mostly exceeded supply is about to become a thing of the past. Bet against this development at your peril.

8

CAPITALISTS ARE CRYING

Companies are facing the prospects of a two-front war: held hostage by competent individuals and under siege by demanding customers. The number one characteristic of a well-functioning market economy happens to be low average profitability. To thrive, organizations must learn to master the arts of capitalizing on competencies and customer creation.

Bubbles burst

We were seduced – again. People like being seduced. Seduction is sexy. Economic erotica. Like Anne Bancroft as the sensuous Mrs. Robinson in *The Graduate*, who in a gentle voice asks the young Dustin Hoffman's character Benjamin, "Would you like me to seduce you?", the future tickled our fantasies. Mankind fell madly in love with money – seduced by the prospects of success. We were all going to come out on top. Seduce me? Yes, please! Open up the pearly Gates. Do it to us one more time. Man has always been and will continue to be an opportunity orgasm addict.

On March 10, 2000, the NASDAQ composite index hit an all time high. It peaked at 5,132 and closed at 5,048 points.[210] In just one decade global stock market capitalization had increased from $9.3 trillion to $25 trillion.[211] Yet, Perkins and Perkins in their book *The Internet Bubble* show that less than 20% of the top 133 dot-coms offered as initial public offerings (IPOs) on the NASDAQ had actually made any profits by mid-1999.[212] Some absolutely flabbergasting assumptions had been built into the valuations of the stocks. When the market peaked, the valuation was based on an average 80% annual growth for five consecutive years – much faster than the historical growth of both Microsoft and Dell.

For instance, by February 2000, if Amazon sales increased by 40% per year during the next ten-year period, that would explain only half of a $64 price per share.[213] The sky was the limit. And the sky knew no limits.[214]

People were so seduced that they did not realize that the magical mystery tour was heading for Death Valley rather than Silicon Valley.

Crash! Boom! Bang! On April 14, 2000, more than $1 trillion in market capital was lost in 6.5 hours.[215] Days of disaster had arrived. Three years later, for stocks that once were worth as much as a pair of sneakers, you could hardly buy a Snickers bar. Reality had caught up with the dreams. We are no longer partying like it's 1999.

The magical mystery tour was heading for Death Valley rather than Silicon Valley.

As we're writing this, the NASDAQ composite index is fluctuating around 1,800 points. Although we have seen some correction in the market during 2003, most people have been living and working inside a 75% downward spiral that lasted for three years. A revolution, as Chairman Mao put it, is not a dinner party.

In the last few years, most corporations – not only the dot-coms – have been under considerable pressure. The wired world has turned weird and some have buckled under the strain. In October 2002, ABB, the Swedish-Swiss electrical-engineering giant lost 64% of its market capitalization - in one day.[216] (And, yes, that is the same company which was lauded throughout the 1990s for its inspired management and organization.) The harder they come, the harder they fall.

The last 50 or so years may very well become known as the period when companies ruled the world. The 1,000 largest corporations still control 80% of world output.[217] Yet, the nature of companies has changed dramatically in recent years. As Peter Drucker has noted, for the first time in history people can expect to outlive the organizations that they work for.[218] The life span of firms, like marriages, is becoming shorter by the day, the minute, the second.[219]

Fortune Global 500 2002

Revenues	Down $281 billion
Profits	Down 56%
Employees	Down 1.3 million

Source: *Fortune*, July 21, 2003.

It was a rude awakening. Suddenly, investors and entrepreneurs were forced to realize that fundamental economic principles were and are still alive. The new economy did not re-write all the basic tenets of economics. From this point of view we had as much of a new economy as we ever had "new physics" or "new biology".

Consider the economics-defying notion of "increasing returns". There are increasing returns involved in the growth of the Internet, but not in Internet consulting. Applying such a "new economy law" to all industries and all situations inevitably leads to disasters. A theory is no substitute for common sense. When you hand people a hammer, they see only nails, but the karaoke world is somewhat more complicated than that. Some of these companies may have operated in real-time, but many certainly didn't operate in the real world.

As MIT academics Erik Brynjolfson and Yannis Baros point out, profitability is maximized by providing the maximum number of goods to the maximum number of consumers for the maximum amount of time.[220] Gloriously simple really.

On the other hand, profits are not maximized by selling yet more plain vanilla ice cream over the Web. A bad business idea does not become a stroke of genius just because you place it on the Net. Profits are based on uniqueness, not the utilization of technology. Neither does simply hiring more intelligent people give companies a sustainable competitive edge. Even in the age of the cosmocrat, profits are about money-count, not man-count.

When you hand people a hammer, they see only nails.

Growth expectations may justify high valuations, but mere growth has never made a company truly wealthy. The value of a firm is a consequence of future expected profits. Period. As a result, the quickest way for management to boost the value of stock-options is not to increase profits but to inflate expectations. And the easiest way to grow really fast is by purposefully sacrificing short-term profitability. In fact, we could all build large corporations in a world where we didn't have to worry about making money. Hire – don't fire.

Profit enemy No. 1.

"During the Internet bubble, it was argued that because the Internet is important, it must be profitable. That does not follow," claims Peter Drucker.[221] Don't get us wrong. We continue to be great fans of e-commerce. In 1995, Web sales amounted to some $436 million. Five years later sales had reached $30 billion.[222] How many companies grew sales by 6,800% in that period? The IT revolution continues and will continue to do so. The infra- and info structure will not simply go away. The bubble was a case of financial frivolity rather than a techno-fraud initiated by juvenile nerds with a Blofeld-complex.

The Net is still a great enabler of new ways of doing business. We will find many future success stories linked to innovative utilization of information technology. Organizations are using new tools to do things that are difficult or even impossible to do in a world without the Internet – such as international aggregation of demand and supply, inviting customers to take an active part in "prosuming" (consumption + production = prosumption) new offerings, and operating in real-time. This will revolutionize industry after industry. Again, opportunities exist in time, space as well as mass.

Information is to an economy what oil is to an engine.

But while IT has created and will continue to create many new business opportunities, from a strictly economic perspective, IT in general and the Internet in particular is probably best thought of as profit enemy No. 1. Perhaps the Net is just too perfect for profit.[223]

The Internet will carry us into a new world of low friction capitalism, in which information will be abundant and transaction costs low. Information is to an economy what oil is to an engine. It lubricates the market machine. It makes the engine even more efficient. It perfects markets.

Indeed, one plausible hypothesis is that the more Web-based and knowledge intensive the business, the less chance there is that any of the profits will end up in the pockets of a company's financial investors. E-commerce enables customers to exert more power and more easily compare prices and so on. Capital is even less of a critical resource in most knowledge-intensive businesses. In addition, companies competing on soft stuff – people, intangibles and competencies – are surrounded by more uncertainty. This equates to more risk. And the higher the risk premium, the lower the stock-market value should be.[224]

The two-front war

To truly understand what is going on and to position ourselves for the future, we must combine the hypothesis that the customer is in charge, with the proposition that talented people now own the most critical means of production. If we do this, the profit potential for the typical business firm is cast in new light. Any profits that can be made after having dealt with demanding dictators must then pass through the hands of core competents. Conclusion? The typical company in the average industry in most parts of the world will face a two-front war. Think Napoleon.

First, they will have to sit down and negotiate salary packages and stock-option plans with the business world's equivalent to Mariah Carey, Michael Schumacher, Julia Roberts and, if they are really lucky, Tiger Woods. They might even have to sit down and talk with groupings of core competents. The top talents may very well link up and form modern versions of the United Artists that Charlie Chaplin and others once started. At the very least, many of them will be represented by agents doing for them what someone like Mark McCormack did for sports-stars for years.

Then, corporations must negotiate prices and discounts with their customers, demanding dictators who may also be bargaining together. Customers are already joining hands. Some 40 retailers in the US with almost 3.5 times the buying power of Wal-Mart have now formed the World Retail Exchange.[225] Talk to them with respect.

Bonus
Stock-option plan

Corner office
Salary package

Discounts
Prices
Delivery time
Quality

The result of all this turmoil is that it will become much more difficult for any firm in any industry to make money. Capitalists may be crying but they shouldn't be surprised. After all it was 1776 when economist Adam Smith noted that low average profits was the prime characteristic of a well-functioning market economy. "The rate of profit does not, like rent and wages, rise with prosperity and fall with the declension of the society. On the contrary, it is naturally low in rich countries and high in poor countries, and it is always highest in the countries which are going fastest to ruin," wrote Smith.[226]

The more efficient the machine of market capitalism becomes, the lower the profits we should expect. In the years to come, for most companies margins will be salami-thin. All other things being equal we should not expect the stock market to boom in a well-functioning global market economy. Competition tends to drive out profits. It may be wise to turn down the music and put the champagne on ice. The karaoke party could very well be delayed – or perhaps even cancelled due to unforeseen competition.

The message to companies is simple: they must establish clear priorities. When customers become more powerful, the value of customer capital increases. If competent individuals become more powerful, the value of human capital becomes higher. Finally, if financial capital becomes less of a scarce resource, the value of such capital decreases. To thrive in this new world, companies must capitalize on competencies and create new customers.

The strange thing is that while it is extremely difficult to create competitive advantages by manipulating financial markets and markets for hard labor, most executives still spend (too) much of their time interacting with investment bankers and trade union representatives. Rather than focusing their energy on buyers of goods or services and suppliers of ideas where the potential for innovation and creation of sustainable competitiveness are much greater, many managers habitually behave like capital and cheap labor were still the most important factors. The time to change is now.

9

WEBS OF WISDOM

Wealth is created with wisdom, but to keep up companies are forced to create knowledge networks that pose new and fundamentally different demands on the organization. Internationalization increases the geographical dispersion of competencies. Hyphenation leads to more diversity. Education boosts the depth of the skills needed while competition simultaneously decreases the durability of knowledge.

The autopsy and the matrix

There is growing recognition and awareness of the power of customers and competent individuals, but actually managing things differently and imaginatively has proved beyond many executives and organizations. Historical hierarchies and boring bureaucracies live on. Corporate inertia is a way of life for many. *Just Do It* remains a neat slogan, rather than a persuasive reality. Most corporations are still running on autopilot. They are using measurement systems that were originally meant for shareholders and tax authorities. Instead of pre-emptive medicine, far too often companies are practicing business autopsy. Organizational solutions still favor the exploitation of givens at the expense of the creation of novelty.

The true irony is that as intelligence and intangibles replace raw materials and capital as the true sources of competitive advantage, certain managers turn to lawyers rather than accountants for advice. They replace one breed not exactly world famous for its creative abilities – possibly excluding Arthur Andersen's Enron team – with another.

The shame of it is that organizational innovations can be extremely powerful. It is said that the first half of the Hebrews' exodus from Egypt to Israel took some 35 years. Then Moses got some advice from Jethro, his father in-law and probably the world's first management consultant, about how to re-organize the Israelites. He followed the recommendations.

The Bible recounts Moses' discovery of an organizational chart: "And Moses chose able men out of all Israel, and made them heads over the people, rulers of thousands, rulers of hundreds, rulers of fifties, and rulers of tens."[227] The second half of the journey took five years.

Since then, organizational innovations have by and large broken things up. In the 20th century we moved from functional organizations to divisional organizations.[228] DuPont did it. GM did it. But, during the 1970s and 1980s, the logic of break-up broke down. Corporations began to realize that much more than one organizational dimension was critical. In addition to products, geography, technologies, customer segments and brands came into play. On top of that, the old cross-functional issues remained. In many European multinationals the local countries were so strong that it was difficult to ensure global economies of scale. Most American and Japanese companies had strong product divisions, headquartered at home, thwarting global learning, local initiatives and flexibility in other parts of the world.[229]

As the competitive landscape evolved, a number of companies started experimenting with the matrix organization. ABB did it. IBM did it. Originally created to co-ordinate large and complex projects, such as putting a man on the moon, the matrix has been called "the most constipated of organizational forms" by strategy professor Henry Mintzberg. It is often slow rather than agile and inwardly focused instead of customer-oriented. Matrix organizations often regard formal organizational structure as a Swiss army knife – a multi-purpose instrument. In reality it is just one of the many tools that we should find in a modern managerial toolbox.

Squeezing all the critical dimensions of the current business world into an organizational structure will only confuse people. On our journeys we came across one company that had decided to make a video of its organizational chart. It was so complex, yet flexible and fast-changing they claimed that it could not be drawn on a piece of paper. Yeah right! Structure should be about clarity not complexity – simplicity not stupidity.

To thrive in a world of competence complexity we must stop believing in developing by dividing. Uncontrolled division leads to corporate cancer. Then, management must stop having so much faith in structural revolutions and revisions and, instead, equip themselves and the rest of the corporation with a new and much more potent medicine against mediocracy. Great leaders know that, as pointed out by our academic colleagues Chris Bartlett and Sumantra Ghoshal, the matrix must be in the mind of the manager.[230]

The new knowledge landscape

You do not need a Ph.D in business administration or economics to figure out that knowledge has always been critical to the success of business firms. It is also true that not all knowledge is strategic. In fact, much is common knowledge, available to anyone. Operative knowledge may help an enterprise get along on a day-to-day basis, but only strategic knowledge can give a competitive advantage. As the Greek philosopher, Aeschylus put it; he who knows useful things rather than many things is wise. In essence, performance equals what you know, what you can teach and what the customers want minus what others know and can teach. Only on the margin can we create profits. All the rest is necessary but not sufficient to create a competitive edge.

What is different now is that the current changes are greatly boosting the economic value of knowledge. As we have seen, individuals and organizations with unique capabilities, have almost unlimited opportunities to leverage these assets across geographical borders.

In addition, the *density* – value/weight relationship – of most successful customer offerings is changing. The material costs of a typical GM car account for only 16% of total costs.[231] Much the same applies to the other automotive companies. One third of the cost of a new Boeing 777 is in software.[232]

Unconvinced? Take a look at the PC on your desk. In 1984, hardware accounted for 80% and software for 20% of the costs, today the situation is totally reversed.[233] Our economy is increasingly weightless. Think about what brainpower really weighs. One pound of Hermes scarf is yours for a mere $1,964.29, cigarettes cost $100 per pound, your typical management book $25-50 per pound, while hot rolled steel is down to 19 cents per pound.[234]

In other cases, bits are replacing atoms. Many customer offerings have already been dematerialized. The production and distribution costs per copy of *Encyclopedia Britannica* in the form of atoms in a book are in the area of $250. For bits on a CD-ROM we are talking about $1.50 (on the Net approaching zero).[235] In fact, in 1999 a dollar's worth of imports or exports weighed on average only 30% of what it did some 30 years ago.[236] Competencies are up; commodities are down.

One pound of Hermes scarf is yours for a mere $1,964.29.

Average price (adjusted for inflation)

	Movie ticket	Burger King Whopper
1980	$2.69	$1.40
2002	$5.81	$0.99
Change	Up 59%	Down 43%

Source: *Fast Company*, July, 2003: *New York Times*, MPAA.

So, if wealth is created with wisdom, how do we create organizations to maximize wisdom? How do we move from promises to performance?

First we must recognize that even in a world of competence-based competition the nature of an organization's knowledge base is not the only thing that matters. As important, or perhaps even more so, is the ability to effectively utilize these resources in the simultaneous pursuit of exploiting current competitive advantages and creating new ones. To thrive, companies need to design and put into practice an organizational architecture that enables them to unleash the full potential of their corporate creativity.

This architecture for innovation, in turn, is dependent on the characteristics of the firm's web of wisdom. To describe this web, the four partly inter-related dimensions of space, scope, skills and speed are useful. The latter two dimensions capture what is usually referred to as the intensity of knowledge, while the first two capture the 'extensity' of knowledge.[237] The actions taken by a company will shape its position in these dimensions and therefore have an impact on its current and future potential.[238]

In all of the dimensions corporation after corporation has undergone significant changes during the last few decades. The kinds of knowledge systems that modern firms need to utilize are simultaneously becoming more geographically dispersed and diverse, cutting across many areas. These networks are also marked by an increasing depth, requiring more and more expertise, while the economic durability – the best before date – of competencies is often decreasing.[239]

Dimension	Driver	Result
Space	Internationalization	Dispersion
Scope	Hyphenation	Diversity
Skill	Education	Depth
Speed	Competition	Durability

Rocking all over the world

The wave of deregulation, internationalization and global integration already affects most organizations – and not only traditional business firms.

The latest Americas Cup in sailing was won by land-locked Switzerland.[240] Russian country & western group Bering Strait recently received an American Grammy-nomination. In a 1999 English Premier League football game between Chelsea and Southampton, the Chelsea squad did not include a single Englishman. It featured players from Romania, Holland, Norway, Nigeria, Uruguay, Spain, Brazil, two French players, and two Italians. (Chelsea won 2-1.)

When it comes to the internationalization of economic activities, the facts are even more mind-boggling. In industry after industry competition has become truly transnational. Insights of various kinds are now more evenly spread across the globe. No wonder that Cisco's John Chambers claims that he'll put jobs anywhere in the world where there is the right infrastructure, an

A modern company resembles a Lego-model. You can take it apart and move the pieces around.

appropriately educated workforce and supportive government.[241] This makes sense, because a modern company resembles a Lego-model. You can take it apart and move the pieces around. Once, activities and units were welded together. Today, successful organizations use Velcro.

Multinational firms face a dispersion-challenge which has many elements. In an effort to use the relative strengths of different local units, some companies (especially ones which are acquisition-generated) have product mandates with global responsibilities scattered throughout

The average level of tariffs in the industrial countries is now less than 10% of the level before World War I.[242]

The total stock of foreign direct investment has increased by some 1,600% in the last 15 years. [244]

The cost of shipping a ton of goods has dropped by more than 70% in the last 40 years. [243]

The turnover of the world's foreign exchange market has risen 50-fold in the past 20 years and during the last 40 years, international trade has increased by some 1,500%. [245]

the world. For example, Sony Music is headquartered in the US, rather than Japan. The internationalization of business functions mostly started with sales and marketing and later included manufacturing. Now it often includes strategic research and development activities. As a consequence of this knowledge dispersion German BMW has one of its concept development centers in California. IBM has 30 software labs around the world.[246] Going abroad used to be a question of ensuring output. Now, it is also a game played to gain valuable input.

BMW also illustrates another important point. While knowledge is increasingly spread across the face of planet earth, it is also progressively more concentrated in a number of hot spots, which vary from industry to industry. Remember the economic impact of gays and bohemians on particular regions. Today five states – California, New Jersey, Texas, New York, and Illinois – account for 43% of all US patents. Indeed, ten cities in the US account for 33% of all US patents.[247] There are Hollywoods for a variety of things. In industries where more than one such cluster of competence exists across the face of earth, successful companies are forced to go international.

But it is not only internal resources which matter. In the age of outsourcing most modern corporations rely heavily on supplier networks that span the globe. In addition to its 30 software centers, IBM has approximately 12,000 suppliers throughout the world wired to its system.[248] Some of them are absolutely critical to the development of new products and services. Organizations combining knowledge from many different fields of expertise are also beginning to realize that sophisticated demand and supply are not always located in the same geographical spot. Companies have to send people across the planet to pick up the latest signals in fashion, design, manufacturing or whatever. Clothing retailer H&M's 80 Stockholm-based designers, for example, travel to Paris, Tokyo, New York and other major cities to check out both catwalks and sidewalks.[249]

Then, there are people. Stars are so extraordinary that you rarely find them in one location. Not all great actors or directors live in Hollywood. Companies refusing to settle for just the Pole Star have to watch the entire sky. And you cannot command the Lennon and McCartneys of the corporate world to move.

Putting two and two together

Scope is not simply a matter of geography. Creation of novelty often requires combining existing things in new ways – hy-phe-na-tion. Federal Express combines mail and flying. "The concept is interesting and well-formed, but in order to earn better than a 'C', the idea must be feasible," a Yale University management professor wrote in response to student Fred Smith's paper proposing reliable overnight delivery service. Smith went on to found FedEx. Amazon pools books with the Net. "Adver-games", which accompany value meals at hamburger restaurants, mix advertising with games.

It is increasingly difficult to separate products from services. Complexity can be mistaken for novelty. Often, the product is merely a container for a service delivery. In the automotive industry, developing and launching a new car requires mixing mechanics with electronics, manufacturing, design, PR, and finance skills. A single firm may of course not have to do all this on its own, but the process still needs to be managed.

We see more and more multi-technology products being born.

We also see more and more multi-technology products being born. Sony Ericsson's P800 mobile phone/camera/PDA/Internet device and Casio's Exilim digital camera, including an MP3 player, are just two examples of such hybrids.

The result is that the borders that once separated industries are becoming increasingly blurred. Just consider the merger of IT and biotech, or IT, media, entertainment and telecommunications.[250] Or, have you heard of "beauty snacks"? The European Commission has already given L'Oréal and Nestlé clearance to market food products designed to improve the appearance of hair, nails and skin.[251]

The way that we actually work is also affected. In product development, being merely technology or customer-driven no longer works. Such push and pull processes are now challenged by genuinely cross-functional efforts in which people from many different parts of the company co-operate. Stories of parallel "rugby" innovation projects and concurrent engineering, especially in Japan, are widespread.[252]

This development also encompasses the people possessing the skills. In Silicon Valley companies, for example, traditional corporate minority groups, such as women and immigrants, are dramatically over-represented compared to traditional US firms. Welcome to Rainbow Inc. The development of new technologies also forces companies to recruit more young people. But there is nothing particularly mysterious about this. It is not a new phenomenon. The average age of the scientists involved in the Manhattan project to develop the first atomic bomb was just 25 years.[253] The young have always been the unacknowledged innovators.

The brain bomb explodes

Competence development adds up. Never before has so much knowledge existed. One issue of the *Herald Tribune* contains more info than someone in the Middle Ages would have been exposed to in a lifetime.[254] And the last few decades mark a genuine explosion in the growth of competences. The US Patent & Trademark Office hands out 195% more patents than it did a mere two decades ago.[255] Since the early 1960s, the number of MBAs graduating annually in the US alone has increased by 1,500%.[256] Even in formerly communist Hungary there are 14 different MBA programs.[257] In addition, spending on executive education is skyrocketing as learning has become life-long.

It is also notable that valuable insights are no longer as concentrated with a few people at the top. Knowledge workers can be found at every level of the modern firm. At FedEx, front-line employees and second-level managers must attend 10 to 11 weeks of mandatory training in the first year.[258] The old saying that the boss no longer always knows best is truer than ever. Now we can all believe it and say it without facing the risk of getting fired. In fact, intelligent leaders admit their ignorance. "I am completely ignorant about three-quarters of the stuff that goes on. And my colleagues on the senior management team? They are 98% ignorant," Michael Gillman, senior VP of research at Biogen, told *Fast Company*.[259] He is not alone..

Beating the best before date

Knowledge has limited shelf life. Therefore, continuous innovation, both revolutionary and evolutionary, is a necessity – possibly an evil one – but still a fact of (business) life. The innovation – imitation – commoditization cycle is picking up speed. As competition gets tougher, knowledge becomes perishable.

Bill Joy, chief scientist at Sun Microsystems, estimates that as much as 20% of the company's technical knowledge becomes commercially useless each year.[260] Companies must cut development time and increase the frequency of new product introductions. They just cannot wait. Organizations are forced to accelerate. Research indicates that the time it takes competitors to imitate has steadily shortened over the last 100 years.[261] Steve Mariucci, former head coach of the American football team San Francisco 49-ers, takes things to the extreme. "I never wear a watch", he says "because I always know it is now, and now is when you should do it".[262] We know what he means.

There's more. It is not only product life cycles that are shortening. The pressure to continuously develop new ways of thinking and working, allowing firms to move faster into the future, is also reaching boiling point. By use of new software allowing it to run tests directly on the computer, Ford Motor Company has cut its average product development cycle from 55 to 32 months. Now, the company is pushing

Organizations are forced to accelerate.

for 24.[263] Spanish clothing retailer Zara takes a fashion idea from the drawing board to the store shelf in 10-15 days.[264] The third largest cement company in the world, Mexican Cemex, has invested some $200 million in a customer information system that allows it to meet a 20-minute delivery window with 98% accuracy. The result is a 35% profit margin compared to an industry average of 21%.[265] Time is worth more money than ever.

The Lego principles

The dominant firm of the 20th century subscribed to the hierarchical organizational model. But while the balance sheet is being wheeled into the ward for long-term patients, the bureaucratic super-model is now on its way to the morgue. This way of organizing builds on a number of important assumptions and principles that are completely at odds with the changes that many corporations are experiencing.

Hierarchical design assumes that competitive advantages are given, eternal and kept within the company. In the world of stability, predictability and linear change, the challenge is one of finding an organizational solution that efficiently exploits this timeless recipe. The theory goes that by building complicated structures, we simplify jobs. When people work on the same and narrowly defined task, learning by doing (or more correctly repeating) results in increased efficiency.[266] Since the recipe never changes, there is no need for people and units to interact once you have found the ultimate solution – the best way in which to divide labor.

The current challenge is to design an architecture based on the principle of recomposition rather than decomposition.

Here's the problem. For how many companies is the creation of new products and services optional? Name five firms currently surviving and thriving as Lone Rangers – without partners or allies? We can't think of any. We all need friends. To give just one example, the number of strategic alliances between biotech and large pharmaceutical companies has increased by 80% in the last five years.[267]

Today, new customer offerings are often the result of companies combining, and re-combining, knowledge across geographical distances, organizational units, technological areas and possibly also across corporate borders – at the speed of light. Imagine this. A recent Philips DVD recorder development team spanned three operating divisions: semiconductors, optical systems, and consumer electronics. On top of that, underlying technological collaboration was carried out with five rivals, including Sony, Ricoh, and Yamaha.[268] If you tried superimposing a neat hierarchical pyramid on teams like that you'd quickly fail.

The message is to forget hierarchy and develop a competitive web of wisdom. And then, accelerate the knowing-doing circle by developing a new organizational solution that utilizes creativity to the max. As our late colleague, Professor Gunnar Hedlund put it, the current challenge is to design an architecture based on the principle of recomposition rather than decomposition – opening up the door of the bureaucracy to let the market come inside.[269] Not only can you dismantle a Lego model, but you can also put the pieces back together again in a myriad of different ways, depending on what you want to create.[270] Anything goes.

Another response to the challenges facing modern firms is to buy more stuff from someone else somewhere else rather than building it on your own. In doing so, internal organizational difficulties certainly decrease – as a firm we can remain local, focused on only one technology, etc. Problems are exported, but they won't disappear. It's a bit like having a drinking problem – by having another bottle you export your worries from one day to another. But just as alcoholics eventually need to deal with things, outsourcing corporations have to coordinate innovation and change at the network level.

In days when the play-it-safe virus is spreading like a forest fire around the world, most companies stuck in the hierarchical logic need to get a vaccination against stability and stagnation, repetition and reproduction. The fact that the bubble burst should not be taken as an indication that bureaucracy is and should be back. Building Innovation Inc. boils down to taking five such shots. Each injection on its own won't do the trick. It's the combined effect of the measures that ensures renewal and competitiveness. When correctly implemented and executed, the Lego principles are mutually supportive and self-reinforcing. The principles can also be applied at the level of an industrial network, a geographical cluster or even an entire region. This is organizational design the Lego way.

Think about Linux, the operating system flexible enough to run everything from a cell phone to a supercomputer and which is now

challenging no less a behemoth than Microsoft. Linux was pioneered by the young Finnish programmer Linus Thorvalds who wrote it as a cut-down version of Unix for the PC in 1991 and then put it on the Web. It managed to draw in talented people by having a strong story centered on the wicked witch of the north called Bill Gates. Everyone could participate in the development. Perspective was secured since the Net does not care about age, gender or color. A ragtag band of volunteer programmers from around the world built it. Linux is the result of a pure meritocracy. The purpose was provided by a powerful knowledge vision focused on open-source programming. Processes were open to anyone – total transparency. Intelligence was distributed. The Internet provided and still provides the info-structure necessary. Persistence was based on not having traditional economic goals. In fact, the point was never to make money from it. Linux is now revolutionizing the way in which software is made. The message is simple. Let go of hierarchy. Lego works.

Not even Innovation Inc. is a Swiss Army knife type of organizational solution.

Dead or alive

Adherence to the Lego principles comes with a caveat. Not even Innovation Inc. is a Swiss Army knife type of organizational solution. It isn't fit to handle any type of situation. It is not for everyone. Short term, for local companies in industries with limited demands for scope, skills and speed, it could be devastating to move beyond bureaucracy.[271] We haven't gone karaoke crazy. This comes with two major qualifications.

In industries that have not encountered significant changes in time, space and mass, hierarchical companies may still out-perform Innovation Inc.. Hierarchy works great under conditions of stability and predictability. No doubt about that. But – and it is a sizeable but – for these organizations, there is a clear risk that eventually an insider or (more likely) a new entrant will change the rules of the game by successfully launching revolutionary strategies. This new recipe will result in successful companies needing a more complex mix of competencies and a different organizational architecture. IKEA did it to furniture. Toyota did it to cars. Southwest did it to airlines.

The very fact that companies use traditional organizational solutions could also inhibit them from launching such revolutionary strategies. The brain-based bureaucracy is an oxymoron on a par with great airplane food.

Undoubtedly, the need to transform both the nature of the knowledge system and the organizational design constitutes a substantial challenge for any leader. It may be wise then to remember the words of Peter Drucker: "One cannot manage change. One can only be ahead of it."[272] Companies can and must invest in shaping their own future.

But departing from the norm means that you've got to have guts. Before you can be creative you must be courageous. "Creativity is the destination, but courage is the journey," says creativity expert Joey Reiman.[273] And we want to emphasize that imagination and innovation are not anarchic. Multi-talented artist Andy Warhol once said: "My paintings never turn out the way I expect them, but I am never surprised."

Innovation Inc. has deadlines on dreams. It is a playground with principles directed by deviants with discipline.

Also be aware of the fact that postponing the creation of a modern web of wisdom and a hypermodern organizational design until you are forced to change only dramatically increases the likelihood of becoming rather than making history. The harsh reality is that either an organization creates the company that will put it out of business, or someone else will. When old institutions crumble: set the new rules, or be ruled out.

What we do know from past research is that successful companies tend to change before they have to. We also know that the last time we went through a major organizational revolution, some 100 years ago, most companies did not change. They failed to adapt and died. No one and no organization is immune to the challenges of our times. Perhaps the Sioux Indians got it right: "When you discover you are riding a dead horse, the best strategy is to dismount."

INNOVATION INC.

Organizations that maximize competencies attract great people to develop a perspective that thrives on diversity. But even deviants need to know who they are, where they are going and be given the incentives to get there. Innovation Inc. utilizes the power of a shared purpose. Creation is not a single voice in the darkness, but a conversation, a process of dialog and discovery. Beyond the quick fix lies continuous commitment to doing things differently. Experimentation requires persistence as much as imagination.

Talent is strange

Innovative organizations with complex webs of wisdom don't need more old style bosses. Instead, they must focus their efforts on drawing in enough talented individuals to ensure renewal. Getting great people on board and then profiting from their skills depends on:

- having a *tale* to tell;
- ensuring talent *transfusion* by increasing individualization;
- *teaming* up competents with complementary characters.

When the scarcest resource is no longer investment but imagination, attracting human capital becomes more important than allocating financial capital. Proper management of the financial function is merely necessary but not sufficient for the creation and protection of a continuous competitive edge.

Competition for good people is truly generic and truly international. Consider logistics giant Federal Express. The company faces tough competition from the likes of DHL and UPS, but it also competes with temp agency Manpower and financial behemoth American Express.[274] Just like FedEx both these companies have half of their employees working on IT-related issues. Whether organizations like it or not, when it comes to the talent market, they are in direct competition with Microsoft of the

US, Nokia of Finland, Porsche of Germany, and Sony of Japan, as well as with biographical tribes like Greenpeace or Amnesty International. They are battling with some of the world's most powerful brands.

The development of increasing bargaining power for women and men with unique skills has not passed business by. When you ask, "What is your company's greatest asset?" managers usually answer: "Our people". They couldn't be more wrong – and we're not thinking about the Dilbert cartoon where people came in ninth, right behind paper clips. Unless you are a football team like Glasgow Celtic or Ajax Amsterdam, or possibly a record company, human capital must be regarded as a liability. Otherwise, companies are practicing a form of intellectual slavery. Organizations do not, can not and should not own their people. Employees are free to stand up and walk out of the office any minute of any day of the week.

Companies simply borrow knowledge from us, very much in the same way as we borrow money from a bank. When there is a loan, there is also interest to be paid. In this case, the interest is called a salary. And if you borrow from the best – people with the hardest currency – you'd better be prepared to accept that these interest rates are on the rise.

In all likelihood, human beings are your organization's greatest liability, but their capabilities also constitute the number one opportunity for the future. To thrive, we must understand that it is the gifted who select organizations – UN, IBM or REM – rather than vice versa. Forget about organization man. Enter opportunistic man and woman.

Tall stories

All corporations need to ask themselves: do we have a (true) story that will seduce stars? Talent and tales go together like love and marriage.

Attraction is emotional and communicative shorthand. And since we are human, first impressions matter – 79% of all college students in the US say that even something as "trivial" as the quality of a potential employer's web site is important when deciding to apply or not.[275]

Everyone who has ever dealt with a company tells their own story.

Stories translate information into emotion.

Potential employees communicate with present employees. The guy who was fired last week won't keep his mouth shut. Customers interact as well. And stories are sticky, for better or for worse. Stories – narratives – are how we remember things. Stories translate information into emotion. Most lists and bullet points are forgotten as we hear or see them.

Markets are basically nothing but conversations. It's all about information exchange. With the advent of modern communications technologies these are increasingly universal conversations. Stories will spread locally and internationally whether we like it or not. Companies can either try to prevent the inevitable from happening or choose to contribute to the conversations. It should come as no surprise that public relations has been one of the fastest growing industries. Corporations should even provide platforms and arenas for discussions – speaker's nets rather than speaker's corners. Doing so, not only enables them to better exercise at least some control over the conversations, but also opens up the possibility of using the information as a valuable input for improvements. Open and transparent communication can foster open and transparent thinking.

So, who is going to manage the story – *Fortune*, the *FT*, Greenpeace – or you?

The trouble, of course, is that messages may not actually be true. We all tell tales. Indeed, the stories being told about regions, organizations, individuals, products and perhaps even racehorses are almost certainly based on completely incomplete information. In many cases they are probably utterly wrong. But this time that is our problem. So, who is going to manage the story – *Fortune*, the *FT*, Greenpeace – or you? Who is willing and capable of taking on the role and responsibilities of the CSO – Chief Storytelling Officer? What's the theme of the story? What is your story? You need something persuasive, something sexy and attractive. Without a story with a fantastic theme you will have a hard time attracting fantastic people.

An additional advantage of having a strong story is that it will attract those (opportunistic) individuals wanting to piggy-back on the organization's reputation to build their own brand called Me, Myself and I.

McKinsey & Company is a great example. Many people, rightly or wrongly, regard it as the most prestigious management-consulting firm in the world. It can charge among the highest fees in its industry, not only for its senior consultants but also for the new recruits. Freshly baked MBAs know that spending a couple of years with McKinsey will not only enable them to learn the tricks of the trade. The simple fact that they were once recruited by this company and can put that in their résumés will also greatly enhance their chances of later landing a top job somewhere else. Like livestock, they are branded for life. Accordingly, McKinsey alumni, headed by IBM's former CEO Lou Gerstner, are spreading like a rash through the business community. The McKinsey story – based on buttoned-down professionalism – is perpetuated by the company's relentless historical success.

Transfusing talent

We all know that human beings are not bulk goods. In the age of the individual we all differ – especially the youthful Generation I. This young tribe is international, informed, informal, impatient, intense and above all extremely individualistic. And since, from a demographic point of view, it is clear that most post-industrialized countries will soon experience a white-haired revolution, more and more companies will have to become adept at dealing with this pool of young me-me-me men and women. Refuse to deal with such talented people and you will end up with an idiocracy.

Talent thrives on flexibility. Individualization implies and demands flexibility. At the innovative Brazilian company Semco, for instance, there are 11 different ways to get paid – ranging from a fixed salary to stock options, royalties and bonus schemes, all of which can be combined in various ways.[276] As an employee, you can take your pick.

Contracts are becoming personal – in business and elsewhere. Some people even seem to use financial instruments like warranties, securities and options when they get married. There is more to come, in any walk of life. The only way senior executives can really understand what people want is by spending time with them. "We run the company so that 300,000 people feel the chairman might enter their world at any time," says Jeffrey Immelt, chairman and CEO of GE. "I spend roughly 40% of my time on people issues; so do our other top leaders."[277]

For those selling ideas, it's also increasingly irrelevant to talk about salaries for hours or days spent. Remember that talent is packaged in units

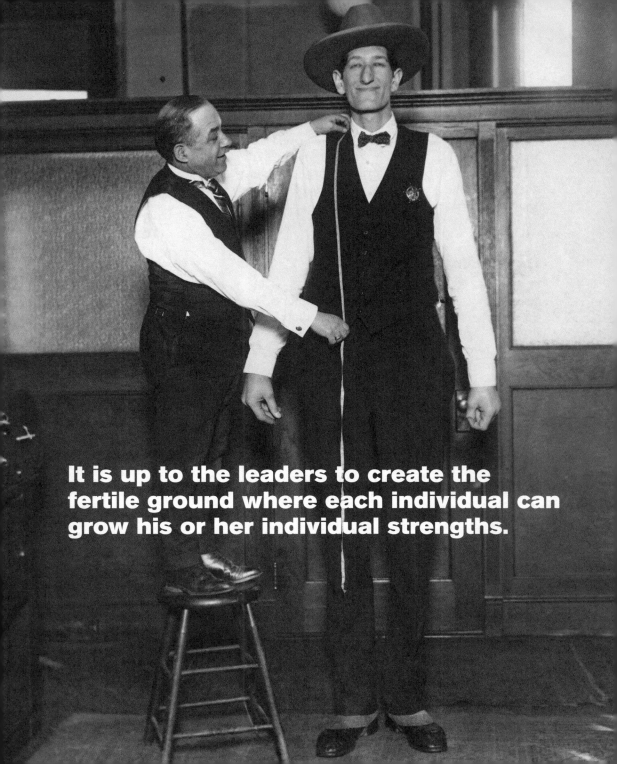

It is up to the leaders to create the fertile ground where each individual can grow his or her individual strengths.

of time. When the difference between the average and the awesomely great is a factor of 1:100 or even 1:1000, organizations will have to pay a fee for work done.[278] Input is nothing – output is everything. In fact, studies indicate that high-performing companies are two to four times more likely to pay what it takes not to lose top-talent.[279] The growing difference between the best and the rest is simply a fact of life.

Shining stars won't settle for mediocrity. It used to be XM (extra medium). Now it must be XMe. Companies have been segmenting customers for years if not decades. Today, they must segment employees. Conformity is the jailer of freedom and the enemy of growth, as John F. Kennedy put it. Curiosity over conformity. We want voice and choice.

Truly recognizing the power of the individual is also a question of letting people do what they are really good at. Focus is everything. Yet, across the world only 20% of all employees working in large organizations feel that their strengths are in play every day. An even greater irony is that the longer people have worked at a place the less likely they are to agree with this statement.[280] Most contemporary organizations are built on two flawed assumptions about people claim Marcus Buckingham and Donald O. Clifton, authors of *Now, Discover Your Strengths*:[281]

1 We can all learn to be competent in almost anything.
2 The greatest room for growth is in the areas of our
  greatest weaknesses.

"People don't change that much," continue Buckingham and Clifton. "Don't waste time trying to put in what was left out. Try to draw out what was left in. That is hard enough."[282]

Tiger Woods is a great golfer but, strangely, he usually hits lousy bunker-shots. How has he dealt with the problem? Living in a bunker? No! By perfecting and refining his main strength, the swing. If it works like a clock, he never has to pay the bunkers a visit.[283] It is up to leaders anywhere and everywhere inside Innovation Inc. to create the kind of fertile ground where each individual can grow his or her individual strengths. Great leaders capitalize on differences.

Personalization also implies being sensitive to cultural differences. Unfortunately, the typical global corporation is still pretty parochial. Part of the reason for this is that they are often a lot less global than you might think. Research by Karl Moore and Alan Rugman found that US multinationals tend to be regional rather than global. Of the US's 25 largest multinational enterprises 22 have more than 50% of their sales in North America. Wal-Mart clocks up 94.1% of its sales in the North American Free Trade Area. General Motors reaches 81%.[284]

Managers need to remember that most people do not leave companies – they leave managers.

Little wonder that cultural sensitivity is not often associated with corporate giants. Far too often foreigners or immigrants are simply regarded as strange. They are marginalized and so, too, are their skills.[285]

Managers need to remember that most people do not leave companies – they leave managers.[286] People love or loathe other individuals – not institutions. Given this, it is absolutely critical to hook up new hires with the best leaders. Conclusion? Individualize or idiocratize!

Teaming up by splitting up

In a karaoke economy inhabited by the merited and the merely mediocre, organizations have to consider how they can build a workplace that harbors both groups. But can you really design such a place? In the sports world it seems you can. Baseball player Derek Jeter is the highest paid New York Yankee player. His team won four World Series between 1996 and 2000 and Jeter earns some $12.6 million per year. The lowest paid player, D'Angelo Jimenez, gets a paltry $200,000.[287]

But how should business manage such differentials? Quite often separating the two groups is the preferred solution. Historically this involved geographical division. Thinkers were recruited at home. Simple, routine jobs were handled in foreign subsidiaries where low-cost labor was available. While this method is still practiced, although it is difficult when strategic knowledge can be found at more than one location, many firms now utilize the power of markets – institutional separation. They buy. Companies use temporary workers employed by someone else, usually people who do routine work. Having temps do such work makes the company more flexible and less vulnerable to fluctuations in demand. Temps lower fixed costs. Temps are variable. But we're not only talking about low-skilled, low-cost blue-collar work. Ernst & Young, for example, already uses accountants in India and the Philippines.[288]

Manpower is a world leader in the staffing industry. In 2001, the company had 400,000 customers worldwide, including almost all of the Fortune 500 companies. With 3,900 offices around the globe, the firm had 22,400 staff employees and 1.9 million temporary workers supplying 780 million hours of work.[289] Companies such as Manpower, with international reach, allow other organizations to practice separation across both national and corporate borders.

In fact, most modern companies need to take a look at activity after activity, process after process, unit after unit, and employee after employee to make decisions about how to position themselves in the two dimensions of geographical and institutional belonging. They need to consider cheaper and better alternatives not necessarily because they like to, but because the harsh reality of global competition forces them to do so.

Yet, all leading organizations need peak-performance not only from the stars, but also from those who work beside the VIPs. And the identity of stars depends on the situation. The work of a custodian or janitor often makes more of a direct impression on customers or people visiting the headquarters of a company than the daily efforts of the CEO. All employees face moments of truth. The real challenge says Marcus Buckingham, is to define excellence in each and every role and then pay on it, award titles on it, distribute prestige on it, and make it a genuine career choice.[290] Human beings are the only irreducible complexity in every company, and anyone who fights human nature will lose, adds Buckingham.

Kissing frogs

Variation is built into modern webs of wisdom – whether it be technical, cultural or another form. Diversity can be constructive or destructive – melting pot or powder keg – but it is always disruptive. For firms doing business in a non-linear karaoke world the disruptive nature of diversity is a source of many opportunities. Productivity helps organizations to survive. Disruptivity enables them to thrive. It opens organizations up so they can go down the road less traveled, the autostrada of originality and difference.

Progressive leaders, on the other hand, are not afraid to kiss frogs.

There is a lot of lip service paid to diversity. The talent pool of the company may be diverse, but the dominant group within the firm – the in crowd – could still be very homogeneous. We have seen many examples of organizations recruiting deviants and outsiders just to place them in corporate quarantine or ship them off to a Siberian subsidiary. Progressive leaders, on the other hand, are not afraid to kiss frogs. They know that one of them could be a prince or princess in disguise.

Innovative companies value the variety of voices. "It's interesting that the strategy everyone is copying came from an industry outsider," says Andy Grove of Lou Gerstner, former CEO and turnaround champion of IBM.[291] Big Blue used to be a white Anglo-Saxon protestant (WASP) bastion, rarely celebrated for its diversity of people or ideas. In January 1996, IBM had only 185 women executives. By December 1999, the number had almost tripled to 508.[292] Things can and do change.

To gain the perspective so critical to innovation, companies need to take on a big combo. They must:

- ensure the *inclusion and participation* of deviants in the strategic decision-making process;
- manage the *decentralization* of power – moving decisions closer to where competence resides.

It's a boy-girl thing

American academic and consultant Richard Pascale argues that survival in nature is dependent on a sufficient degree of mutation and variation. You never know in advance exactly which set of genes will be most likely to survive. When the world was hit by the bubonic plague – the Black Death – some didn't die. No one really knew why, but variation enabled certain people to live on.

Variety in turn is ensured by sexual reproduction. You mix two beings into a new and fundamentally different one. The alternative, parthenogenesis (cloning) does not result in any mutation or variety at all. We know this. Variation works. Still, at many companies the clones continue to be in charge – Star Wars II reincarnated – or, as Pascale colorfully calls them, "the enemies of sex".[293]

One of the main objectives of any corporation must be to create novelty. In order to move from words to action, we must let the diversity of organizational members be reflected in top management teams. Academic research is unusually clear in indicating that zero diversity kills creativity. Sameness breeds more of the same and yet more.

One of the main objectives of any corporation must be to create novelty.

The trouble is that sameness rules among senior executives in the typical organization. Take a look at a picture of an average board of directors in Europe or North America and you become bored of directors. So many uniform white men dressed in dark business uniforms, so many WASPs you could start a hive. In most other parts of the world, the only thing that is different is the color of the guys, suits and ties.

Some time ago, one of us did a presentation with a well-known elderly European industrialist. When checking in together at the venue, he told a story about how his wife had embroidered his name in the back of his trench coat. She had finally tired of him coming back home from the office or conference center with someone else's trench coat. Since they all looked the same, the only way to tell them apart was to put his name in it – just like at any daycare center.

Successful management
teams must reflect
the complexity of the
karaoke world.

We are not suggesting that all companies necessarily need to go over the top. They don't need to exclusively hire oddballs, nerds and people with beards that are so dirty and scruffy that it's difficult to tell the front of their face from the back of their face.

In fact, this is not at all what we are talking about. We are not thinking about having people dress up as someone else. No theater, make-up, nor plastic surgery. Transparency will take care of all imposters. We are merely suggesting that successful management teams must reflect the complexity of the karaoke world – its competents and customers. Remember that on the bottom of river mainstream we find mediocrity.

Visiting the top 10 list of what books people working at certain companies and within specific industries buy on Amazon.com reveals another dirty little secret. While most people pay obligatory lip service to the importance of perspective, the scary truth is that a majority of people at most companies within a particular industry tend to read exactly the same books. Transparency is revealing. At the typical engineering company, books about Jack Welch, Six Sigma and business process re-engineering seem to be in vogue. At investment banks analysts hoping to beat the index tend to read the same books with the same models. While we are certainly competing on recipes, using the same recipe as all the others will not do. Karaoke copycats look alike – read alike – think alike. And as General George Patton put it: "If everyone is thinking alike, then someone isn't thinking."

The disappointing reality is that most organizations disdain diversity – especially at the top. The implications of most recent studies on careers suggest that if you really want to make it, there is only one (almost) safe bet: Be born as a white male and get a partner who stays at home to take care of the kids (alternatively, be gay but for God's sake don't tell anyone at work).[294]

Some time soon the penny must drop and things really will change. Nowhere is this clearer than in the treatment of women within corporations. "Women in the United States have created 9 million businesses and 27 million jobs, but people refuse to speak to us as economic engines, they see us only as consumers," says Nell Merling, founder and president of Strategy Communication Action.[295]

Why do companies need more female executives? In most other walks of life, she is already in charge. Consider the following figures for percentages of spending decided by women: family groceries 80%, family travel 80%, family medical 70%, family automobile 55%, family insurance 55% and so on.[296] Compare these stats with the numbers of women executives. Unfortunately, many contemporary companies do not mirror the complexity of the real world, but rather the stupidity of single-mindedness. Perhaps as a consequence, in 1999, more American women worked for women-owned businesses than for Fortune 500 companies – the largest companies in that country.[297] One would have hoped that we had come further from the reality of 1914 when a Berlin professor allegedly claimed that, "Brain work will cause women to go bald."

Individualization and competence-based competition imply the fall of the homo organization and the rise of hetero corporations. Otherwise groupthink, constipation and decline are the inevitable results. No individualization = no innovation. No innovation = no tomorrow. Women of the world unite.

Thrills at the fringe

Having a perspective on things also means relying more on the periphery – geographically and organizationally. To get a good viewpoint corporations have to be on the edge. The fringe really is the thing. Rapid decisions need to be taken closely to where critical, in-depth knowledge resides. The time from detection to solution and execution must be reduced. In a disruptive world, self-renewal is dependent on anticipation rather than prediction.

To enhance the anticipatory capabilities companies need early warning systems. Skilled people are like radar-screens. Power needs to be located where the action is. As former US Vice President Al Gore put it, most organizations encounter change at their edges, not at their centers.[302] Similarly, Martin Sorrell, CEO of the ad-agency WPP Group, says: "The people at the so-called bottom of the organization know more about what's going on than the people at the top. The people in the trenches are the ones in the best position to make critical decisions. It is up to leaders to give those people the freedom and resources that they need."[303] This is real grassroots-leadership.

Read our lips: Centralized planning no longer works. A more decentralized and delayered approach is required. IBM once had 27 layers from top to bottom. At latest count the maximum number of levels was seven.[304]

Academic Karl Weick has been studying high-reliability organizations (HROs) – firefighters, nuclear plants – for years. This is what he has to say about organizations that are always at risk but rarely make a mess of things: "Managers at these organizations keep their attention focused on the front line... HROs also defer to expertise, and they refuse to simplify reality... Leaders must complicate themselves in order to keep their organization in touch with the realities of the business

In the United States some 41% of all middle managers are female, whereas the equivalent numbers in the UK, Europe, and Japan happen to be 29%, 18%, and merely 6%, respectively.[298]

In the US only 4% of all top managers are female, and in Great Britain, Europe, and Japan the equivalent numbers are 3%, 2%, and less than 1%, respectively.[299]

A mere 2% of the executive directors in FTSE 350 companies are female. Just four of those companies have a female chief executive and only 6% of the non-executive directors are women.[300]

A shameful 6% of CEOs slots in Internet companies financed by venture capitalists were held by women.[301]

world."[305] Weick's advice is plainly put: simplify the organization and complicate yourself.

Coming up with one great idea requires that you to have thousands of workers thinking and dreaming. Sensing and making sense can and should no longer be the preserve of a few managers at headquarters. "It does not make sense to hire smart people and then tell them what to do. We hired smart people so that they could tell us what to do," says Apple's Steve Jobs.[306]

At the same time, corporations must continuously boost the brains at the borders. Decentralization without education is just foolish. Education without decentralization is equally ridiculous. Information without action is just overhead, one executive told us. And boosting overhead certainly does not create profits.

Pass the map

In the old world, control and co-ordination were based on legal authority and formalization. No more. The situation is that experts in various fields need to know about the general direction from those in charge before things change. These specialists will then often control the skills necessary to come up with the answers required. Whether they like it or not, leaders must rely increasingly on such talented individuals.

The Bronett Brothers who head Cirkus Scott admit that this isn't straightforward: "Leading a group of individualists is not always that easy, especially not if some of them are animals."[307] When companies encounter the simultaneous impact of internationalization, hyphenation, education and increasing competition they must practice something more sophisticated than management by rules and regulations. Imposed standardization only results in an inability to innovate across borders – whether these are geographical, organizational or technological. Indeed, this may be one of the reasons why a company such as McDonald's is in trouble. Any lack of variety across space leads to limited diversity and disruption and, as a result, minimal innovation.

The time from
detection to solution
and execution
must be reduced.

Adhering to the Lego principle means developing a strong purpose providing direction. The idea is not new. "He whose ranks are united in purpose will be victorious," wrote the father of strategic thinking Sun Tzu. But it is more relevant than ever. Creative corporations need;

- a shared *idea;*
- a clear *identity;*
- and *incentives* that shape behavior.

Some 35 years ago during the Vietnam war the Vietcong had all three, the US forces none. These few mutual principles secure co-ordination while still allowing for flexibility.

The big idea

All organizations need a shared idea of why they exist, who they are, and where they want to go, but those with complex webs of wisdom even more so. People with different cultural and organizational backgrounds, with different skills and mindsets, need a shared idea that channels and focuses the disruptive forces of the system. Even talented individuals need a light that guides their search for the unknown and the unseen.

A vision is truly the perfume of the mind.

The result? Companies must develop principles that inspire and motivate people – ideas that excite and energize the work place. Nokia is there to "connect people". Simple but stirring. A vision, as business writer Harriet Rubin puts it, is truly the perfume of the mind.[308] Smell the difference.

Ronald Reagan knew the tricks of this trade. According to former presidential advisor David Gergen, Reagan "recognized that to stir people, you must give voice to their own deep desires, inspiring them to believe they can climb mountains they always thought were too high".[309]

In a karaoke world leaders must provide vision to everyone in the organization. They must tailor their vision so it strikes a chord with talented high achievers. They must connect with people in disparate cultures and nations. They must connect inside and outside the organization. Vision is power. "Man is what he believes," claimed Russian author Anton Chekhov.

Even the biggest of ideas need to be communicated and then communicated again and again. Reimer Thedens, Chairman and CEO of OgilvyOne Worldwide, tells a story of how the Christian churches in Singapore came to them saying: "God has an image problem. Can you help?"[310] Among other things, Reimer and his team used SMS messages that could be targeted to specific people and certain points in time. Some of these messages read:

- "Thank ME, it's Friday!" GOD
- "Even I rested on the 7th day" GOD
- "Want to come to my house today?" GOD

It is critical to communicate ideas persuasively, simply and repeatedly. Great companies, great leaders and great entrepreneurs delight in simplicity. They focus minds on the things that matter through a simple, persuasive vision. IBM, for instance, has built a strong knowledge vision around "e-business", later expanding the concept to "e-business on demand" – delivering technology like a utility. "It was about appealing to the pride of 320,000 people to go to the next level," says CEO Sam Palmisano.[311]

Have you ever heard of DNS? Probably not. It stands for Digital Nervous System. This was Microsoft's attempt to dominate the e-business territory. The company ran ads featuring DNS. Mr. Gates even wrote a book about DNS. The problem for Bill and the rest of the people at Microsoft was that e-business turned out to be a much more powerful idea.

Keeping it simple is harder than it seems. It is easy to become distracted, to be taken in, to become carried away. Keeping faith with straightforward practices and principles is the preserve of the chosen few. Think of Warren Buffett and remember that simple doesn't have to mean simplistic. The master investor was unimpressed by the dot-com boom. He seemed out of step with the times. But he was right. Buffett has stayed resolutely faithful to his deceptively simple investment theories for decades. It works so why elaborate. Successful leaders often explain what they do with persuasive simplicity. Short is sweet.

Hire attitude

People are not only individualists. They also want to belong. Much research on culture treats individualism and collectivism as two end-points on a continuum.[312] Yet, the firm of the karaoke future is neither individualistic nor collectivistic. It must be both. You + union = *younion*. Egos together; an individualized community; strong personalities kept together by a shared purpose.

Firms with a future will use this fact to their advantage. To prevent Cacophony Inc. from becoming Chaos Inc., they will build an organizational community or tribe where people share a common identity. "Firms will not manage the careers of our employees, they will provide opportunities to enable the employee to develop identity and adaptability and thus be in charge or his/her own career," say the authors of *the New Protean Career Contract*.[313] When people have little time for anything outside work, it should come as no surprise that they bring religion and quasi-religious beliefs to work. This development is merely the logical extension of what we usually call corporate culture. The future will see an increasing focus on using vision, storytelling and every other tool at the leader's disposal to build organizational tribes.

The easiest way to get people to share your values is to hire those who

already do. So we expect to see more and more organizations recruiting people with the right attitude and then training them in skills. We have always fired people for having the wrong attitude – "John was a great programmer – too bad he liked to walk the corridors in a leopard skin leotard". Nothing strange about this fact. Great leaders have many different characteristics, but they are usually sacked only for the absence of two: character and judgment.[314] It is time to accept the full practical consequences – before things get out of hand.

Look at organizations with strong cultures such as Hell's Angels, Virgin, the Manchester United supporter's club, or Nike. Imagine Hell's

Imagine hiring them for skills and then training them for attitude.

Angels hiring for skills and then training them for attitude. These organizations simply do not believe in the idea of bringing in people with the right skills and then re-programming their value systems. Values first.

Why? Well, the half-life of knowledge is coming down so fast that if you recruit someone with relevant knowledge today, three months down the road these skills may be obsolete. Bill Joy at Sun is not the only one working at a company where the shelf life of competencies is decreasing.

Another element is that it is easier to change our skills than our basic values – pretty obvious to anyone who has ever tried to live with

Values are magnetic. Values attract.

someone else. This also implies that from the point of view of building and then keeping a tribe together, there are no better or worse sets of values. Values are just different – an organization for each individual and an individual for each organization.

The great thing is that if you get enough like-minded (not single-minded) people on board, processes tend to become self-reinforcing. "People here like to invent, and as a result other people who like to invent are attracted here," says Jeff Bezos of Amazon.[315] Values are magnetic. Values attract.

A strong identity also helps to retain good people. For most McKinsey consultants, with a few notable exceptions such as management guru Tom Peters, even if you are among the best of the best, leaving the company would not necessarily enable you to charge higher fees as a free agent. Ex-consultants would have to do business without the legitimacy of the McKinsey brand stamped on their forehead (and invoices). Brands are uncertainty reducers. And, in the consulting business (as in most other industries) customers are often willing to pay a hefty premium for what is perceived as the best corporate comforter around. Few executives ever got fired for hiring McKinsey.

But hiring people for attitude also means that you have to articulate your values. Successful Italian grocery chain Unes has four such core corporate values:[316]

- Love your customers and fellow workers.
- Have a positive approach to the future.
- Always think about new ideas.
- Tolerate frustration.

If all this is critical to the atmosphere and competitiveness of the company, how do you translate these values into the actual recruitment of people? We promise you this, CVs and traditional résumés will tell you very little. Multiple choice questions will tell you even less.

The downside of all this is that clans easily evolve into cults. What may begin as an effort to select people based on a handful of attitudes, norms and values, can easily turn into processes focused on selecting out individuals. Instead of having one lowest common denominator, new characteristics and standards are continuously added. The end result is that you are left with an extremely homogeneous group that looks down on or even despises outsiders. Cults exclude people, obey heroes, become dogmatic and develop a crocodile syndrome – no ears but a really big mouth. From a societal point of view, real problems occur when the cult starts developing its own moral philosophy, at odds with the rest of the world. It happened to David Korresh and his followers in Waco, Texas. It happened to Chancellor Helmut Kohl and the CDU in Germany, and it will probably happen again. Beware.

Give me one good reason

If you have a diverse tribe of true believers in pursuit of a clearly communicated vision you must then work out the right rewards and incentives to continuously promote innovation. Companies must reward sharing rather than keeping; creating as well as exploiting knowledge. If we want to bring together a company that is spread out across space, we need not only local bonuses but also ones based on global sales or profits. If knowledge creation across divisions and functions is critical to the development of competitive advantages, organizations will have to start

Projects, and particularly international ventures, should be run by the organizational equivalents of sumo wrestlers.

rewarding the transfer of competencies to other parts of the organization. One company that we have worked with even has a scheme to reward "human exports". Headquarters basically subsidizes the temporary transfer of local stars to other parts of the network. If speed is important, rewards must also capture the rate of renewal. A laudable first measure, now quite commonplace, is to base bonuses not only on sales, but on sales generated by new products.

At many companies, rewarding the development of new products and services also implies strengthening the role of project managers vis-à-vis the line management.[317] Far too many teams where creative work is carried out suffer from having lightweight project leaders. Critical decisions are still taken by senior executives in the line organization. And if project leaders are made of the real stuff, they are often promoted away from projects into (apparently) more important positions. Projects are no solution if they are crippled into operational impotency. Instead of lightweights, projects, and particularly international ventures, should be run by the organizational equivalents of sumo wrestlers. Real projects capable of forceful action, rather than committees for casual conversations, must have considerably more power than is the case in most contemporary companies. It is not only salaries and bonuses, but prestige that matters. Without giving up the idea of paying for exploitation while merely praying for creation, we won't get any result.

Dedicated to dialog

To drive innovation companies need the proper tools and arenas where such processes can occur. It doesn't make sense to bring in new people and then put them into fundamentally unchanged processes. In a competence-based economy, dialog is the new basic unit of work. No dialog – no development. To successfully create, exploit or even destroy knowledge, organizations need a process-platform made up of three components:

- an organizational *memory;*
- a shared *language;*
- and sophisticated communications *channels.*

First, let's look at organizational memory. Information and information flows increasingly define what an organization is and is not. Or as Robert Reich says: "A *company* will be best defined by who has access to what data and gets what portion of a particular stream of revenues, over what period of time."[318] But unless the company knows what it knows, it is predestined to be a place with pockets of individual creativity rather than an intelligent corporation. Yesterday, the general manager or CEO was supposed to know who knows who, who knows what, who knows how and who knows where. Innovative companies need a design where more or less everybody knows who, what, how and where – where the whole is reflected in all parts – a holographic organization.[319]

Growth, particularly in space, increases the probability that opportunities and solutions may be located at different places. In fact, if the solution exists in France, people in Japan may not even see the opportunity. With rising complexity it becomes more difficult to keep track of, and update, the map of competencies. This reasoning is also valid for resources located outside the legal boundaries of the firm, such as knowledge controlled by customers and suppliers. Efforts focused on increasing knowledge awareness must be more actively managed. Firms capable of creation by combination need a memory that extends beyond the individual.

Innovation is often a question of searching for the white spaces – territories yet to be explored – *terra incognita*. At many corporations, such solutions may actually already exist, but the lack of a well-functioning organizational memory means that no one, or at least very few people, are aware of them.

For instance, what is the percentage of ideas that failed last year that could work today? What about ideas from five or even ten years ago? How many employees remember them? The situation resembles life before Christmas when people buy new decorations for their Christmas trees, only to later realize that they already have all the decorations they need. In a business setting, as in a family, high turnover of people does not help build a great memory. Innovative organizations need at least a core group of people that stick together for quite some time and are in it for the long term.

Successful companies use a professional and systematic approach for handling their most vital resources. A knowledge memory should include a detailed inventory of core competencies and competents. It must cover both the stock and flows of knowledge.

To truly boost shareholder value corporations must work hard to transform the knowledge and skills of core competents into core competencies. Successful firms excel at turning human capital into structural capital – in the form of systems and procedures, routines, etc. This latter type of capital basically equals all the stuff left at the office when people leave at five o'clock. While from the outlook of the corporation, human capital is best thought of as a liability, structural capital is definitely an asset. By actively collecting, codifying and communicating the knowledge of critical employees to the rest of the organization, the firm enables any part of the company to utilize the entire body of knowledge. Knowledge = power. Shared knowledge = power[2].

But in the karaoke world, people also have a responsibility to themselves. As single individuals we must transform the structural capital of the organization into our own human capital. To ensure employability men and women must vacuum clean their current work place for ideas and information.

There is one small problem with creating a learning organization. Learning works great when change proceeds in a nice, neat, predictable and linear way. Managers we meet would like nothing more than to work in an age in which the environment did not constantly interfere with their strategies, but they are also intelligent enough to realize that acting as if things were stable would be self-delusional. Whether we like it or not, we are forced to do business in discontinuous times. The past is no longer always a good predictor of the future.

Companies must, therefore, also learn to forget. They must delete to develop – destroy to build. We have to make sure that we get rid of the old to make room for the new. The corporate memory must be equipped with an erase button. Quite often doing so is easier said than done. "The greatest difficulty in the world is not for people to accept new ideas, but to make them forget their old ideas," claimed the super-economist John Maynard Keynes.[320] Philosopher Bertrand Russell went one step further by claiming: "The resistance to a new idea increases as the square of its importance." In an organizational setting, getting rid of the past is particularly difficult since many senior executives are at the top because they are experts at what was important yesterday.

Talk talk

To share knowledge people also need to speak a common language. Conversations are contingent on common codes of communication. International communities such as medical doctors, Jews, overseas Chinese, gypsies or the Catholic Church have all relied on, and some still rely on (among other things), a shared language to act as a force of integration and unity. Research actually shows that people are bound together more by verbal conflict than by verbal agreement (or at least immediate agreement which is a sign of lacking communication.)[321] This idea may sound counterintuitive but spend a Sunday dinner with an extended Italian family and you'll get the point.

Even so both verbal conflict and agreement require a shared language. In practice, for most modern companies this means making sure that all individuals with strategic roles speak English. For some nationalities this procedure may be a bitter pill to swallow. But even the French are going down this route. Cement giant Lafarge expects all managers to speak English and offers language classes.[322]

The language question extends beyond the tower of Babel issue. People in different divisions and departments need to communicate. Effectively combining competencies requires a shared definition and understanding of key concepts and words, whether these are CRM, TQM,

The language question extends
beyond the tower of Babel issue.

Six Sigma, or more specific technical terms. A shared language bridges the different parts and thought worlds of the company (possibly including partners outside the firm). This is yet another reason why executive education has exploded during the last few years. Management training is not limited to the expansion of knowledge, but also serves to unify use of words, corporate grammar and mindsets.

From this perspective, digitization offers the second truly global unification of language. In addition to the language of mathematics, we now have one more world standard. But the entire language matter also puts a restriction on companies hoping to be ultra-innovative. They have to be relatively narrow.[323] Innovation Inc. is no conglomerate of unrelated businesses. There is no point in hoping that thousands and thousands of talented people with a variety of skills will come up with new ideas if they are not capable of communicating with each other.

Push me, pull you

To get processes moving Innovation Inc. needs a pull-oriented "info-structure". Such a communications platform enables the different parts of the organization to inform themselves on a need-to-find-out-basis. It is based on total openness, giving all units and employees full access to all information. On-demand-learning systems are knowledge bazaars where units and single individuals can share, search and shop around for ideas. A traditional push-logic, where the CEO and his or her team are responsible for informing the rest of the organization on a need-to-know-basis, will not do. Again, the forces of transparency and openness become visible. With more open intranets and Internets, old lines of communication and authority can be short-circuited. Information does not have to travel via the top of the hierarchy anymore. Anarchical? In theory perhaps; in practice not necessarily so. Actions are carried out within the realms provided by the purpose.

The critical importance of face-to-face communication should not be downplayed. Not all knowledge can be easily codified or articulated.

Information can lose meaning. For instance, research shows that based on everyday learning average 17-year olds learn some 5,000 words per year. They live it, eat it and breathe it. In this case learning refers to understanding the meaning as well as the practical use of the words. Learning based on abstract definitions from a dictionary, on the other hand, is limited to 100-200 words per year. Such learning also results in people producing sentences like "Mrs. Morrow stimulated the soup" – not only wrong, but exactly wrong.[324] Transferring certain types of knowledge requires face-to-face communication and human interaction – the context grants meaning.

So creative organizations practice socialization, though not in the Marxist sense. Innovation Inc. understands the power of place, even in the face of rapid internationalization. Innovative corporations co-locate people from different parts of the world (including partners) – for longer or shorter periods of time. Meeting face-to-face every now and then makes it possible for individuals to productively use e-mail, video-conferencing, and phone calls during periods when they are geographically separated.[325] Know-who is critical in that it helps talent to locate other carriers of competencies. Not only that. It also enables them to judge the relevance and quality of information.

Friends are much more efficient than acquaintances in performing collective tasks.

Socialization means having people working in teams, spending time together after work, attending corporate training programs, etc. Over time, such groups develop tacit – silent – knowledge. The members of the team will know things that they cannot tell.[326] Tacit knowledge enables them to communicate without words. In fact, research suggests that friends are much more efficient than acquaintances in performing collective tasks.[327]

Increasingly tacit knowledge is what companies are left to compete with. Anything that can be articulated or put on a piece of paper will be distributed, broadcast to the rest of the world. In many cases, this diffusion will happen within minutes rather than days. As soon as something can be articulated it can also be imitated. And if it can be imitated, companies cannot make too much money on it. Remember that economics and business is the science of scarcity. Almost by definition, stand-alone pieces of articulated knowledge are not scarce. Tacit knowledge, on the other hand, is sticky and does not diffuse with the same speed. Whisper it: the future of competitiveness may well be silent.

Socialization increases tacit knowledge that in turn works as talent handcuffs.

The existence of tacit knowledge also brings a bonus for corporations in that it makes it trickier for people to walk out the door with their skill-sets intact. Part of the body of knowledge of a specific individual will be nested in a network of relationships with existing colleagues. Anyone threatening to leave can therefore only bring some of their own skills with them. For instance, it is obvious from the solo albums of Mick Jagger and Keith Richards, that the Rolling Stones magic is lost without Charlie and Woody being in attendance. This also explains why many recruitment agencies prefer to outplace entire teams rather than single individuals.

Socialization increases tacit knowledge that in turn works as talent handcuffs. This not only transforms human capital into structural capital, but also increases the likelihood that people will stay with the firm for longer periods of time. And keeping the team together is critical for companies competing on innovation.

The rules of creation

Any corporation needs to do two basic things. It must exploit what is and create what is not (yet). For as long as we can remember, business life has been built around short outbursts of creation and long periods – often decades – of exploitation. We exploited natural resources, exploited technologies and exploited people. It should come as no surprise that companies are good at exploitation. Some of them have hundreds of years of experience.

In sharp contrast, most of us are not very good at creation. Our corporations are not designed for it. And most individuals are not trained for it. Still, all organizations must uphold this fruitful balance between the exploitation of givens and the creation of novelty.

Two main forces make it difficult to maintain the balance. There is a built-in resistance in most human beings to the unknown and uncertain. This need for uncertainty reduction is of course more prevalent in some cultures than in others.[328] Our main point here, however, is that acts of creation are always less certain and obvious than those of exploitation. The consequences of such activities are also more remote in time.[329] People like to play it safe. We continue to exploit.

Research by Stanford's James March and others suggests that over time organizations learn how to allocate resources between the two types of activities. This balancing act has short-term as well as long-term effects. The feedback loops from exploitation tend to be quicker and more precise. Learning processes therefore generally improve exploitation more rapidly than creation. As time goes by, exploitation will crowd out creation.[330] We spend more and more of our time and resources exploiting the recipes of the past.

The fact is that most influential management ideas only tell us how to become even better at what we are already good at. The re-engineering frenzy, for instance, is all about boosting efficiency within an existing frame. Hierarchical organizational design boils down to organizing for repetition rather than renewal. So far, much of management theory and practice has been obsessed by making good use of what already is. Studies by McKinsey consultant Richard Foster also show that between 1917 and 1987 only two of the Forbes 100 companies generated a return better than the market average.[331] Newcomers practice innovation. Old-timers focus on repetition. Exploitation Inc. was and is built for continuity – not change. Also remember Einstein's definition of insanity: doing the same thing over and over again and expecting different results.

Against this backdrop, we should not be surprised that history is littered with examples of companies that failed because they got trapped by their own success as exploiters of a particular competence combo.

They fell into a competency trap.[332] This is the argument at the heart of Clayton Christensen's *The Innovator's Dilemma*. "Good management was the most powerful reason they failed to stay atop their industries," writes Professor Christensen.[333]

Success can also be its own worst enemy. Many individuals and companies have to face the winner's curse.[334] "The day you believe you are successful is the day you stop being successful," says Herb Kelleher of Southwest Airlines.[335] Michael Porter of Harvard Business School even claims: "The best companies are always worried."[336]

To beat off the forces crowding out creation, companies need to develop:

- *experimentation* routines,
- a greater *tolerance* for failure,
- and a climate of *trust.*

Experiment or extinct

The traditional recipe for success told us to focus our attention on strengthening the core to maximize return on short-term investments. For innovative firms this is not enough. The prime task is not to perfect the known but to create the unknown and the unseen. This has two consequences. Creating the unexpected means looking in "uncalled for" places and investing in "unnecessary" communication platforms and links. In effect, the organization must also have longer-term perspectives. Innovation does not require perfection but persistence. "It's not that I'm so smart, it's just that I stay with problems longer," said Einstein.

Strategy guru Gary Hamel claims that companies fail to create the future, not because they fail to predict it, but because they fail to imagine it.[337] Successful ideas and products often arise from searching beyond what is currently rational. Frida Kahlo knew this. Wolfgang Amadeus Mozart knew this. Ernest Hemingway knew this. Most successful painters, composers and authors are very familiar with this principle. Ditto for innovative companies – 3M with post-it-notes or

Instead of playing grown-ups, it is time for grown-ups to start playing.

Dyson with vacuum cleaners. Conclusion? Put purist economic goals to one side and take on multi-rational goals. Instead of playing grown-ups, it is time for grown-ups to start playing. But bear in mind that play can be hard work.[338]

Innovation takes time. It is not an efficient activity. Creation involves repetition, trial and error, and experimentation. Slack is a prerequisite for innovation. More planning won't do the trick. Indeed, **Speed really isn't everything.** more and more planning eventually creates paralysis by analysis. And most academics now agree that while analysis can certainly help us avoid developing truly bad strategies, it will not aid us in creating great strategies.

We are left with intuition. Professor Karl Weick defines this as *compressed expertise* – our own intuition and the intuition of others.[339] Perhaps that is why the banking magnate JP Morgan once observed that, millionaires don't believe in astrology, but billionaires do.

Innovative companies also work hard to construct corporate speed bumps. They know that speed kills creativity. $I = T^3$. Innovation equals Time To Think. As the *Harvard Business Review* eloquently observed: "When creativity is under the gun, it usually ends up getting killed."[340] Speed really isn't everything. "Brains don't speed up," notes Intel's Andy Grove.[341] And as little as Chopin's "One Minute Waltz" becomes twice as good just because you play it in 30 seconds, can we evaluate innovation by efficiency.[342] The most efficient innovators are usually quite inefficient.

Masters of mistakes

To master innovation, companies need to change from having a focus on making *no* mistakes to an emphasis on making new mistakes. Only such a culture makes it feasible to pose stretch goals that trigger not marginally better, but completely different ways of doing things.

Winners make more mistakes. Screw up or prepare to be screwed. Or as IKEA marketing manager Benny Hermansson puts it: "If you don't make any mistakes, you must be asleep."[343] At IKEA, mistakes are expressly allowed since they trigger learning and lead to new ideas and possibilities. Forget the myth about the great and lonely genius. Innovation is mostly about mileage rather than one big bang. Double Nobel laureate Linus Pauling notes that: "The best way to have lots of good ideas is to have lots of ideas and throw away the bad ones."[344]

Strategy used to be described as a process of ready, aim, fire. In the nanosecond 1990s it became ready, fire, aim. Today the version preferred by MTV's Beavis and Butthead tends to dominate: fire, fire, fire. David Kelley, founder and CEO of the product design company IDEO claims that: "Enlightened trial and error outperforms the planning of flawless intellects."[345] You do, then change, and then you do and change again.

Maybe, as *Harvard Business Review* editor Tom Stewart suggests, in addition to mission statements, companies also need *permission* statements.[346] Failure happens. "The cure – to encourage people to always ask for permission – is worse than the disease," adds Amazon's Jeff Bezos.[347]

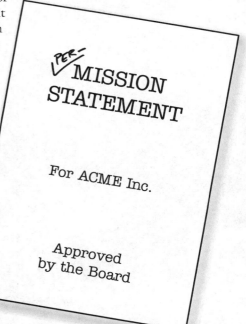

Failure-tolerant leaders, say psychologist and former Harvard Business School Professor Richard Farson and author Ralph Keyes, break down barriers separating them from others, engaging with people on a personal level. They don't praise or criticize, but analyze. FTLs don't have any problems admitting their own mistakes. They institute a climate of collaboration, rather than competition. But more than anything else they move beyond traditional definitions where failure is regarded as the opposite of success. They treat the two outcomes of experimentation as complementary.[348] Or as Thomas Alva

Collaboration requires trust.

KARAOKE CAPITALISM INNOVATION INC.

Edison once put it: "I have not failed. I've just found 10,000 ways that won't work." FTLs are constructive. Have always been and will always be. Cicero wrote: "I criticize by creation – not by finding fault." The statement still holds true.

Inside the temple of trust

All future social organizations aspiring to be creative must be based upon the principle of trust, whether they are nation-states, rock bands, voluntary organizations, football teams, or business firms. Innovation means that from time to time we must re-shuffle the Lego pieces. Some of these pieces are ours, but others will belong to someone else – inside or outside the corporation. Collaboration requires trust. Without trust organizations can't design and use the kind of open info-structures that are so critical for dialog and development. Trust not only facilitates co-operation but also reduces contract and monitoring costs.[349] Yet many contemporary organizations are fear factories rather than temples of trust.

The opportunity rests with the fact that trust was once taken for granted – now it's up for grabs. We used to trust authorities for no other reason than the fact that they were at the top of the system. Now, we can trust anyone and trust no one. Trust has to be earned.

Studies show that three things are absolutely critical in determining whom you actually trust: competence, care, and character.[350] Developing trust is not a quick fix. It is, says Manfred Kets De Vries, "a very delicate flower – one that takes a long time to blossom and is easily crushed."[351] Over time people learn to trust you for your ability. You must also constantly prove your compassion and generosity. As if this was not enough, companies and individuals cannot afford any blemishes on their integrity. Recall why leaders are fired: lack of character and a lapse in judgment. Trust-development is a matter of sticking to a number of principles proving your character. A leader who does not believe in people cannot expect too much knowledge creation. Such leaders only produce anti-trust. From an innovation point of view, they are bad news dressed in shoes. Trust-boosters will prevail. Trustbusters will perish.

11

THE HOLY GRAIL OF BUSINESS

From Microsoft to Picasso and Michael Jackson, temporary monopolies have found the way out of the karaoke bar. But the old recipes no longer work. Great technology and modern organizational solutions are all necessary but no longer sufficient in the race for industry leadership. In a capitalist world of economic Darwinism, survival and success is a question of being fit or sexy. The new winners compete on rational and emotional innovation – exploiting market imperfections and the imperfections of man.

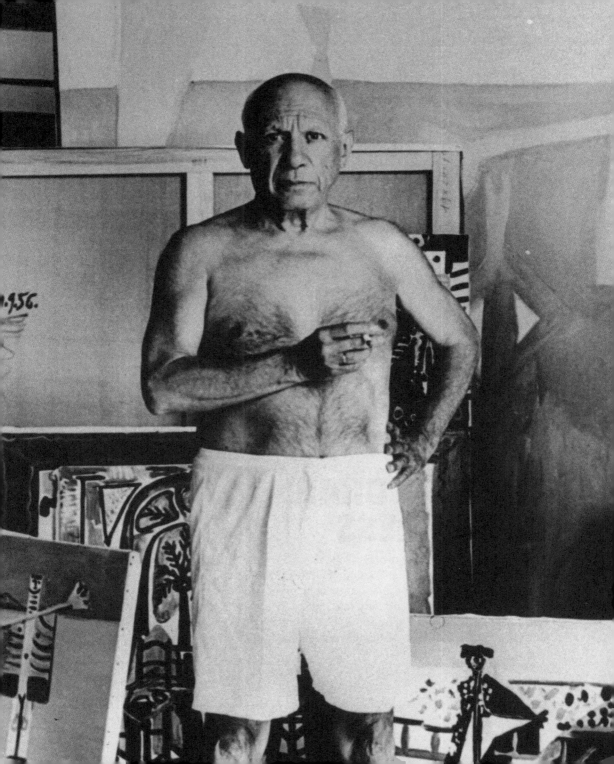

Moonwalking monopolies

What do Michael Jackson, Pablo Picasso and Bill Gates have in common? They are, of course, all legends in their own right. But now think about what made them famous. Think again, because their stories hold the key that may help unlock the hidden door to competitiveness. These three icons have revealed the secret of success. Each of them has found the Holy Grail of commerce. They have created and exploited recipes that gave them temporary monopolies.[352] For a short moment in time and/or space they were (and, in the case of Bill, *is*) unique – the only ones.

Look at Michael. Mr. Jackson was the only one who could sing with an extremely high-pitched voice and moonwalk, simultaneously. The temporary monopoly made him world famous.

Picture Picasso. He drew paintings of people who looked like they were made out of mutated Lego pieces. His temporary monopoly eventually made him rich. The story goes that a famous art critic complained to Picasso at a museum reception asserting that his wife certainly did not look anything like the women that Pablo painted. What does she look like then, asked Picasso? The critic turned around and pointed toward an 18th century painting of a beautiful woman. So, she is only ten inches tall, replied Pablo. "Everything you can imagine is real," he once noted.

Microsoft is another great case in point. The software colossus has a rock solid temporary monopoly. In fact, this phenomenon partly explains why the company needs to spend so much time in court these days. (The rest of us should probably hope to spend some more time in front of a judge. Time spent in court can be a sign of success in the age of karaoke capitalism.)

Sometimes, we meet executives who say: I just love competition. How sad and disappointing. If you are a manager and seriously in love with the concept of competition, you should probably quit your job now! Go work for the anti-trust authorities, or do something completely different, just as long as you are no longer in charge of a company. Great businessmen and women should loathe competition. They should simply adore monopolies and fall head-over-heels in love at the merest sight of one.

Corporations exist for the simple reason of continuously and creatively crushing competition.

Indeed, they are trained to do so. They are rewarded to do so. Be warned. Do not believe anything else. Corporations exist for the simple reason of continuously and creatively crushing competition. They are created to fight the spirit of free enterprise. To avoid destructive competition, successful entrepreneurs practice creative destruction. They destroy through building. It is this very sequence of creative destruction resulting in temporary monopolies that ensures development and economic growth in a market economy.[353]

And behind these temporary monopolies we always find an innovation – Sony's Walkman, GM's multidivisional organization, the Tetra Pak and so on. Note that we are talking about innovations and not inventions. It is the process by which ideas are translated into the economy that is so critical.

Research shows that it is innovation and innovation alone – and not necessarily technological innovation – that drives above average shareholder returns on a sustained basis at both industry and organizational level.[354] In the long run, it is the ability of an individual or a group of individuals to think a thought that no one else has thought before and then successfully turn that idea into reality that separates the best from the rest. The unseen and the unknown do not have any competitors. And don't forget that the principle is essentially the same at the level of single individuals such as Picasso and Jacko.

Sure Thing Inc.

The creation of novelty is no longer optional. But organizations face three additional hurdles.

The first is associated with the very definition of innovation as something limited in scope to products and company resources. Now the process is changing into a much more sophisticated creative game.

The second challenge is that traditional sources of competitive advantage are no longer as powerful. There is nothing strange about this fact. Competition makes historical advantages lukewarm – always has and always will. Not even great innovators or innovations are immortal. The vampires of business eventually die. There is no such thing as a bulletproof competitive advantage. Sure Thing Inc. does not exist.

Indeed, one of the basic laws of physics can be applied to business: over time, any matter and every matter turns into (not spreadsheets but) spread shit. To bring things together again you must add energy. In effect, companies are condemned to an eternal search for new fountains of youth.

The third hurdle is related to the fact that on the whole we have given up on the principle of nurture and are building a society where the laws of nature rule. Innovation used to be focused on Mr. and Mrs. Average, now the Extremes rule the world.

A few years ago a lot of people claimed that IT was the new answer to our prayers for increased profitability. And information technology certainly opens up the opportunity to do business in entirely new ways. Having

Does access to a toilet provide any sustainable competitive advantage?

concluded that though, let us ask something. Back at the office, do you have access to a toilet? Probably. Now, let us ask a second question: does this provide any sustainable competitive advantage? Probably not.

Like water and sewerage, plumbing and toilets, IT in general, and the Net in particular, have become necessary but no longer sufficient for the creation of a sustainable competitive edge.[355]

One hundred years ago electricity was the big thing – a very efficient way of transporting energy. In recent years, the talk of the town has been the Internet – a very smart way of transporting information. But as soon as something becomes available to all players all over the world, no company in any industry will ever be able to create as much as one sustainable competitive advantage by only having access to that something.

It is true that information technology lowers costs. An average bank transaction costs $1.25 with a teller, $0.54 with a phone, 24 cents using an ATM and on the Net we are down to 2 cents.[356] The problem is that all other companies can also utilize these new savings.

What a lot of corporations fail to realize is that IT is not a core capability, nor will it ever be one. The core of any company needs to be firmly founded on a unique value proposition to customers. IT is an enabler – nothing more and nothing less. It is infrastructure, electronic plumbing in the corporate washroom. Karaoke copying the others does not lead to sustainable competitiveness.

But still blind optimism rules. "Last year we invested $3 million in this new web solution and in three, four years time we're going to reap all the benefits," managers confide to us with cheery misplaced optimism in every syllable. This is a bit like opening up the annual report of a company, and halfway through the CEO's letter to the shareholders, you read: "Last year we installed 38 new mensrooms and next year, by God, we're really going to kick ass." Of course, you need toilets. Otherwise the company may end up pretty constipated. But when PC=WC, access is no longer enough.

In fact, in most industries, technology has become like the air we breathe and the water we drink – available to all players and no longer a source of differentiation. It no longer makes companies or products

Technology doesn't make you less stupid; it just makes you stupid faster.

unique. There are some exceptions – in pharmaceuticals and high-tech for instance – but, in general, great technology is necessary but no longer sufficient for the creation of sustainable competitive advantages. Techies should also remember what Thornton A. May, chief psychographer at Toffler Associates, says: "Technology doesn't make you less stupid; it just makes you stupid faster."[357]

And yet, many companies still continue to compete on the basis of their technology – moving further and further into the darkness of the tech-tunnel. This confuses and sometimes offends customers. According to one survey, the gadgets perceived as most difficult to understand in 2003 are the digital camera and the handheld electronic organizer.[358] Or consider the names of some of the hottest new technologies in consumer

No one can outsource the creation of competitiveness to someone else.

electronics. To the impressive list of GPRS, MP3, WAP and megahertz, we can now add *FireWire* and *Wi-Fi*. These two terms are certainly improvements compared to their original technical names of 1394 and 802.11b, respectively, but they say absolutely nothing about benefits to consumers.[359]

With technology failing to act as a differentiator, many firms try to compete on new organizational or managerial solutions. They embrace TQM, JIT, Kanban, MBO, MBWA, ISO 9000, ISO 9001, ISO 9002, ISO 9003, ISO ninethousandwhatsoever, Six Sigma or BPR (COA – competing on abbreviations or acronyms?) with something approaching abandon. Make no mistake, for a short period in time or space, these innovations will make a few companies tingle and glow. The power of these ideas was once immense. They made Japan one of the wealthiest places on planet earth. Many traditional companies have survived because they have been, and still are, experts at playing this managerial and organizational game. In all likelihood, most of us work for, buy stuff from, perhaps even lead or own stocks in such masters of management. That is the good news. Here comes the bad.

McKinsey & Company exists. Boston Consulting Group exists. Accenture exists. Cap Gemini Ernst & Young exists. Roland Berger Consulting exists. Aided by this cadre of consultants, all of your competitors are also re-engineering, re-focusing, re-structuring, re-organizing, re-newing, re-vamping, re-, re-, re-, re-, re-... For anything from $1,000 to $10,000 per day you can buy as much organizational and managerial knowledge as you'd ever need. You can fill the office from floor to ceiling with such information.

But so can your competitors.

Not only that. Managed by the same cadre of standardized MBAs these companies are all using identical recipes for success. We should know. We both work at a business school. And, we promise, most business schools around the world share a dirty little secret: They all use the same books. It's Michael Porter's *Competitive Strategy*, the Free Press 1980. It's Philip Kotler's *Marketing Management*, 11th edition by now – with study guide. It's Brealey and Myers in finance. It does not matter if you get your MBA in Boston, Birmingham or Bombay – same old books. How on earth can MBAs then be expected to make a difference?

Copying others is no solution. Similarity does not result in success. Sameness still sucks! As Nissan's CEO and turnaround champion Carlos Ghosn puts it: "You don't build your character by doing what everybody else is doing" – not even in the promised land of karaoke itself.[360]

The trouble is that far too many companies have placed their bets on the assumption that someone else is going to supply them with a sustainable competitive edge. Unfortunately, some of them have stopped thinking and instead become consulting junkies. But listen up – self-proclaimed gurus may not like this one. No one can outsource the creation of competitiveness to someone else. We cannot buy a competitive advantage from the über-guru of all management gurus Tom Peters – not that he would ever claim that he sells such – or any other external advisor. IBM is a great company but it can't provide other organizations with a sustainable edge. And you certainly should not expect us to supply corporations around the world with temporary monopolies. All this information is available to all players on a truly international market. In a karaoke world competitiveness is not for sale.

As noted by Professor David Teece, competitive advantages at the level of the firm can flow only from the ownership and successful deployment of non-tradable assets.[361] The very second that a particular asset is available in a market, it is also potentially accessible to all your competitors and therefore worthless from a commercial point of view. But Professor Teece is only partly right. Competitive advantages can indeed and do often arise from the combination and re-composition of tradable assets into unique bundles – hy-phe-na-tion. Therefore, it is the task of people within companies, quite possibly in cooperation with others, to start putting two and two together in innovative ways.

Monopolies of the future

So, what are successful companies actually doing – if technology spreads like poison ivy and managerial innovations diffuse internationally and instantly? What are modern monopolies made of?

What's the deal with Wal-Mart – the US mega-retailer that brought K-mart down to its knees? In 2003, *Fortune* named Wal-Mart the most admired corporation in the world.[362] One day of sales in 2002 – $1.42 billion – were larger than the GDP of 36 countries. Its estimated yearly growth is equivalent to the size of Dow Chemical, or one PepsiCo or one Microsoft. If the anticipated $2 billion that the company loses through theft each year could be incorporated as a business it would rank at 694 on the *Fortune 1,000*. A 2002 McKinsey study even showed that more than one-eighth of US productivity growth between 1995 and 1999 could be explained by the retailing giant.[363] All this is impressive (and frightening, some would say), but what is the secret behind the success of Wal-Mart?

A respectable manufacturer of rubber boots and toilet paper now totally dominates the cellular phone industry

Switch worlds. What is pop star Madonna doing? She certainly doesn't have the best voice. She is a decent but definitely not the best dancer. For sure, Madonna has a lot of "cred" (at least before the movie *Swept Away*), but how can we explain her iconic status?

And, meanwhile in Finland, what are the guys at Nokia up to? A company that not so long ago was a respectable manufacturer of rubber boots and toilet paper, now totally dominates the cellular phone industry – selling five phones every second.[364] Nokia accounts for 10% of Finland's GDP and more than 50% of the value of its stock exchange.[365] Is the company successful because it possesses groundbreaking technology that its competitors cannot get hold of – some ingenious little gadget that a guy called Pekka invented back in 1995? Do you think Jorma Olilla, the top-guy of Nokia, has stumbled upon an absolutely amazing book on marketing, branding and design only available in Finnish? No, this must be it. Nokia is probably located closer to the future. There is a one-hour time difference between Finland and much of the rest of Europe.

Don't get us wrong. Of course companies need the best technology available. They need to pioneer new organizational solutions and management systems. In more and more industries, global presence is mandatory. All of this has become necessary, but it's no longer enough. So what are Singapore Airlines and Easy Jet; Gucci and H&M; Dell and Apple actually doing? What is the fabric of contemporary temporary monopolies? What are the strategies which work in a saturated world where nature has replaced nurture as the guiding principle and where abnormality has overcome normality?

Fit & sexy

To fully grasp what is going on, let's go back to nature. In 1859, Charles Darwin published his famous book *On the origin of species by means of natural selection*.[366] Darwin argued that evolution could be portrayed as a process marked by the survival of the fittest. Species produce far more individuals than can survive to procreate. Individuals have different features. Those that manage to grow to adulthood and procreate will populate the environment with offspring having those features – physiological or behavioral. These features can involve traits such as maturation speed, running speed, dietary requirements, size, aggressive qualities, cooperative tendencies or color.[367] In Darwin's words, "... multiply, vary, let the strongest live and the weakest die." The ability to survive boils down to adaptation in relation to a changing environment. Superior species evolve over time. The church was outraged. The scientific community was fuming.

But poor Charles did not rest on his well-evolved laurels. There were things that he could still not explain – like the male peacock's tail. It did not seem very fit – not even to Darwin. In fact, from a fitness perspective, the tail actually provided a competitive disadvantage – easy to spot and cumbersome to carry around. Darwin went back to the drawing board. Twelve years later he published the less known *The descent of man, and selection in relation to sex*.[368] Fitness, claimed Darwin, did not explain it all, fertility also came into play. Courtship was critical. He divides sexual selection into *female sexual selection* (or female choice) where the female picks a male for a specific quality and *male combat sexual selection* (called male-male competition) where males compete physically for the opportunity to mate with a female. In both cases, *she* decides.

In nature, survival and success is a question of adaptation and attraction.

Together, survival of *the fittest* and *the sexiest* explained evolution.[369] Now, people were really upset. This may disappoint a few of you but an interesting and related side issue to this is that over time, and at least for man, sexual selection appears to have shifted its primary target from body to mind.[370]

From Darwin to Wal-Mart and Apple. In nature, survival and success is a question of adaptation and attraction, but what does all this have to do with corporate strategy?

Consider the following. During the 20th century, most great social experiments were based on the principle of nurture. The state rather than the market ruled. Under such conditions natural selection did not always work – (economically) inefficient companies could (and some still can) survive with the help of government subsidies. But, in a double economy of market mania without a flourishing middle-class and mass-markets based on the laws of nature, something happens.

The business environment has changed. We have witnessed a transition from an information desert to an information jungle. Markets rule. There are no longer any safety nets to protect the inefficient. Nature strikes back. Corporations must adapt.

Also people have changed. We have moved from collectivism to individualism. Now, some of us have more or less endless choice. We are slowly beginning to realize that human beings are emotionally rather than rationally wired. When surplus and sentiments rule success becomes a question of courting the customers.

We have witnessed a transition from an information desert to an information jungle.

Consumers with too much cash and others in desperate need may make up the ingredients of a pretty scary society, but this does not necessarily represent a bad combo of customers for business. Successful companies have always adapted to their times. In reality, truly great companies do not settle for merely adapting. They know that either you set the rules or you will be ruled out – make history or become history. The true revolutionaries of business have realized that as the Bell-curve has burst into binomiality the shape of things to come will change. The future is pear-shaped.

Business is not rocket science. More pocket science. In a capitalist world, all economic activities boil down to interactions among men and women on markets – economic entities and the environment. From a strategic standpoint, man and markets are the only things you need to care about. But when both the environment and the economic entities change, new strategies are called for. Innovation has always been and will always be a question of creating and exploiting imperfections – monopolies. Perfection drives out profits.

In karaoke capitalism there are only two ways in which organizations can build sustainable competitiveness. Either we exploit market imperfections or the imperfections of man – supply-side and demand-side innovation, respectively. The former strategy means practicing rational innovation by creating unique business models that are well adapted to the new business conditions, while the latter builds on emotional innovation in order to create moods that attract and addict customers. Model companies are designers or parts of value-creating networks. Mood competitors are providers of experiences. Rational innovation is often directed toward the low-end niche of the double economy, while emotional innovation generally makes the most of differences within the group of high-enders. In a world of information mania market models are fit. In the age of individual choice moods are sexy. The executive summary? Move away from the middle.

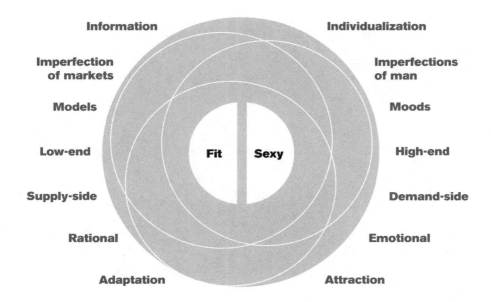

12

MODELS WITH MINDS

In the age of information mania, fitness boils down to using markets to your advantage. Model companies exploit imperfections in the form of transactions, trust or talent. Becoming a super-model starts with creating a unique customer value proposition and developing the core competencies that will enable us to master the model. Then we must get complementary capabilities from world-class partners around the globe. Taking the next step requires leveraging our unique recipe across new customer areas, applications and marketing channels.

Models Inc

There is no doubt about what used to be fit in the 20th century. A single corporate model has dominated business life for some 100 years. Our parents and grandparents may have worked for firms applying it. Business students were forced to read about it in textbooks and case studies. We all bought products from organizations using it. The vertically integrated industrial company was the model – one for all and all for one.

This was a corporation where most activities were carried out internally. The firm made what it sold. Unlike today's Nike and Timberland, back then, if you sold shoes you also made them. Not only that. To ensure input, many companies practiced backward integration. Henry Ford and others pioneered the model some 100 years ago. Henry made cars. In cars there is quite a lot of metal. So, the company invested in mines. At that time there was a lot of wood in cars, so Ford bought forests. What about rubber? Inevitably, the company owned a few rubber plantations.

This made sense. Keeping it all in-house worked well when information was a scarce resource and markets were under-developed. But when the environment changes, we have an entirely new ball game, one in which Henry Ford would be as comfortable as Tiger Woods playing ping-pong.

Information is now plentiful. And, when we leave the information

More or less all the pieces that were once kept in-house can now be bought from someone else.

desert behind us and enter the information jungle, markets begin to destroy the hierarchies that formed the backbone of vertically integrated companies. Information is to the welded Vertical Corporation what termites are to houses and climate changes to dinosaurs. Markets feed and breed on information. And when markets become more efficient, the vertically integrated company becomes an instant, spectacular misfit in the new economic landscape.

More or less all the pieces that were once kept in-house can now be bought from someone else. You no longer need a rubber plantation. Under such conditions certain corporate species must develop new strategies or they die.

To succeed companies must use transnational and hyper-efficient markets to their advantage – whether they are markets for activities, processes, components, people or parts. We have moved from a world of building to one of buying. Synergies are out. Outsourcing is in.[371] Executives used to believe that 2+2=5. Now it is 5–2=7 because the more non-core activities you place outside the firm the higher the value you can generate.

The model is catching on. It is estimated that the number of companies outsourcing manufacturing almost tripled between 1998 and 2000.[372] ABB recently outsourced 90% of its IT to IBM. "Today more than 50% of our products do not touch a Cisco factory or employee, it just gets magically assembled and shipped and the customer does not even know we never touched it," says Howard Charney, Senior Vice President of Cisco.[373] Karaoke magic doesn't require Roy & Siegfried or David Blaine, just some fresh thinking.

This means that any company in any industry must start thinking about strategy from scratch.

The good news is that even in this world of market dominance there is still room for companies. While markets feed and breed on information, organizations feed and breed on ideas. Markets do not innovate. Corporations do. Organizations do not exist merely because they minimize transaction costs. Success is also a question of maximizing value-creation – satisfying real customer needs in innovative ways.

The make-up of models

Companies, both new and old, are decomposing and recomposing traditional value-chains – replacing what used to be welded with Velcro. They are taking them apart and putting them together in a variety of different ways. Instead of controlling a supply-chain, some of them are designing demand-chains. They manipulate with the boundary of the firm. They focus and leverage. They work together with customers and suppliers in new ways. Model innovators will do just about anything to create a business model that is an efficient, self-reinforcing provider of unique customer value.

It may all look confusing, but there is a clear logic behind the corporate workout that leads to model-based fitness. Building a modern business model capable of thriving in an information jungle boils down to thinking creatively about the answers to four critical questions:

- What do we want to do for what customers?
- What world-class things can we do on our own?
- What can world-class partners do better than us?
- What potential for growth exists and where?

The answers to these questions make up the main building blocks of a competitive business model.

Customer value proposition	Core competencies	Complementary capabilities	Critical options for the future
Exclusivity / Execution / Elasticity			

The making of models

Any successful model must start with a unique *customer value proposition* – a hypothesis about the bundle of benefits that a single person or an organization wants badly enough to pay for. This proposition must be clear to, and communicated to, employees, customers, as well as shareholders.

Companies going after the low-end niche of the double economy must choose between two basic options. Either they offer customers more value for less money or a little less value for a lot less money. IKEA and Wal-Mart, for example, both exist to enable ordinary men and women to buy what used to be the privilege of rich people. Or, as IKEA used to put it: not for the rich but for the smart.

Adding value may represent a number of different things depending on the circumstances and the focus of the model. In some cases, it could mean saving time for over-worked individuals with double jobs like Pizza Hut, McDonald's, Burger King and many others. In other cases aggregating demand to allow customers to use their collective bargaining power, such as Wal-Mart does, could be the answer. In a sense, that company acts like the professional procurement department for millions and millions of consumers.

Of course, activities that add little value to a target group of customers are simply omitted from the offer – like at self-service gas stations. Typically, these are activities that made sense when companies were going after a flourishing middle-class but are simply expensive and redundant extras for people with less money.

Take Amazon, Home Depot and Ryan Air. Amazon offers the consumer a much wider selection, reviews, free samples, gift vouchers, top-lists, suggestions on what other items to buy, etc., at a lower price than your local bookstore. Home Depot combines the prices and selection of superstores with the service level of specialty hardware stores. Ryan Air, and many other low-cost airlines, offers airfares that are sometimes almost ridiculously low. "Air travel should be like a bus journey around Europe," says Michael O'Leary, CEO of the Irish airline.[374] But these companies offering less for a lot less do not exactly pamper the customers. Just listen to Herb Kelleher of Southwest Airlines, the firm that invented this low-price model – trying to become the "greyhound of the sky". "If we are going to treat the customer as cattle, we might as well develop a business model for cattle, no reserved seating, no meals, no fancy lounges, and no in-flight entertainment," says Herb.[375] It works.

The Dilbert strategy of finding dumber customers rather than developing better value propositions won't work.

In a world dominated by consumers more empowered than ever, the Dilbert strategy of finding dumber customers rather than developing better value propositions won't work. On the contrary, creating a viable value proposition could mean saying no to certain customers by saying a strong yes to others. In the early 1960s, Wal-Mart basically copied the recipe for discount retailing, but unlike his competitors, Sam Walton put his stores in "little one-horse towns which everybody else was ignoring".[376] Nice move Sam. This temporary monopoly in space has now lasted for some time and came from the simple idea of seeking out rural towns that were both far away from the cities in which competitors had located, and too small to support more than one large retailer.[377]

Mastering the model

The second aspect of modeling concerns the *core competencies* that enable the company to master the model.[378] This requires an inside-out perspective rather than one that takes the nature of the industry or business environment as the point of departure. Often it is, and should be, the starting point of the strategy-making process. The core customer group and the value proposition is a consequence of who you are, what you know and what you can do for them.

Together with the answer to the question of cooperating with others, this procedure also signifies the main departure from the dominant logic of the vertically integrated company. Model companies leave the traditional way of working behind by either themselves moving closer to a market solution, exploiting other imperfections, or by being part of a business system that shares many traits with that of the market.

The opportunities and challenges opened up by the move into an information jungle simply make the recipe of the past unfashionable. Firms must focus on knowing, doing or owning only those things that are unique, world-class and valuable to the specific group of customers targeted by the core value proposition. In all likelihood, these are few rather than many. Now, more than ever, organizations need to follow the advice of the Greek philosopher Socrates who said that it is better to do a little well than a great deal badly.

From this perspective, there are three basic types of competitive business models. Companies either own:

- the *concept;*
- the *customer;*
- and/or specific *capabilities.*

Indeed, prosperous organizations or networks of partnering firms often use a potent mix of these elements to dominate their territory. This reasoning is true not only for traditional business organizations. Consider opera. La Scala in Milan and the Metropolitan in New York own the customer. Going to these venues guarantees that you will (in all likelihood) not be disappointed (except when realizing how much it costs to get in). Composers such as Guiseppe Verdi or Giacomo Puccini are (despite being dead and possessing echoes of Sinatra's comeback) concept owners. The stars, Luciano Pavarotti or conductor Zubin Mehta, control the critical capabilities. All these players are successful, approaching the opera industry from different angles and with various competitive advantages. In fact, they are complementary – parts of an international opera ecosystem in competition with other clusters, whether these are local opera houses, the record industry, Broadway musicals, or DVDs.

Many successful model companies are network orchestrators.

Many successful model companies are network orchestrators. They own the concept and exploit transactional imperfections. These corporations realize that in certain cases it is better to buy than to build things in-house. In industries dominated by hierarchies, network orchestrators introduce the power of markets.

Dell and IKEA are great examples of this logic. The Dell direct-to-the-customer model operates as a flexible broker of parts. Dell lets the consumer design his or her own PC. The company operates in real time on information provided by the customers. It runs on-line auctions for more or less all components with its suppliers. By doing so Dell not only makes sure that it gets great prices, but also avoids building up costly inventories in a fast-changing industry where stock has a lot in common with fresh fish – it loses value really fast. But Dell does not give customers limitless choice. Instead it limits the number of options per choice and, by doing so, makes customization manageable.

IKEA's flat-pack-home-assembly model is also based on standards enabling the customer to take over activities that were traditionally carried out by the furniture company. IKEA is like a spider co-ordinating a web of relationships. Both these companies of course rely heavily on partners supplying standardized parts and components.

The second model company is that of the *relationship builder*. These firms are not customer led, but have a focus on leading the consumer. They even try to own the customer. Think Mastercard and Visa. Trust is the market imperfection that these players are aiming for. Loyal customers equal more business. Loyalty, in turn, is based on trust. Relationship builders charge a premium for their ability to reduce perceived uncertainty. They profit from the fact that we all worry about being deceived and swindled by those we are doing business with – especially when information is asymmetrically distributed. Obviously, trust is more important in service where the seller usually has more of an information advantage. When you go to the barber you can't really look at the customer offering until it may be too late. As the service content increases in most industries, trust also becomes more of an issue – and an opportunity for all organizations.

At the heart of the Amazon value proposition lies the exchange of information for customization. Every time people surf the site and buy stuff, they (voluntarily or not) hand over a lot of information to Amazon. The company is not merely selling stuff over the Web. It is in the business of building *buyographical* relationships – confidence-based contacts that can later be used to sell other things to these consumers. When buying stuff from Amazon we trust that we will get low prices, probably not the lowest, but still low. We trust that what we have ordered will also be delivered. We trust its promises of secure shopping when using our credit cards.

Or look at the highly successful Internet auction-house eBay where you can sell and buy everything from cars to real estate. In 2003 at least 30 million people will buy and sell stuff on eBay. More than 150,000 entrepreneurs will earn a fulltime living selling things on eBay. More automobiles are bought on eBay than at the No.1 US dealer

IKEA's model is based on standards

AutoNation.[379] But the company is not merely a broker. It provides a platform for selling and buying things over the Net, but not only that. In fact, eBay is the industry. This is one of the reasons why the company is so successful. But how did it become the industry? Well, eBay is designed in a way that enables reputation and relationships to evolve over time as customers interact with each other and with the site. Indeed, when trust is abused people simply send in reviews that destroy the credibility of the bad apples. eBay allows the bidders to see the reputation history of all sellers. Instead of fighting transparency, the company uses it – it goes with the flow. Amazon's ranking of all products takes advantage of the same basic idea. Open architecture again. Reputation and relationships in turn lead to trust.

But the secret behind eBay is not only linked to being an enabler of trust. Decisions about the number of activities it performs have a direct

This material has been reproduced with the permission of eBay Inc.
COPYRIGHT © EBAY INC. ALL RIGHTS RESERVED.

impact on the cost structure and also constitute a cornerstone of its model.[380] After the auction eBay lets the buyer and seller take care of the logistics of payment and shipping. The firm is never in possession of what is sold and therefore does not carry any inventory. This means no transportation costs and credit risks. The model obliterates overhead. The brilliance of eBay is that it provides the tools that enable the customers to build the company.

Finally, there are the *capability specialists* that essentially complement the others. They own unique competencies within particular processes, technologies or activities. We have already mentioned Manpower which dominates the staffing industry with its recipe for **Talent provides a market imperfection.** renting out temps. Or consider firms such as Flextronics and Solectron, which use their talent in manufacturing to enable other companies to outsource a number of activities traditionally kept in-house. Talent provides a market imperfection. Unlike the stuff sold on markets for capital, hard labor or raw materials, knowledge is differentiated. Competence and carriers of competence can be unique.

We find capability specialists all over the place. In a world of increasingly large competitors, biotech company Genzyme, for instance, specializes in so-called orphan drugs – those that treat just a few thousand patients with rare diseases. $1,000 invested in this company 10 years ago is now worth $4,665.[381] Or consider Forest Labs, which licenses and relentlessly promotes promising drugs from mid-size foreign drug-makers lacking the skills and muscle to market in the US.[382]

Look at consulting firms like McKinsey and Accenture. In addition to selling trust that is weaved into some of the best corporate comforters around, these companies, and a number of their competitors, also have micro-monopolies on certain types of talent. By having strong identities they attract competent individuals with particular traits – stamina, strategic thinking or whatever. The same reasoning is largely true for investment banks such as Goldman Sachs and UBS Warburg.

Any model competitor needs at least one solid base or source of competitiveness. Many companies that revolutionize industries do so by gaining first mover advantages in one of the three dimensions – like Dell in exploiting transactions. In certain cases firms develop initial advantages characterized by increasing returns – such as Microsoft with its software. This enables them to thrive and survive for a longer period of time. Eventually, however, more or less all corporations are forced to move on.

Strategic renewal usually starts with efforts to refine the initial advantage. Jeff Bezos of Amazon, for instance, quickly realized that the company needed to operate its own warehouses to ensure the customer experience and get good prices from suppliers. The firm was forced to build new capabilities to complement the original concept. Ultimately, continued success becomes a question of entering an entirely new advantage cycle. Ideally, this means exploiting other market imperfections in addition to the original advantage that gave birth to the firm. Successful companies need to create strategy spirals where the end of one advantage cycle also marks the beginning of a new one.

Successful companies need to create strategy spirals

There is nothing strange about this. The logic can also be applied to human beings. Consider Oscar-winning actor Tom Hanks. Initially a capable comedian he developed his skills as a drama actor. Later, he started directing movies and eventually produced the *Band of Brothers* series with Steven Spielberg. His reputation as a great actor had positive spillover effects on the series for which he owned the concept. You can trust Tom.

Extreme and extended profits are usually dependent on a model that covers all three bases on market-based competitiveness. Either this means that a single company exploits all three dimensions simultaneously, or that it is part of a hypercompetitive business ecosystem capable of doing three things simultaneously. Such 3D-models are prosperous since they are generally much more difficult to imitate. This limits competition. The transaction part also lowers costs while the trust and talent dimension simultaneously increase revenues, opening up a great profit gap.

Network Orchestrators
Concept – Transactions

Relationship Builders
Customers – Trust

Capability Specialists
Competencies – Talent

But there are clear dangers in trying to keep all three sources of competitiveness in-house. Such a system of mutually supportive strengths can and do often create lock-ins. Leaders of such companies may feel that they cannot change in one of the dimensions because that would cancel out the other advantages and destroy systems-balance. Inevitably, however, innovation sweeps the rug from under their feet. IBM and its experience with the mainframe business is a classical example of a company painting itself into a corner.

Fuzzy logic

This leads us to the next component of a business model: the activities that a company decides not to do on its own but which are still essential to its value proposition. Today, you either use world-class co-operation partners to supply such or you perish. The boundary of the firm is becoming increasingly fuzzy as partnerships bring in both customers and suppliers, and deal with gaining input as well as securing output.

Consider MasterCard. Its business model focuses on customer ownership and exploitation of trust. It processes millions of credit card transactions every day. But the firm has only 1,000 employees with 800 in data processing.[383] The rest is left to the network of affiliates and partners. Network orchestrators in particular, as well as relationship builders, take on a role similar to that of a curator in the art world. Rather than protecting the internal and permanent collection of the company – historical resources and activities – their task is to pick the best players, regardless of who they are and where they work, given the specific nature of the value proposition. Designing the business model resembles running the art biennial in Venice. Curators determine both who and how these players should relate to each other.

In addition, customers can function as valuable partners. Think of how millions of consumers helped to build eBay. At the core of a concept-based business model often rests the elimination of waste – non-value adding activities that are exposed by increasing transparency. Both Ryan Air and EasyJet avoid travel agent commission by dealing directly with the customer. This may seem to imply that the companies take on extra activities, but in reality it is more accurate to describe it as leaving certain processes to consumers – think IKEA and self-assembly.

This requires a standardized interface. EasyJet introduced Internet ticketing in 1998, and four years later sold some 92% of its tickets over the Web.[384] Ryan Air reached the same level of Net sales back in 2000, cutting marketing, sales and distribution costs by 62% in the second half of that year alone.[385]

Partnerships cover two broad strategic areas: ensuring input or securing output.

Input can have a focus on either exploitation or creation. When it comes to exploitation, outsourcing manufacturing of standardized components or even entire products is now commonplace – in the automotive industry, the fashion industry, the electronics industry, in just about any industry. H&M, for instance, farms production to some 900 suppliers in Europe and Asia. This enables it to move a garment from sketchpad to store in three weeks.[386]

Ensuring creative input is more demanding. Working with other companies on creating the unknown requires that the firms are willing and able to apply the Lego principles to their partners. In practice this means moving beyond standardization and planning to co-ordinating activities through mutual adjustment. Strong relationships need to be established not only at top-management level. Differences in the respective organizational architectures also need to be aligned, at least on a project level. For example, people need common ideas, ideals, identities and incentives. As a result, most examples of successful creative combination occur where the two firms share a history of collaboration. Co-operation is a learning process. Experience results in routines for leveraging knowledge and a climate of trust minimizing secrecy and cheating.

But gaining valuable input is often not enough. When international competition intensifies it is also increasingly difficult for a single firm to dominate an entire market. More and more companies have been forced to realize that the old saying is true; if you cannot beat them, join them. Alternately, have them join you. Sony's experience with the Betamax video format is a well-known example of failing through less than splendid isolation. The company had the best technology in town, but refused to license it to the others and underestimated the necessity of having great content available. Apple had a similar experience. Or as a former top executive at the company once told *Business Week*: "Apple had an ice cube in the desert and everybody wanted it. They could have licensed it to anybody. Now all they've got is wet sand."[387]

We need knowledge to be able to outsource knowledge.

In contrast, Nokia says that it "firmly believes that open standards are vital to the future success of the communications industry. The substantial effort and resources the company puts into GSM standardization has contributed to its success and this philosophy continues for 3G".[388] The company has a significant presence in most standardization bodies. Standards not only simplify the co-ordination of joint development, but also secure market acceptance for new products and solutions. Experience the power of open systems once again.

It is also worth noting that it is extremely difficult to be a great buyer of complementary competencies if you do not have any knowledge about the stuff you are acquiring. Friedrich Nietzsche pointed out that a man has no ears for that to which experience has given him no access. We need knowledge to be able to outsource knowledge.

The glorious anatomy of super-models

The last few years have seen many companies, which once claimed that they had great new business models, failing miserably. When it comes to business models skepticism is healthy. Building a great business model is merely the first step. It is our experience that models fail for three primary reasons; lack of *exclusivity, execution* and *elasticity*.

Exclusivity is the ultimate test of the value proposition and whether the competence network exists to turn the promise into practice, performance and ultimately profitability. Successful models deliver a unique bundle of benefits using a matchless mix of activities and competencies that is difficult to imitate. The creation of temporary monopolies is dependent on the existence of demand but also on limited supply for as long as possible. Wealth creation necessitates plenty of customers with needs and few competitors capable of similar deeds. Getting one out of two things right simply won't do the trick.

While exclusivity largely revolves around the effectiveness and endurance of the model, execution boils down to efficiency and consistency. To succeed companies must do the right things right and the elements of the model must be mutually supportive and self-reinforcing. Execution means implementing the strategic imperatives in each and every aspect of the operation. It also includes co-ordinating activities with the complementors. Mind though that execution only does the trick if the model is exclusive. Otherwise, the end result is that things just go to hell faster.

In the case of Wal-Mart all this has meant a strong focus on cost reductions through innovation in areas such as purchasing, logistics and information management.[389] Wal-Mart store managers have the power to lower prices, but not to raise them.[390] Now, that's what we call a permission statement.

At the heart of a low-cost model, such as EasyJet's, are a number of principles capturing the capabilities necessary to fulfill the promise of the value proposition.[391] EasyJet managers mention two critical principles: asset-sweating and auction-pricing. It is absolutely essential

Models fail for three primary reasons.

that its planes are as full as possible and flying as much as possible. To achieve this, the company uses variable pricing based on demand.[392] Unlike many other airlines where you can get last minute bargains, EasyJet makes it cheaper for those who buy early and then gradually begins to raise prices. Again IT is the enabler. The company uses a sophisticated yield management software pricing system.

For EasyJet one implication of its focus was to start charging for the coffee it serves on flights. This enabled the company to earn a few more bucks. But it also led to less coffee consumption so that passengers do not have to visit the toilet as often. EasyJet then removed one of the toilets from each of its airplanes and instead put in extra seats so it could carry even more passengers. Some would call it cynical. Another interpretation would be that it's just clever – efficiency and consistency in one neat package. "We don't aspire to be all things to all people. We do one thing very well at low cost," says Phil Jones, Chief Technology Officer at the company.[393]

Finally, elasticity concerns the flexibility and adaptability of the model – over time, space and mass. While companies should avoid compromising the underlying logic of the value proposition, other aspects of the model must be open to change. Leaders of super-models decide what should never be changed and then feel free to change just about everything else. These organizations are completely fixed and flexible at the same time. Nothing besides the core is sacred. Dell could never sell computers via retailers since this would violate the very core of its direct-to-the-customer logic. But the organization was flexible enough to pioneer using the Net rather than telephones to interact with customers.

Similarly, great models must be able to adapt to fluctuations and differences in demand and customer preferences. The EuroDisney experience is a telling example.[394] People back in the US expected Europeans (and in this case particularly the French) to behave like the folks back home. And boy, were they wrong! The revenue side of the model did not work as they had predicted. For instance, people expected to be seated at exactly the same lunch and dinner hour, rather than grazing all day long at various restaurants as the Americans did. As a result, the facilities became over-loaded, creating long lines of angry, hungry and frustrated visitors. The turnaround of EuroDisney required changing more than ten key elements of the model to fit this new cultural context.

Lastly, in terms of mass, the border between the organization and the rest of the world may change. As markets continue to conquer hierarchies, or companies figure that it is better to keep activities internally to boost value innovation rather than pursuing transaction cost minimization, activities are outsourced or brought back home.

Fit for the future

Once the basic properties of the model are in place, it is time to start thinking about how to gain momentum. While the business model could be thought of as the DNA of an organization, the stock market value of a company is also dependent on its ability to create options for the future – new customer offerings. All organizations need to have an on-going dialog to develop a point of view about how the creation of value may change in the years to come, including how it possibly migrates throughout the value-chain. And we mean all companies.

A behemoth like Coca-Cola may well have a 50% global market share in the cola market, but it has only a 2% market share in the global consumer beverage industry.[35] There is potential to rethink things. Always. Jack Welch of GE did just that by urging his managers to redefine their industries or markets so that they had less than a 10% market share.[396] Perspective matters – some even claim that it is worth 50 IQ-points.

The hypothesis about an imaginable future serves as a point of departure for leveraging the value proposition and the value-creating network. In essence, model-based growth is three-dimensional, covering areas, applications and access – adding customers, content and marketing channels.

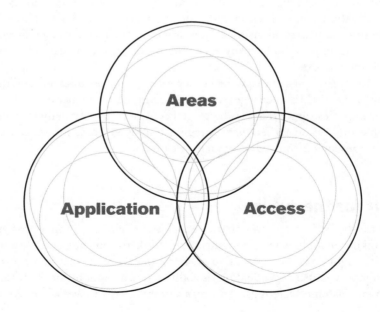

Growing the area means opening up for new types of customers, adding new countries, or attracting different communities. Dell, for instance, has expanded internationally while also being among the first PC makers to go after large corporate accounts. Amazon has recently added professional supplies, such as industrial, medical and scientific supplies, to its roster of products. Cosmetics giant L'Oréal uses its global marketing machine to buy local brands and then launch them internationally.

Application-based growth concerns content. EasyJet is now complemented by EasyCar, EasyInternet Café and EasyCinema. Its model seeks to revolutionize industry after industry. For example, an EasyCar rental center literally equals one person in a van with a laptop connected to the Internet operating in leased space at a parking lot. "I believe we've removed half the cost base of Hertz and Avis by eliminating people and lots," notes Stelios Haji-Iannou, founder of the company.[397] In addition, EasyCar will charge you $15 extra if the car has not been washed when you return it (80% of the cars are returned pre-washed).[398] The logic is simple and beautiful: clean assets are easier to sweat.

Or take the retailer GAP that has extended its offer to consumers by applying its core capabilities within merchandising and brand marketing to now include Banana Republic, Old Navy Clothing, GAP Kids and Baby GAP. With a little help from Tiger Woods, Nike has done to golf what it once did to basketball. Dell recently added its own brand of printers and ink cartridges by entering a partnership with Lexmark. Other partnerships include EMC for storage gear and EDS for systems integration.

Leveraging access means adding new marketing channels. During the last few years, for many traditional companies this has meant enabling the customer to get access to the offer over the Web – clicks and mortar. In an effort to fight off Amazon, Barnes & Noble launched b&n.com, departing from its traditional model of large physical bookstores where people can linger for hours and take a latte while flicking through the books. Meanwhile, Amazon, on the other hand, was true to its core idea of building buyographical relationships on the Net rather than real-world bookstores. Not all growth is great. If expansion is not aligned with the core of the strategy there is a clear risk that eventually the model becomes flab rather than fab.

13

MOODS THAT MATTER

In a world of mood swinging markets, understanding feelings lies at the heart of business. In the age of the individual and endless choice, success is based on letting go of the notion that people are rational creatures. Masters of mood exploit the imperfections of man by seducing or sedating consumers. They know that our brains are emotionally wired. These companies are master story-tellers selling sinovations. Mood monopolists understand that either an organization creates a brand or it is banned. Design is their new competitive weapon.

Moods Inc.

Do your customers faint with joy, excitement or sheer unadulterated pleasure when they see what you have to offer? How often do you need to perform the Heimlich maneuver to revive them? Mastering moods is about creating such positive wow-experiences. Emotional enterprises must excite, energize and enthuse their customers. In an age where collectivism has given way to individualism, survival of the sexiest is a question of understanding how the human mind really works. Woo them, then wow them.

Much of management, in practice and in theory, has been based on an underlying belief in rational man. If we can only come up with more and better arguments based on reason, we can convince people to buy our stuff. Forget it. While most people try to act rationally, in reality we are all emotionally wired. Neoclassical economics is wrong. People are not always calculating and selfish. Our preferences are not given and eternal. Do you know anyone capable of leaving their emotions at home when they head off to work or go shopping? Studies by Nobel laureate Daniel Kahneman show that supposedly rational individuals are perfectly willing to take a 20-minute drive to save $20 on a $200 VCR, but not prepared to walk five blocks to save $40 on a $2,000 cruise.[399]

Research in neuroscience now suggests that the brain's limbic system, which governs our feelings, is much more powerful than the neocortex that controls intellect.[400] Whether we like it or not, the traffic instructions that God or evolution provided our brains with are pretty clear: emotions always have the right of way.

Our minds work like this for some pretty good reasons. When a tiger approaches you don't have time to think about the fact that the universe is really big and expanding. Survival first. Or as Professor Karl Weick puts it, people think narratively rather than argumentatively or paradigmatically.[401] Emotions lead to action, while reason only results in conclusions. As Insead's Manfred Kets de Vries says: "An ounce of emotion can be more effective than a ton of facts."[402]

Still, many organizations and managers throughout the world appear emotionally bankrupt, incapable of addicting customers. They are managing organizations selling nightmarish commodities rather than sexy dreams. They have been trained to be nothing else. They have been told to do nothing else. And they are rewarded to be anything but emotional. These people have been to so many training programs and read so many business books that they have overdosed on logic and reason.

In the process of growing up we unlearned most of our right-brain skills.

Executives are not alone. In fact, says Manfred Kets de Vries: "In the process of growing up, we (all) *unlearned* most of our right-brain skills."[403] The challenge for mood monopolists is to create an emotional experience that some of us cannot refuse. Only then will these firms be able to reach above average profitability. In effect, managers of mood must become more like Captain Ahab in Herman Melville's *Moby Dick*. "Ahab never thinks, he just feels, feels, feels."

Competing on models is largely a question of looking for similarities within the low-end niche of the double economy. Competing on moods is the opposite. There are three solid reasons why people buy products and services: practical, social, and emotional. Increasingly, in the karaoke world of choice social and emotional needs are taking over. Mood monopolists thrive on differences. And in a binomial society where people with capital and competencies have more or less endless alternatives, we should expect customers to differ. As a consequence, companies and leaders of business must create, provide, and fulfill our dreams. We can't tell you exactly what these dreams are about, but rest assured that in the age of the individual they come in vibrant technicolor and glorious surround sound. Everyone dreams in color.

Dreams die hard. Legendary Swedish advertising guru Leon Nordin – who dreamt up the Absolut bottle among other things – talks about the five perpetual dreams of mankind:[404]

- eternal life
- eternal youth
- eternal richness
- eternal virility
- eternal happiness

These categories explain 99.9% of the spam you receive. Success has always been and will always be about coming up with innovative ways to satisfy the basic urges of people. Dream-centered competition is generic – dream against dream, organizations around the world in a total global battle for a share of customers' money and minds. The church competes with Herbalife. L'Oréal is up against Nike and Coca-Cola. Banks and insurance companies are fighting it out with lotteries and bookies.

E(motional)-business

Mastering the management of mood means engaging all the senses of man. It may no longer be enough to satisfy the needs of consumers. Perhaps, it is more relevant to talk about customer desires or the ability to surprise potential buyers and help them become successful. Sometimes it takes the business community a while to realize just how different we all are. Remember that it took the automotive industry close to 100 years to figure out that women are not small men. Millions, perhaps even billions, of dollars were spent on marketing research to end up with this brilliant insight that may well take another 25 years to implement.

To prosper, Moods Inc. centers its attention on being a de-commoditizer. It uses different tools to capture the attention and interest of customers. It exploits the imperfections of man – the fact that our gut reactions are emotional rather than rational.

Apple's Steve Jobs was asked what distinguishes the company's Mac OS X operating system. He replied: "We made the buttons on the screen look so good you'll want to lick them."[405] He did not utter a single word about megahertz and gigabytes – buttons that look so good that people will want to lick them. Jobs is a true CEO – Chief Emotional Officer. He is out to make a dent in the universe. The iMac was the same story. Apple claims that around one third of the people who bought an iMac did not previously own a computer.[406] "They were talking about the iMac in a language usually reserved for small, fluffy animals and close family members," says Jonathan Ive, head of Apple design. While few customer offerings have a life, all great products and services have a soul. Lick the competition.

All great products and services have a soul.

iMac

Many organizations have already moved from mainly producing things that you can touch to adding a human touch. Alberto Alessi, CEO of the eponymous Italian company, argues that they are not manufacturers, they are mediators between the expression of creativity and the real things that touch people's hearts. Sir Richard Branson of Virgin sometimes claims it is feelings – and feelings alone – which account for the success of the Virgin brand in all of its many forms. Mood matters.

Capturing the emotional human being is a question of figuring out the secret wishes and deep desires of people – addicting customers. But there's more. Our society is marked by individuals loathing the negatives as much as loving the positives. In medicine, experts claim that people are more interested in removing pain than adding joy. Similarly, in business, we are more willing to shoulder risk to avoid losses than to make gains. Mood strategies, therefore, can also focus on the reduction of negative feelings. Management of mood is a question of seduction or sedation. And we're not talking about a one-night stand; you must constantly seduce or sedate. Customer relationships are in need of constant reinforcement. "What have you done for me lately?" is what customers (and pop star Janet Jackson) are asking. We're talking about a love affair.

Sinovation

From a biological point of view, human beings are essentially animals. Genetically speaking, the difference between an average person and a pygmy chimp is about 1.5%.[407] Over time, we have painted a layer of varnish on this animalistic body of man. This finish consists of norms and values, codes of conduct and behavior. Man became a "moral animal" as suggested by American author Robert Wright.[408] But it is a thin coat of varnish. Indeed, in our age of deregulation and fragmentation – or moral meltdown as some would put it – the layer is beginning to crack. When tempted, man has always been and will always be prepared to rid himself of the mask of morality.

Such behavior is increasingly socially acceptable. Managers of mood know this. Successful emotional enterprises already exploit this. To many of these companies, innovation equals something that looks more like "sinovation".

"People have always been immoral, shiftless, self-gratifying, good-for-nothing shits," observes the suitably entitled www.deadlysins.com. In economics and business we usually refer to this as opportunism. Yet, for ages, man struggled to find a conceptual framework to operationalize our spiritual shortcomings. In the 6th century, Pope Gregory the Great made a major break-through when he nailed it down to seven deadly sins. Since then, with one exception, these sins have stood the test of time (what is now sloth started out as sadness.) Time is the ultimate test, so the list should be a reasonable proxy of human imperfections (perfection or imperfection of course depends on your vantage point). It is interesting to note that, as far as we know, the concept of deadly sins hardly exists in the other major world religions (although greed, for instance, is definitely regarded as a sin in Buddhism) which all seem more focused on what people should do rather than what they shouldn't do. (Something similar could be said of the Bible's New Testament.)

Many of you are probably more familiar with the sins from the blockbuster movie *Seven* rather than from all the years spent at Sunday school but as a moral refresher here are the magnificent seven:[409]

Pride   The excess belief in one's own abilities that interferes with the individual's recognition of the Grace of God. The mother of all sins. (Also known as vanity.)

Envy   The desire for other's traits, status, abilities or situation.

Gluttony The extravagant desire to consume more than one requires.

Lust   The excessive craving for the pleasures of the body.

Anger   Manifested in people who spurn love and opt for fury. (Also known as wrath.)

Greed   The desire for material wealth or gain, ignoring the realm of the spiritual.

Sloth   The avoidance of physical or spiritual work.

Around each and every one of these sins, there are clusters of highly successful corporations built on exploiting our weaknesses – some explicitly but most implicitly. If you want to experience all sins at once, we suggest that you take the first available flight to Moscow, Las Vegas or Sun City in South Africa and get a suite at the Gomorrah Inn. Sins are seductive.

The sins provide themes for stories created to lure and snare customers into buying the experience. Therefore, just about any customer offering can be positioned in seven different ways. The sinful story envelops the product and service. Often, the experience is a (mostly) socially acceptable

Man has always been prepared to rid himself of the mask of morality.

surrogate for the real thing. Consider anger. We can't have people running around the streets killing each other, but that does not mean that fury has been exterminated from the face of planet earth. Rather than shooting your real world enemies, computer games such as DOOM enable you to let off some of the steam. Or go and play some paint-ball. Combine two peccadilloes and you can be even more successful – hyphen-sin-ovation. The computer game *Tomb Raider* mixes lust and anger. We have been told that the heroin, Lara Croft, is recognized by more people around the world than His Holiness the Pope.

We gamble because our lives have become overly predictable and safe.

Sins are deeply rooted in the karaoke society that we have created. As the American author and columnist Dan Savage puts it, we gamble not necessarily because we are greedy but because our lives have become overly predictable and safe. Despite recent tragedies, for many people in the information society, risk and excitement are scarce resources. Similarly, people indulge in sloth in response to stress caused by increasingly hectic schedules.[410]

The 7S-moods.

Stories about pride deal with issues of exclusivity and accomplishment. Companies wanting to create experiences centered on vanity must help people believe in and respect themselves. At its best, this leads to self-esteem. At its worst, self-importance and arrogance is the end result.

Both approaches can be equally commercially successful. American Express Platinum cards, gold airline loyalty cards and membership of seemingly exclusive clubs, are all about making people feel proud of themselves. By letting people know that they belong to a select group, you tell them that they have moved closer to God. In the world of business schools, God lives right next to Boston's Harvard Square.

Building a tribe of pride is a question of invitation, rejection and co-production. Accomplishment-stories often center on making people

37% of Brits claimed that they wanted his portrait on the new 10 pound note.

pleased about their own contribution. By involving them in the experience they can take pride in the production of things rather than merely being relegated to the role of a passive consumer. Consider the New York marathon. The runners are customers as well as the stars of the show. The prize you get after having finished the race differs depending on your time. We are not all created equal. Talk shows and rock concerts operate under similar principles.

Envy can be exploited in at least two different ways. The first type of tale tells people that they have a chance of joining those who are apparently luckier, wiser or more attractive. Basically, all ads use envy in one way or another. "If I could only be more like Tiger Woods." You can if you buy a Tag Heur wristwatch. Tales of envy are especially effective if they can be linked to iconic personalities.

People are more susceptible to envy soccer star David Beckham than a pair of football boots. This explains Adidas' offer of a £100 million lifelong promotional deal to Beckham. This is what happens when you have someone who is so popular that 37% of Brits claimed that they wanted his portrait on the new 10 pound note.[411] Mr. Beckham transcends geography, ideology and religion. He is even featured on the fundament of a Buddha statue in the Pariwastemple in Bangkok.[412] Stars tell a story. Most products don't. Stars sell (out).

The other type of story deals with delight over other people's misfortune. Look at tabloids in general and the British ones in particular. Celebrities may be rich and famous, but people take malicious pleasure in learning about their drinking problems, weird sexual habits and nervous breakdowns. If we can't have what they have, we want them to have less than us – in at least one area of life. Mood monopolists exploit the fact that we all want to get the last laugh (at someone else's expense). There is a small version of Shakespeare's Iago inside us all.

Next on the list is gluttony which can be interpreted literally or figuratively. Fast food companies, manufacturers of snacks, candy and chocolate all try to persuade people that the road to happiness leads to the stomach. The US food supply already provides some 3,800 kilocalories per person per day. This is almost twice as much as required by many adults.[413] Recent research suggests that we are in the process of giving up the concept of regular meals and have instead started grazing like cows and horses.

Moving on, there are post-gluttony strategies by which companies create stories linking gluttony to envy, pride or pain – mixing seduction and sedation. Look at weight watchers, lean cuisine and cosmetics companies. Charles Revson, founder of Revlon, once remarked: "In the factory we make cosmetics, in the store we sell hope."[414] The ultimate

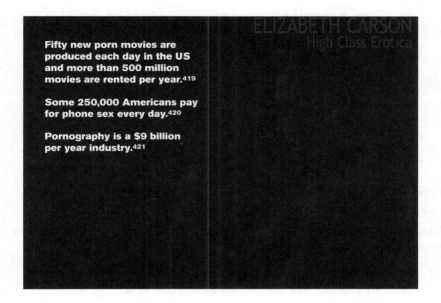

Fifty new porn movies are produced each day in the US and more than 500 million movies are rented per year.[419]

Some 250,000 Americans pay for phone sex every day.[420]

Pornography is a $9 billion per year industry.[421]

ELIZABETH CARSON
High Class Erotica

exploiter of the post-gluttony syndrome is probably pharmaceutical company Pfizer. Its Lipitor tablet is the number one prescribed cholesterol-lowering pill in the United States and the best selling drug in the world. Over 18 million Americans have been prescribed Lipitor to help lower their cholesterol.[415]

Gluttony is also aligned with the conspicuous consumption of the cosmocrats – remember the pearls and the yachts. People in the West and elsewhere live in the most consumption-crazed society since the Roman Empire. The trick is to convince people that the good life revolves around shopping – redemption by retailing.

And then there is lust. This is largely obvious. The Internet porn business is valued at $1 billion by Forrester Research.[416] Internet porn generates substantially more than 70% of all the revenues earned by online content providers.[417] The sites set up by female sex entrepreneur Danny Ash have more than 3 million visitors per month. She has 20,000 subscribers paying $19.95 per month and a profit margin of 35%.[418] You can win with sin.

And sex sells other things as well – from cosmetics and clothes to cars. Sigmund Freud was right. Desire is a strong human driver. By looking at the number of book titles available on Amazon you get a clue about how strong a driver sex really is (and also about how the world in general works). In May 2003, 6,365 books covered stress while sex was included in 20,428 titles. For exploiters of lust, the challenge is to turn the customer offering into the equivalent of a swinger's party experience.

Human beings, and especially the male species, are wired for anger.

What does your company sound like, feel like, taste like, smell like?

Guns and ammo sales in the US, as well as the American thirst for vengeance through lawsuits, are clear example of this phenomenon. To thrive on fury, companies need to provide stories centered on a message of risk-free tension. Action movies, for instance, allow people to deal with rage in a "safe" way. You can pretend to be the Terminator without any risk of being terminated or sent to prison. Computer games make the experience interactive. Or consider music. A concert with death-metal band Entombed is all about wrath. Along the way all of our senses are assaulted. PlayStation, Nintendo and Xbox games, as well as most movies, have soundtracks. We all know what Intel sounds like, but what does your company sound like, feel like, taste like, smell like?

Certain sport events also function as post-modern primal therapy. We gather the tribe and fight verbal wars with our enemies (although these confrontations occasionally get out of hand). A less physical way of exploiting anger is to position the experience so that it takes a strong stance against something that disturbs people. Greenpeace, Amnesty and Save the Children Foundation are but three of these socio-political customer complaints departments for people who are no longer prepared to put up with what they deem wrong.

Meanwhile there is always greed which lies at the heart of our Christmas Carol capitalist society. Greed has even become something of a virtue. Now, we can all be Scrooge. Banks and investment funds already know and exploit this fact. In Las Vegas, the construction of casinos has been elevated to an art form. Architects follow strict rules to draw in people closer and closer to the womb of Mammon. Artificial light makes sure that people lose track of time.

More interestingly, one could argue that globalization per se leads to increasing opportunities to exploit greed. Our world is now full of people who have left their old homes in the pursuit of happiness elsewhere. These new arrivals leave their history behind. Their name and title no longer means anything. In terms of social status they start from scratch. So, what is the fastest way to gain recognition and build social status at a new place? By being really nice – like the Ingalls family from *The Little House on the Prairie*, living the heavenly virtues every day. No way. Start amassing material wealth. This phenomenon, in part, probably explains why the US is so materialistic. It is a country of immigrants eager to improve their status vis-à-vis the neighbors.

The challenge is to make people feel good about doing nothing.

Exploiters of greed create experiences that function as status symbols – stories that focus on the individual rather than the community; stories that attach meaning to money; stories linking accumulation to abundance. We are the guardians of our customers' financial dreams, says David Pottruck, co-CEO of Charles Schwab.[422] As a consumer you should remember that your punishment in hell will be that you are boiled in oil. "It's the finest, most luxurious boiling oil that money can buy, but it's still boiling," notes the keeper of deadlysins.com.

Sloth is about physical and intellectual laziness. Such experiences are by definition mind numbing. Think soap operas. Think also of all-inclusive holidays with special clubs that take care of the kids and much more. The challenge is to make people feel good about doing nothing. Another type of story revolving around sloth positions it as a reward for hard work. It's ok to pamper yourself since you have been praying by working for so long – you're worth it. Go directly to the Banyan Tree spa in Phuket without passing go.

Heaven & hell

Sinovation is not only a question of what stories you produce. There is a difference between what a company does and how it does it. Companies can pursue a strategy that is either sacred or sinful. You can pursue this strategy in a way that is either virtuous or villainy. That is, corporations can do sinful things in a virtuous way and sacred things in a villainous way. Combine these two dimensions and you end up with four typical organizations – ranging from Heaven Inc. to Hell Ltd.

We are living in contradictory times so don't be surprised when we tell you that the *Dark Angel Enterprise* may well be the company of the future. Such corporations have cultures which emphasize the importance of care, control, courage and candor. They create, promote and sell sin, but without necessarily hurting anyone else (possibly with the exception of religious zealots).

This hypothesis may annoy the "virtuecrats" of the world. But, is sinovation really any worse than organizations pursuing virtuous business

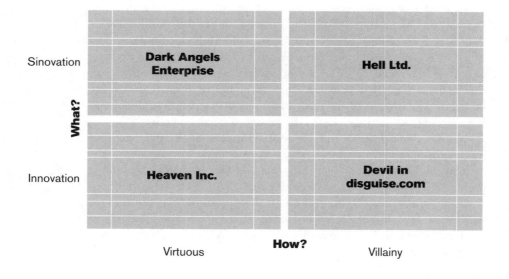

opportunities in a sinful way – polluting the air and water, using child labor, bribing government officials, etc? On the other hand, fat kills people. Obesity is recognized by the World Health Organization as one of the top 10 global health problems.[423] There are many people with an alcohol, drug or gambling problem. The social ramifications are great. You judge.

For now, suffice to say, in a transparent society it will be much more difficult for companies and individuals to hide the ways in which they are doing things. Capitalism has always followed the law of least resistance. Emotional innovation is demand driven. We get the kind of companies and customer offerings that we deserve (or are). Capitalism is merely a mirror of our aggregated selves. Legislating against human nature would essentially be like trying to pass a law against gravity. Though many people would like to fly, it was the Wright bothers and not the Supreme Court that solved the problem. "Good people do not need laws to tell them to act responsibly, while bad people will find a way around the laws," said Plato (who knew more than most about sin). People are human. "Gravitation can not be held responsible for people falling in love," suggested Albert Einstein. Case closed.

Create a brand or be banned

The rich and famous can make their choices. But, in this age of abundance, ambiguity often follows. People are drowning in an ocean of uncertainty caused by infinite choice in a world of surplus and excess. It is increasingly difficult to figure out your own preferences. What do my friends and colleagues say about my choices? How will I be able to evaluate all the alternatives? Should I buy now or wait for the next generation? Sound familiar?

And human beings hate uncertainty. We are all control freaks. Lack of perceived control makes us sick. It causes anxiety and stress. We love certainty and so we seek guidance from brands. Brands are the perfect commercial answer to the schizophrenic nature of human beings – our wish to simultaneously express our individuality and our need for belonging. Brands mean that we don't have to think, just act. The brands do the thinking for you. Brands are seductive and sedative.

But mood companies and their ad agencies now face a very different reality. There is increasing fragmentation. During the last decades the fastest growing brand category in many industries has been labeled "other".[424] It is no longer relevant to talk about a "youth culture" because there are so many of them. A brand like Levi's, for example, is under threat. In the age of collectivism Levi's focused on building a name based on a specific product. Now, it has to face a group of customers with very different lifestyles.

The second brand buster is surplus. In an excess economy attention is a really scarce resource. Organizations may even have to pay for it. Today, a company will underwrite your monthly car payment if you permit it to put an auto wrap around your car.[425] In the future you may very well be driving a rolling billboard. Another challenge is caused by increasing transparency. In a striptease society the days of faking are over. The messages that you are sending have to be authentic – true stories. Finally, there is the question of schizophrenic man.

Brands fulfill the dual needs of belonging and being different

Let's consider a true story. Some time ago, one of us spent a weekend in Paris with his wife. Strolling down Avenue de Montaigne in the fashion capital of the world, he was approached by two young Japanese women. They asked him if he would be willing to go into the Louis Vuitton store and buy them a bag with a special pattern and color. They were under the mistaken impression that the store had a limit of one bag per customer. The two women handed over 700 Euros, and told him that they would be waiting two blocks away (so no one in the store would be able to detect their cunning deception). Alas, the bag was out of stock.

The story illustrates a couple of important points.[426]

No.1. Brands rule. The women were perfectly willing to trust a bald Swede dressed in black with 700 Euros, just for the prospect of getting their hands on the LV bag.

Before mating can start people dress up in brands – they buy their own feathers.

No.2. They were very particular about the specific pattern and color of the bag. They even had a color copy of a page in the LV catalogue that they had brought all the way from Japan. It was absolutely critical that the bag was of a kind that they couldn't get hold of at home. It simply had to be different.

Brands fulfill the dual needs of belonging and being different – hyper-individualism and tribal collectivism. Today's consumers are more complex (or sophisticated perhaps) than those of yesterday. They do not settle for either/or when they can get both.

Brands are not only capable of uncertainty reduction. They also serve the purpose of attention expansion – attraction by association. All individuals are competing for attention. They want to be noticed, recognized or even admired by other people. During the last few years, research in evolutionary psychology has taken an interest in Charles Darwin's theory of sexual selection.[427] He claimed that male peacocks developed their colorful tail to court female peacocks more effectively and thus ensure the survival of the species. Female peacocks do not regard the males as unfit or ridiculous because they have a useless though beautiful bunch of feathers sticking out of their butts, but find the strength of their genes – as expressed by the feathers – attractive.

Design is about truth, love and beauty.

The same is true of human beings. Note again though that the argument of evolutionary psychology is more about Beethoven than Brad Pitt – brains rather than beauty (not implying that Mr. Pitt is not also super-smart). Researchers claim that the development of the human brain – our ability to enjoy and create music, art, literature, etc. – must be understood from the outlook of sexual rather than natural selection. Success is therefore a question of getting beautiful minds to connect. Companies must court customers with offerings that trigger a positive emotional reaction.

The outside still matters of course. Before mating can start people dress up in brands – they buy their own feathers. Those with enough cash and choice design their own personalities and identities – their own brand. But from this evolutionary perspective, our obsession with what society defines as attractive is about rationality rather than vanity. Wearing Donna Karen or Helmut Lang is a peacock's tail feather. Man is programmed and predestined to procreate. Here, we do not have a choice.

Design an experience or expire

Masters of mood are familiar with the peacock principle. They know that sexy products enable you to thrive. The best brands are instantly identifiable. Survival of the sexiest does not imply that such customer offerings have longer product life cycles but rather that a steady stream of sexy things ensure the survival of the firm behind them.

Distinct design is the primary weapon. Recently, the *Financial Times* reported that "Ericsson lost $2.3 billion on mobile phone handsets last year because its products are ugly".[428] Michael Weinstein, CEO of Snapples, notes that his company is no longer in the soft drink business. In reality, it is a player in the fashion business, "which is a constant world of new products, flavors and packaging, pitched to consumers who want the latest thing".[429]

Companies are in the fashion business not because they like it, but because their customers want them to be in it. Customers expect to be wooed and wowed by design. They want the latest and brightest peacock feathers and they want them now.

And we find great design in the most unexpected places. Slovenian white-goods company Gornje, for instance, collaborates with legendary design-house Pininfarina which has fashioned car-classics such as the Alfa Romeo Spider and Ferrari Testarossa. Great design is global. Swedish architects/designers ClaessonKoivistoRune have designed the new cultural center in Kyoto, Japan.

Aesthetics play an important role in evoking strong feelings. Most people take technology for granted these days. What they want are products that seduce. Attracting the emotional customer is not a question of superior price or performance. Remember that great technology is mostly given – necessary but not sufficient. How many contemporary customers do you think do reversed engineering on their DVD-players, PDAs or PCs? Design is about truth, love and beauty and, increasingly, about whether a business has a sensational strategy or the same strategy as everyone else.

"Design is not done with rules, but with intuition. Intuition never lies," says the leading British designer, Jasper Morrison.[430] To some this is frivolous indulgence, a world away from the realities of the bottom-line and quarterly capitalism. To them, design is mere decoration rather than pure meaning. Successful companies tell a different story. Furniture retailer, IKEA, proclaims its vision of "good design, good function and good quality". The American airline JetBlue announces that its priorities are "simplicity, friendly people, technology, design and entertainment". This corporation has 3,100 employees and a market value that is greater than the combined value of Northwest Airlines, United and US Airways that together employ some 175,000 people.[431] "Customers really respond to products that involve new thinking and connect with their souls," says Ron Jonson, former vice-president of Target, the low cost retailer with some 1,000 stores which works with renowned designers such as Michael Graves, Isaac Mizrahi and Philippe Starck.[432] It successfully competes with giant Wal-Mart not by being cheaper but by being different.

Design is the only thing that differentiates one product from another in the marketplace.

Industrial design is an increasingly rich source of differentiation. "We won't make things cheaper than the far-eastern nations, but we can make things better through design and innovation," says British designer Sir Terence Conran.[433] Robert Hayes of Harvard Business School echoes similar ideas by claiming that: "Fifteen years ago companies competed on price. Now it's quality. Tomorrow it's design."[434] A good price/performance relationship is necessary for any company in any industry but no longer sufficient. Getting that stuff right buys you a ticket to sit close to the ring, but it will not win the fight. E-motional business is about improving the *money/meaning* relationship.

Inevitably, some companies have been exploiting emotional economics and the power of design for many years. "At Sony we assume that all our competitors' products will have the same technology, price, performance and features. Design is the only thing that differentiates one product from another in the marketplace," says Norio Ogha, former Sony CEO.[435]

The fear and the attraction of design lie in its infinite possibilities. Design is a fact of life – though not always appreciated – and all embracing. It concerns all aspects of the organization, from branding to how we deal with customers and colleagues – the office architecture, the stores, packaging, sales people, etc. Just like firms can grow the business model, companies can leverage the business mood. Armani and Calvin Klein now both have home collections of towels, bedsheets, plates, glasses, and other domestic mundanities. In addition to its watches and jewelry, Swatch has entered the automotive industry with the Smart Car through a joint venture with Mercedes Benz. Shape and form touch all aspects of business and life. Successful mood companies must, as a result, design an emotional experience.

The moment of truth when people actually buy things is also affected. Without a doubt, shopping will increasingly be online. So the way we think about real-world shops will change dramatically. Until recently, we designed, built, manned, organized and decorated shops to sell stuff in them. In an economy where sales almost always equaled physical presence (though let's not forget the Sears catalogue) this was reasonable and sound. Rule: optimize shelf-space. With the introduction of e-commerce, things change.

It's time to wake up. A real-world bookstore, or any other store for that matter, cannot compete with a virtual one in terms of availability, price, convenience, etc. With the advent of mobile Internet, people can even bring their own cash register in the phone to the store and have a look at the product (touch, feel, listen, smell, taste – all the stuff that really matters – grown-ups, not only young kids, are tactile) and then search the Web to find the best deal.

The result for those in the real world is that they must compete on real world advantages. IKEA has a catalogue that is distributed to millions of households, but the real deal is the store displaying ways of decorating the home rather than single pieces of furniture. In the years to come, a lot of manufacturers of goods will be forced to set up shops to show stuff – and a lot of shops that just sell stuff produced by someone else will be forced to close down operations (or reincarnate on the Web).

The new rule is to optimize the emotional experience. How? Well, what about adding elements of aesthetics and entertainment? If all customer offerings contain an aesthetic element, and they do regardless of whether they are beautiful or ugly, we should consider them as pieces of art. Where is art displayed? At museums and galleries of course. Visit the Guggenheim in Bilbao and learn something about the shop of the future. Prada, Gucci and others may already have done so. Just look at how products are displayed at their stores. Myron E. Almon III of the highly successful cosmetics company Sephora even claims that "when our customers stroll down Fifth Avenue, we want them to say to themselves, should I go to the Museum of Modern Art, or should I go to Sephora?"[436] Making your mind up will become harder and harder.

And, if you want to add some entertainment, go to an amusement park. But hurry up. We predict that many face tough times. Why pay to go to your local theme park when it's free (or you will actually be paid) to play around with the latest video games or whatever by those who make them? Instead of the storeowner telling you: show me the money. You tell them: show me what's funny! Look at how people seem to enjoy themselves at a Sharper Image store. Or, why not combine it. At Nike town, Marion Jones' running shoes are displayed as modern age Mona Lisas while you can watch her and other sports stars perform on giant video screens. Companies interested in having a future must focus or combine aesthetics and entertainment. Remember what Raymond Loewy, the father of industrial design once said. The most beautiful of forms is that of a rising sales curve.

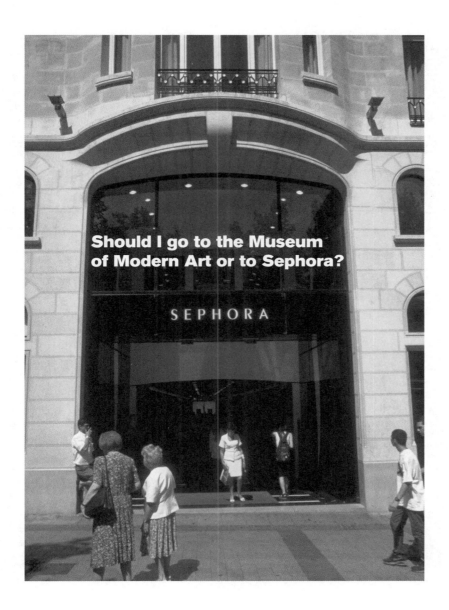

Should I go to the Museum
of Modern Art or to Sephora?

SEPHORA

14

MANAGING MOODY MODELS

Excellent companies need to combine the strengths of models and moods. To truly thrive, organizations must be fit and sexy. Re-inventing innovation means realizing that the future will always arrive as a surprise unless we create superior customer experiences by taking intellectual leadership over a value-creating network. The time has come to stop re-engineering and start re-energizing our organizations.

Roulette time

The time has come to place your bets – models or moods?

But there is a small problem. As soon as someone says either or, true entrepreneurs will see this as an invitation to do both. We fear that few companies will truly thrive on 100% models or moods. Darwin was right. To succeed, you have to be fit and sexy – combining substance and style, functionality and fashion. Fitness is a question of adaptation. In the age of information mania this means exploiting market imperfections. The sex thing is about attraction – making the emotional connection. When individuals rule, this boils down to exploiting the imperfections of man. We want to emphasize, however, that we are talking about doing both, not striking a balance. It's fitness x fertility, rather than staying in shape + sex.

Southwest Airlines invented the low-cost airline business model, but that does not tell the whole story. The stock exchange ticker for Southwest is spelt LUV. Its slogan? "The airline that love built." Flying with Southwest you are liable to hear announcements such as "There may be fifty ways to leave your lover, but there are only four ways to leave this aircraft... ", or "Smoking in the lavatories is prohibited. Any person caught smoking in the lavatories will be asked to leave the plane immediately." The website of Southwest even boasts, "Time flies when you're having fun".

Or let us revisit Wal-Mart. It certainly has a great business model, but the culture of the company also displays strong elements of mood. According to Professor Richard S. Tedlow, its founder Sam Walton had a "special genius for transforming anybodies into somebodies".[437] Wal-Mart is a tribe.

As little as these model companies would survive without moods, would Moods Inc. thrive without exploiting market imperfections? Nokia makes sexy mobile phones, but in addition it also operates an efficient business model. The company has a very low cost-structure. Fit and sexy. Driving a BMW car is a great experience, but it is an experience dependent on a sophisticated network of companies interacting to produce it. F&S. eBay has a unique business model, but auctions also add excitement to the shopping experience. Apple's iPod looks great, but the on/off button still needs to work. We could go on and on.

As we have seen, intelligent enterprises realize that the scope of innovation has grown much larger. In fact, the truly great ones have been responsible for expanding and cultivating this new innovation landscape.

Reinventing innovation

As soon as you mention the word innovation, people tend to think about nuts and bolts, mad scientists and laboratories. They think Q. For many people, innovation equals technology. This is not necessarily so. Administrators can be innovative. Innovation is all-embracing and stereotype-defying. [438]

Once upon a time, innovation used to be a question of what we did in-house. The creation of novelty really was the preserve of engineers and scientists – men and women in white coats carrying around test tubes. Then we added suppliers. Just think about all the stories of the Japanese automotive industry during the 1980s. Now many organizations also include customers in the development of new products and services.

Harley-Davidson offers the ability for a 43-year old accountant to dress in black leather, ride through small towns and have people be afraid of him.

Creating a superior business model is increasingly a question of being the mastermind behind a value-creating network – a model innovator. Either you design the new puzzle or you'll be left puzzled. Just ask the people at HP/Compaq about Dell.

As if this is not enough, innovation also used to be a question of products. Then it became products plus services. Now, we are in the business of having to create an emotional experience for the customer.

Just listen to the Harley-Davidson executive who claims that the company offers "the ability for a 43-year old accountant to dress in black leather, ride through small towns and have people be afraid of him".[439] Similarly, Frederick W. Smith, chairman, president and CEO of FedEx notes that: "We thought we were selling the transportation of goods, in fact we were selling peace of mind."[440]

The future will always arrive as a surprise to companies that see innovation as something that pertains only to the product and activities that are carried out within the organization. Those companies will be under constant attacks by incumbents and traditional competitors using the entire stage to surprise and delight customers. Anyone is a potential threat. So all companies need to worry about how many nukes are pointing at them right now. The advice is simple: corporations either re-invent innovation or they risk becoming punch-drunk boxers forced to say, "We didn't see it coming".

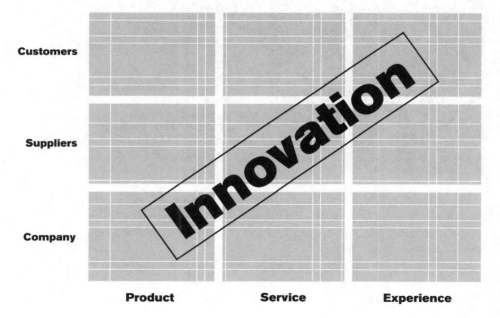

KARAOKE CAPITALISM MANAGING MOODY MODELS

Successfully navigating the new innovation landscape requires orchestration and improvisation. Companies need to run simultaneous strategies. Strategies have to be simultaneous from the point of view that they must run them internally as well as together with partners; combining exploitation and creation; making use of markets and man; capturing supply and demand-side innovation; pursuing rational as well as emotional imperfections; being fit and sexy. To cope, leaders of leading organizations must have split vision.

Re-energizing the corporation

To get to the future first, companies need speed. From physics we know that velocity is a function of mass and energy; the greater the energy and the lower the mass, the higher the velocity. Translate this to the business world. The 1980s and 1990s were largely devoted to processes of *demassification* – downsizing, outsourcing, lean management, etc. Companies re-engineered themselves into hyper-efficient competitive weapons. Managers were told to focus on core competencies and create a knowledge-based organization where IQ could flourish. Meritocracies replaced bureaucracies. So far, however, most companies have by and large neglected the other variable in the function.

"How prompt we are to satisfy the hunger and thirst of our bodies; how slow to satisfy the hunger and thirst of our souls," noted Henry David Thoreau some 150 years ago. Now, the time has come to start re-energizing our organizations. The future does not only lie in front of excellent companies. It must also rest within them – in the heads and hearts of its people. While tomorrow's winners may well be the "empires of the mind" that Sir Winston Churchill once talked about, they still need a sense of spirit – *energy* through *emotion*.

Easier said than done. Far too many executives are now in the process of "organizing enterprises that are destructive of the things people most care about, like quality of life or good relationships with people we work with, or good relationships with our family, or long term sustainability," according to management writer Margaret Wheatley.[441] Ensuring and enabling change in a brain-based organization is not a question of rearranging the boxes and arrows. A while back, Steve Ballmer of Microsoft pointed out that the company had probably gone through too many re-organizations. Now, the challenge was one of re-missioning people rather than re-organizing them.[442]

Our notion of re-energizing the corporation is slightly more sophisticated than turning managers into an unlikely combo of cheerleaders and preachers. Consider this. Competition in the high-end niche of the job market used to be a question of security and salary. Then we swapped security for stock options. Now, we are in the business of having to create an emotional experience not only for customers, but also for talented individuals.

Companies used to be consumers of competence. Today, they must be both co-creators of competence *and* providers of personality. Once it was money for mastery. Now, it must also be meaning for membership. The relationship between employer and employee becomes both transactional and relational. In the future firm, people have a calling as much as a career. Here, the true stars are non-profit organizations such as the Red Cross and Amnesty International. How many people at a typical business firm would show up for work tomorrow if they didn't get paid a single dime? Today's talent demands money and meaning, value and values. To thrive, companies must learn how to master the art of combining skill and soul.

All extraordinary achievements depend on passion – in sports, art, politics, business, etc. Certainly, successful companies have core capabilities that determine what they can do. Most organizations also have core opportunities reflecting what is possible to do. But more important than anything else are the core compassions, what people in organizations actually care about doing. Modern corporations definitely compete on competence, but not competence alone.

Knowledge is to a firm what gas is to a car. Fill it up, but remove spark plugs and it still won't move. Without passion we will not get any innovation. Know how and know who are small things compared to

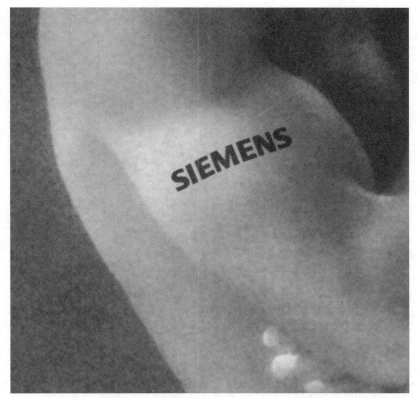

SIEMENS

If you can love a schnauzer you should be able to love your company, should you not?

know why. Leaders face the challenge of transforming *bureaucracies* into *amorocracies*. Bureaucracy came from the French *bureau*, meaning office. The new organization comes from the Italian *amore*. It is an organization based on passion and love. In such firms, all people have a P&L responsibility. Why is it important that all employees have P&L responsibilities? Listen, as always, to Homer Simpson: "If adults don't like their jobs, they don't go on strike. They just go in every day and do it really half-assed."

Over the top and too excessive? Perhaps, but then recall that our brains are emotionally wired. For those of you who are married – why did you say yes to your spouse? Great price/performance? Perhaps he or she is extremely reliable – a human version of the Energizer bunny? Or maybe the power of knowledge got such a grip on you that you ran a pre-wedding IQ test. Unlikely. Most likely you got married because you love(d) your spouse.

In fact, most important relationships in our lives are characterized by love. We love football teams – Bayern Munich or Juventus. We love our hobbies. We love our spouses (at least in the beginning). We love our pets. So, do you love your employer or suppliers? If human beings are capable of loving a schnauzer they should be able to love companies. The real acid test is how many people – colleagues and customers – are dedicated enough to tattoo your corporate logo on their biceps (or elsewhere).

The 10 commandments of karaoke leadership

The costs of bad leadership are on the rise – for politicians, executives and religious leaders, as well as for the rest of us. Leaders are indeed becoming more like pop stars. But they appear to display more similarities to one-hit wonders such as Pseudo Echo than long livers like The Who and Rolling Stones. Today, you can be extremely successful and still have a short life expectancy. Executives everywhere feel the heat. CEOs make more money than ever before but the stakes are high and uncertainty levels are becoming higher by the year. CEOs appointed after 1985 are three times more likely to get fired than those appointed before 1985.[443] Some 35% of all *Fortune 100* companies replaced their CEOs between 1995 and 2000.[444]

Twenty years ago leadership expert John Kotter claimed that most companies suffer from being over-managed and under-led.[445] Time has proven him right. So it is good news that the entire concept of leadership is undergoing dramatic changes. Gone are the days when the leader was supposed to be a combination of John Wayne and Albert Einstein. Karaoke leadership comes with a healthy dose of realism. Leading the way means living by the ten commandments of karaoke leadership.

✳✳1✳✳

Thou shalt not display your feathers to demonstrate
your all round brilliance and beauty.

The first secret of karaoke leadership is that it comes accompanied by minimal ego. "Talented people are less likely to wait their turn. We used to view young people as trainees, now they are authorities," Ed Michaels writes in *The War for Talent*.[446] So, leaders must ask themselves if they are really prepared to surrender their own egos to others. No less a sage than leadership guru Warren Bennis argues that true leaders revel in the talent of others.[447] Great leaders even have a special talent for spotting talent. "Mediocrity knows nothing higher than itself, but talent instantly recognizes genius", noted Sherlock Holmes author Sir Arthur Conan Doyle.

As Nelson Mandela points out, a true leader is like a shepherd, he stays behind the flock, letting the most nimble go on ahead, whereupon the others follow, not realizing that all along they are being directed from behind.[448] As a result, great leaders need to uphold a fruitful balance between self-confidence and self-awareness. Too much of one or the other and people are bosses – not leaders.

Dee Hock, founder and CEO emeritus of Visa International, says that if you seek to lead you should invest at least 50% of your time in leading yourself, your own purpose, ethics, principles, motivation, conduct, invest at least 20% in leading those with authority over you, and 15% leading your peers. "If you do not understand that you work for your mislabeled subordinates, then you know nothing of leadership. You know only tyranny", claims Dee Hock.[449]

2
Thou shalt not walk unto the wilderness blindly, but open your eyes and those of others.

The second factor is the realization that leadership is no longer a position but a process. As a leader of change you need to set the direction, determine the distance and be clear on timing and pace. It is a question of knowing why you are changing, where you want to go, how fast you want to go, when you want to go, how far you want to go and persuading people to come along. Karaoke leaders inspire followers. They know that you inherit subordinates, but you earn followers.

"If people are afraid to help their leaders lead, their leaders will fail," says Wharton professor Michael Useem.[450] We are not only genetically a lot like primates, we are also socially not that different. "The attention structure of the primate group, not the distribution of resources, will tell you who is the leader. It is not who gets the most bananas, it is who gets looked at," argues Lionel Tiger, anthropology professor at Rutgers University.[451] Leaders attract and are attractive.

We all make a difference, whether we like it or not. Recent research by Daniel Goleman and others suggests that feeling are contagious – positive more so than negative.[452] The limbic system is characterized as an open loop. It relies heavily on connections. So, the moods of leaders affect the emotions of people around them. In fact, you cannot avoid making an emotional impact. Every organization has a mood. Therefore, leaders better make sure that it is the right feelings that they are evoking in men and women around them. Smile and the world smiles with you.[453]

3
Thou shalt not count the pennies at every turn.

The third characteristic of karaoke leadership is that successful leaders are not in business solely for the money. The money is certainly good if you are a top CEO but the really great ones aren't there for the cash.

Leaders who are totally focused on making money at all costs tend not, in the long run, to be successful. Henry Ford remarked that a company which only makes money is no sort of company at all. He was right. For successful leaders money is a by-product of doing the right things.

The corollary of this is that the leaders who succeed have a broader notion of why they are in business. They have values. They know what they stand for, what is important and this is reflected in their expectations of their colleagues and employees.

"When I hear corporate leaders refer to values and culture as "soft" issues, I wonder what they regard as being "hard"," says Randall Tobias, former CEO of the American pharmaceutical giant Eli Lilly.[454] "In my experience, cultural beliefs are the heart and soul of all business matters. More than heroic working hours, more than pay incentives, certainly more than strategy alone, shared beliefs, values, can be the key to unleashing the talents of all the people in an organization. Values can be the very foundation of success."

✻✻4✻✻
*Thou shalt value values and live them purely
and unequivocally every day.*

Strong values nurture a strong culture. So karaoke leader factor number four is that leaders create companies that have distinctive and robust cultures. Successful leaders live the values of the company and continually set the culture. When Wal-Mart CEO H. Lee Scott Jr. recently took part in an annual media mogul summer camp in Sun Valley, Idaho, he stunned the others by explaining that he drives his own small car and, when traveling, he and another executive always share a room at inexpensive hotels.[455]

The role of the CEO is not to charm investment analysts or to seek out ever bigger acquisitions. The job of the CEO is to keep the culture and values of the company on track. But a corporate culture cannot be invented. All organizations have cultures, for better or for worse. And you can't change them over a day. Instead as noted by Larry Bossidy, chairman of Honeywell, culture is a consequence of the way you run the place and your performance.[456]

Look at sports. The best teams do not necessarily have the best players (but often they have the best leaders). Over the last decade, Manchester United has won many games in the final minutes sustained by their culture of success as much as by their ability. Their culture is shaped in the image of their leader, Sir Alex Ferguson. Cultures come in all shapes and forms, but the truly great ones always encourage people to commit to the organization and its goals. Culture comes from the top.

** 5 **
Thou shalt loveth all and all will love you back.

The fifth habit of karaoke leaders is that they are people people. "I offer you peace. I offer you love. I offer you friendship. I see your beauty. I hear your need. I feel your feelings. My wisdom flows from the Highest Source. I salute that Source in you. Let us work together for unity and love," commented Mahatma Gandhi on the roots of leadership. Increasingly, successful leaders will be judged by the success of the people around them. "The questions are, one, how can I make this guy successful? And two, how do I get out of his way?," says Larry Bossidy.[457] In a world where talent is the most critical resource leaders have to be good with people. Consider some of the key leadership tasks: *selection* (of people), *expectation* (defining and communicating goals and objectives), *motivation* (of employees and partner organizations), and finally *amplification* (making individuals grow). In one way or another they all deal with people.

Linked to this is the fact that successful leaders are persistent and powerful communicators internally as well as externally. Internally leaders talk to the people who work with them and who work for them. Unfortunately, many managers lack a true and authentic interest in such matters. "Executives tend to want to avoid direct conversations with lower level employees because they're afraid it will just turn into a complaints session," says the consultant Leslie Kossoff, author of *Executive Thinking: The Dream, the Vision, the Mission Achieved*.[458] "As a result, even in the days of Managing By Walking Around, executives and their support staff members created these interesting tours of various departments, divisions, etc. that were most like staged events, or warp speed walk-throughs, than anything of substance."

But there are exceptions. Sir Richard Branson is known for giving his private telephone number to each and every employee of Virgin, and then asking them to call him if they have any problems or ideas.[459] Alan Jones, group managing director of TNT Express, sets the tone of the company by constantly writing personal notes to people.[460] It shows that he knows that they have done well (or not); it shows that he is on the case; and it shows that he cares. If you receive a personal note from the MD you are likely to pay attention – and tell other people about it.

✱✱6✱✱

Thou shalt know the inner-most sanctums of your
customers as well as your own backyard.

And then there are customers. The best leaders don't just have a vague idea what goes on in the minds of consumers; they intimately understand their needs, aspirations and behavior. They spend time with customers.

"There's a lot of talk about the company getting close to the customer, but for the most part, the more senior the executive the less real customer contact they get," reflects Leslie Kossoff.[461] "Part of the problem is that even when they get customer contact it is so structured and pre-arranged that the executive doesn't get the opportunity to truly speak to and learn from the customer. It is treated far more as an event than for learning purposes."

The need to communicate with customers is emphasized by Adrian Slywotzky, a senior partner at the global strategy consulting firm Mercer Management Consulting and co-author of *How to Grow When Markets Don't.* "Those conversations lead to the opportunities that have enabled growth innovators to grow at 10% or more, while their industries are growing at 2 to 3%," says Slywotzky. "In terms of culture, it's not just the CEO spending time with customers in non-ceremonial conversations, but most layers of management spending time with customers. The deeper and more multi-level your relationship with your customer, the better you'll be able to identify and understand their unmet needs."

✳✳7✳✳
Thou shalt cast out the rule book of bureaucracy.

Karaoke leadership characteristic number seven is that leaders minimize the rules. Key to this is the realization that corporate politics kills communication. People keep information and bright ideas to themselves or communicate with a select few. The best leaders encourage and enable people to share information and ideas naturally and continually. So the onus is on constantly communicating to ensure that the message gets through.

Unfortunately, some organizations have re-created themselves as nanny states such is the size of their corporate rulebooks. Rules stifle. Companies with strong cultures and a clear sense of values do not need a behavioral bible inspired by Stalin. How people behave is understood. Unencumbered by rules, people tend to get on with the job.

Of course, the most famous example of a company without rules was American utilities company Enron. The greatest corporate failure of modern times hid its misbehavior behind the façade of being a freeflowing entrepreneurial company that gave executives the freedom to express themselves. This is laudable but, as Enron proved, it has to be backed by a strong sense of values and integrity among corporate leaders. Enron had neither.

✳✳ 8 ✳✳
*Thou shalt giveth out carrots as you would
have carrots given to you.*

The eighth characteristic of effective leaders is that they reward and recognize behaviors they wish to encourage. They acknowledge great work. "People want to be caught doing things right and affirmed as a human being," says Ken Blanchard, author of *The One Minute Manager* and a host of other bestsellers.[462] "Recognition is a human need. How do you know if you're doing a good job? Most people say if they haven't been shouted at recently then they're doing a good job. People in organizations are still getting beaten up for not doing what they didn't know they're even supposed to do."

Some leaders have taken recognizing good work to a new level. Take Yum! Brands, which owns Kentucky Fried Chicken, Pizza Hut, Taco Bell and the Long John Silver seafood chain. It has 850,000 employees in 100 nations. Its aim is, obviously, to put a yum on everyone's face.[463]

A lot of the company's energy has been directed into recognizing exceptional work. When people engage in behavior Yum!s chief executive David Novak wants to see, he hands out floppy chickens with the person's name on it and what they've done. Every manager at the company now has to have some form of personal recognition. When one of the company's top franchisees died, he was buried with his floppy chicken.

✳✳ 9 ✳✳
Thou shalt not engage in acts of self-congratulation.

Karaoke leaders never, ever rest on their laurels, no matter how impressive their laurels might be. Great leaders have an appetite for change. They never sit still. Whether things succeed or fail, they learn from it and move on. Look at Microsoft. It is restlessly creative. It innovates, launches and then goes back to the beginning. It is a perennial state of reinvention. Bill Gates is too curious to engage in self-congratulation.

Change does not necessarily mean reinventing the organization. Not all development comes in quantum leaps. An evolution everyday can cause a revolution. Therefore, also execution is important. Or as Larry Bossidy puts it: "Getting things done isn't tactics, it's the heart and soul of a company... It produces satisfied customers and repeat business, higher operating margins and earnings per share. Leaders who do not pay attention to how their companies get things done are running companies that don't do things well."[464]

Change can also mean encouraging and enabling people to think and behave differently. When he became CEO of Eli Lilly, Randall Tobias introduced rewards for failure for one year to encourage people to back their hunches. "Historically there had been no benefit in taking a risk – though we made it clear that you couldn't build careers out of failure," he says.[465] "Almost every corporate breakthrough or technological advance has come about because of change taking place. So the biggest skill is willingness to be open to take advantage of change."

As part of this Tobias encouraged Eli Lilly personnel to look at other businesses for inspiration. And so the pill makers went to see the candy makers. "It wasn't a question of copying M&Ms but of looking, being more open minded and creative about where we look for ideas. It is commonsensical. We have a desire to over-complicate things," Tobias reflects.

10

Thou shalt depart toward the door before
you are forced or asked to do so.

The final characteristic of highly successful leaders is that they quit when they are ahead. We asked Michael Critelli CEO of the $4.4 billion turnover company Pitney Bowes how long a CEO can remain effective. "Ten to 13 years for our size of company is optimal," he replied.[466] "Beyond a certain length of time you get to believe that you can't be replaced so it is best to leave when you are still on top and still fresh."

The trouble is that leaders have a very poor track record of leaving office with good grace and their reputations intact. They cling on to power as surely as the most Machiavellian of politicians or arrogant of sports stars. It is difficult to let go – especially if you are a huge success. Kicking the habit is the final challenge for the successful leader.

15

BREAKING FREE FROM KARAOKE

In the world of karaoke capitalism we can choose or lose – as societies, organizations and individuals. There is a price to be paid for prosperity. Capitalism, like communism, comes at a cost. Do we want capitalism with a cause or a curse? Developing the character of capitalism while still creating wealth means accepting individual responsibility. We must look inside. Success is based on leaving the copycats of the karaoke club behind. Accept no imitations; accept no limitations.

The real world

Chance, choice, cash and competence make the world of karaoke capitalism go around. We don't all agree. We don't all get a back-stage pass to enter the front-stage of the karaoke club. We don't all have the same options, the same amounts of capital or the same capabilities. Welcome to the human race! The character Merovingian in *The Matrix: Reloaded*, even states that choice is merely "an illusion created between those with power and those without". Whether you like it or not, we too are being pushed into a split vision society – regions, organizations as well as individuals.

The pundits would probably tell us not to worry. Man is ingenious. Needs trigger innovation – always have and always will. When there is a problem, there is also a solution. And there are solutions aplenty. The flavor of the month is Sidenafil Citrate and Fluoxotine Hydrocloride – aka Viagra and Prozac. For some, Viagra and Prozac are the only things left. They are the dream team. We have moved from funk soul to junk soul brothers. These pharmaceutical partners help us to realize the dreams of our times. Indeed, when push comes to shove, they increasingly constitute what we understand to be the good life.

Feel the goodness! Prozac is food for the modern soul – the little pill that provides that something special for the spirit by preventing the brain from reabsorbing too much of the neurotransmitter serotonin.[467]

And by increasing blood flow to explicit body parts Viagra is the food of love. Play on.[468] Too frivolous? Just consider the historical sales-figures. These drug buddies are among the best-selling pharmaceutical products ever in the Western industrialized world. Forget idealism, the good life weighs only a few grams, but costs its weight in gold. In fact, that's understating things just slightly. Viagra costs $11,766.00 per pound; gold merely $4,827.20 .[469]

The good life weighs only a few grams.

The enormous profits that the drugs have brought to Pfizer and Eli Lilly are alluring. But there's more to this blissful mix than profits and pharmaceuticals. The intriguing and important aspect of the success is what it tells us about society, and about the future. Any kind of success is just a reflection – a mirror – of something. The only question is what this something happens to be.

The smallest things can have the biggest side effects. Think about it. If the intended consequences behind the consumption of block-buster pharmaceutical products capture only a small fraction – one, two three, seven or eleven percent – of what truly drives people in our times, then we must surely come up with new ways by which to motivate, inspire and lead these horny and happy wannabes.

Free to choose or lose

Look in the mirror. What do you see? While unfettered individualism increases the possibilities for people to grow, it also means more loneliness. Viagra certainly boosts performance but it does not produce relationships – perhaps that explains why we need Prozac. People not

The new socio-economic landscape

capable of finding their fellow tribesmen and women have replaced local identity with isolation in a global village of seclusion. Individualism is both rewarding and demanding. Karaoke capitalism at best results in liberty and opportunity. At worst, the bi-product of increasing individuality is selfishness and loneliness.

Freedom, a term often used in a rather loose and one-sidedly positive way, is a complex concept. There are at least three different types of individual freedom: the freedom to think, talk and take action. The new elite enjoys and relishes full freedom. The rest of the human race is at best free to think and talk, but certainly not to take action. Abnormality results in apartheid. This is the comeback of the class-society.

Freedom is just
another word
for nothing left
to lose.

In fact, the more skilled companies become at managing models, moods and talented individuals, the more they will contribute to increasing the pace of this transition into a double economy – a place with luxury for some and low-cost stuff for the rest; a labor of love and a whole lot of work depending on who you are.

If we are indeed re-entering a world based on the laws of the jungle, companies in countries with less of a focus on nurture will get a head start. In business we usually refer to this as first mover advantage. Organizations based in the US, home of the most passionate market evangelists, now have this opportunity. Note that we said companies based in the US. Any company in almost any part of the world, is free to set up operations in this creative cluster of capitalism.

We can look forward to a roller coaster shaped future where cosmocrats and commoditents live, work and consume side-by-side. Enterprises applying the normal strategies and structures of the past will simply not survive living off an increasingly marginalized middle. In effect, our economies, enterprises and lives are being reformed.

Janis Joplin once sang: "Freedom is just another word for nothing left to lose." The reality is that we are all condemned. Those with competence or capital are condemned to freedom – as Jean-Paul Sartre and other existentialists suggested – the freedom to constantly have to choose.[470] They do stand a chance. Those who are forced to live their lives by chance are simply condemned – freedoomed – at least in economic terms.

In karaoke capitalism markets rule. Individualism reigns. Forget about your private life. The new reality is one in which we have privatized life and all our relationships – personal and professional. Everything is potentially for sale, everywhere, and at any time of the day. Resourceful people call the shots. Madonna was right. We are living in a material world.

There is only one little problem. Is this what we want? "I saw the best minds of my generation destroyed by madness," wrote beat poet Allen Ginsberg.[471] Are we willing to risk seeing some of the best minds of our generation destroyed by markets without meaning? If not, the time to howl is now.

The egos have landed

Big Brother is gone, except on our TV screens. The responsibilities are ours. While freedom is limited to the individual, we believe responsibilities extend far beyond single human beings. It seems reasonable that the more freedom an individual enjoys, the more he or she should accept responsibility for the totality.

More than 2000 years ago, Aristotle divided all selling and buying activity into *aeconomica* (thereof economics) and *chremastistiké*.[472] The former activities concern "housekeeping" or the maintenance of a well-run state, while the latter have to do with the sheer making of money. According to the philosopher, *aeconomica* is natural. *Chremastistiké* is not. But, today it appears as if the unnatural has become the most natural thing to do. Slowly but surely the un-normal has been normalized.

One Swedish krona (Skr) invested on the Stockholm Stock Exchange in 1979, was twenty years later worth on average 90 Skr.[473]

Some 85% of the value of the stock-market gains during the 1990s went to the wealthiest 10% of the people In the United States[474]

Approximately 40% of the vogue of the stock market gains went to the wealthiest 10% of the US population.[475]

People with competence can and do take new freedoms of unprecedented proportions. Capital charges on and capitalists are in charge.

Freedom means that you can command. The only real tax exempt in Sweden over the last few years has been for the really rich. Since 1997, 16 billionaires (in Skr) owning more that 25% of the votes in publicly traded companies no longer have to pay wealth tax on their holdings.[476] A social democrat government passed the law. Remember that in the karaoke world the left is likely to back not only workers but also capitalists. For politicians, the harsh reality is that either you meet these demands or the mobile just move on. And if this can happen in Scandinavia, it's bound to happen elsewhere.

With increasing freedom and individualization, the potential for excessive-elite behavior is rising. "It is not that humans have become more greedy than in the past generation... It is that the avenues to express greed have grown so enormously," said Federal Reserve Chairman Alan Greenspan in a speech to Congress.[477] For once, Freud was wrong. As with Orson Welles' *Citizen Kane*, greed is an effect of nurture rather than nature. Now, the egos can run disastrously riot. (This may be related to the complete absence of a discussion of what makes for a good life beyond dying rich.) Or as Henry David Thoreau once put it: "Men have become the tools of their tools" – shaped by the structures we first shaped. Material progress does not equal moral progress. If nothing changes, moral meltdowns are here to stay – infectious greed as Mr. Greenspan called it. It may seem unlikely, but the Enron boys did have something in common with the L'Oréal girls – they all thought they were worth it. Welcome to the *egoconomy*!

On towers, temples & town squares

The theoretical father of bureaucracy, Max Weber, once claimed that a social system can be coordinated in three different ways: by the sword, the purse or the word.[480] Either you coerce and threaten people, pay them in cash or try to convince them. The 20th century saw examples of all of these instruments being used. We moved from the sword of Hitler and Stalin to a society dominated by those with money – Getty and Soros. Eventually we ended up in the knowledge-based world of Gates and

No matter where we look it appears as if cash is still king.

Dell. But no matter where we look it appears as if cash is still king. And in some parts of the world the swords are still red with blood. "We have just enough religion to make us hate, but not enough to make us love one another," claimed author Jonathan Swift some three centuries ago.

The use of pistols, purses and pens largely correlates with the traditional means of control used by the rulers of the tower, town-square and temple, respectively. Kings and dictators ruled and still rule by controlling the military Democratically elected leaders use laws and the police to enforce certain behavior. Markets boil down to money – co-ordination by cash. Finally, the values present in religion or any other ideology – from the boy scouts to Baader Meinhof – usually concern the interpretation of a text or spoken words that are used to get people moving in a certain direction.

The use of pistols, purses and pens correlates with the means of control used by the rulers of the tower, town. square and temple.

A sustainable society must achieve a balance between the town square, the temple, and the tower – the economic system, the ideological system, and the regulatory system. Simply put. The town-square ensures efficiency. The temple guarantees empathy and/or ethical behavior. The contemporary tower, depending on who's the tenant, provides pre-conditions for egalitarianism and/or entrepreneurship by designing the legal framework and tax system.[479] The past also teaches us that when one of these systems becomes too dominant – the Vatican in the middle-ages, the communist party in the Soviet Union – things can and do go terribly out of control.

The world of karaoke capitalism is definitely dominated by the town square. And the town square of all town-squares – the US – is the powerhouse of the world economy.[480] Just compare the United States with other major industrial countries in terms of GDP per capita and economic growth.

The US is successful among other reasons because of its ability to create and foster new companies. If you take a look at the 25 largest US firms toward the end of the last century, eight of those companies did not exist or were very small in 1960. Compare that to the situation in Europe, where the largest 25 companies were all large already back in the 1960s.[483]

Turnover is high not only of companies, but also when we look at wealthy individuals. Every year, Fortune publishes a list of the forty richest people under forty, in the US and the rest of the world. In the 2002 list, seven out of the top ten Americans were entrepreneurs who had founded companies (the eighth was Michael Jordan, the basketball player, an entrepreneur in his own right). Outside the United States, in contrast, six of the top ten people had inherited their fortunes; three were Russian business tycoons starting off in oil; and the final individual was a Japanese IT entrepreneur.[484] In the US, the ugly duckling can indeed become a swan. The American dream implies that you can choose. You can indeed be a winner – at the center of the town square – but you can also lose. In America you are never better than your last gig.[485]

The US brings to the table a unique combo including a spotlight on innovation and entrepreneurship;[486] fluid and flexible markets for labor and capital; weak trade unions and central government; low taxes with limited progressiveness; a strong focus on a culture of individualism that accepts a lot of uncertainty; and a clear, committing and communicated story – "the American dream". These make up a national business model that the US has improved, perfected and implemented throughout the (young) history of the country. The American dream is a story that attracts certain people. The United States of America is an idea, not a country in the traditional geographical sense. We may admire the dream or feel appalled by it – love it or loathe it – but people outside the US cannot ignore it.

In 1970 the US led the pack by an average 31%. In 1989, this figure was down to 10%, but during the 1990s something happened, because by 1999 the US once again had increased its load to more than 22%.[481]

While during the last few years many people have been amazed by the enormous growth figures from China, it is wise to remember that in 1998 when the growth in jobs in China largest cities was 4.1%, jobs In Las Vegas grew by 8.5%.[483]

Europe, on the contrary, suffers from keeping on defining itself as a geographical area, rather than a community based on a genuine idea. There is a great scene in the blockbuster movie *Gladiator*, where after the battle in Germania, Maximus, played by Russell Crowe, meets up with the Emperor who wants him to make Rome a republic again. Marcus Aurelius says, "There was once a dream that was Rome. You could only whisper it. Anything more than a whisper and it would vanish... it was so fragile." To keep up, perhaps Europe needs to think more of developing a "Euro vision" than having the yearly Eurovision Song Contest? Instead of another super state we need to develop a shared state of mind – a story that attracts certain people born elsewhere. Rather than reflecting on a past that no longer exists, Europe needs to look to the future. And karaoke copying the US won't work. Europe will never beat the States in the contest for being Mr. and Mrs. American of the year, nor the next decade.

The more positive story, for both Asia and Europe is the net effect of the Internet. The productivity gains from information technology implementation are potentially much greater for them. It is not only that they are lagging behind. In Japan middlemen that can now be circumvented dominate many industries. In Europe most industries are fragmented since competition at least on a pan-European level has not

Instead of another super state we need to develop a shared state of mind.

been as tough as in the US. But fragmentation will no longer be as much of a drawback when these companies can cooperate in IT-enabled networks. Consider how well the pan-European effort Airbus is doing in competing with American Boeing. In essence, Europe lags behind the US among other things because of structural inefficiencies. As soon as Europe can sort these out it could well become the next powerhouse.

The US market model works especially well in times of disruptive change since it thrives on uncertainty. It is based on circulation, rather than permanence – a more typical trait of the European system. It is also clear that the genuine market model, with no or only minor adaptations, now appears to become dominant design in many other parts of the world. Our planet is becoming one gigantic market-square. And here we are getting to the heart of the matter. Total town-square dominance comes with pros and cons.

If the last 100 years of human history has taught us anything, it is that states need markets.[487] Just look at what happened to the Soviet Union. But markets also need states – though not necessarily nation states. Commerce is a bit like water in that it will flow wherever it is allowed, and sometimes where it is not allowed. MIT's Lester Thurow notes that "any society that values order above all else, will not be creative, but without the right degree of order, creativity disappears as if into a black hole".[488]

In the long haul, it is difficult to see how a deregulated knowledge-society can do without forceful and democratically elected bodies. "If socialism failed, it was for political, more than economic reasons; and if capitalism is to succeed it will be because it finds the political will and means to tame its economic forces," says American author Robert Heilbroner.[489] Not only that, to produce long lasting value, capitalism needs values. Modern monarchs, markets and morality must act in symbiosis. The regulations of yesterday need to be substituted with something other than raw self-interest.

Think about this. Are we adopting a system where more opportunity also by design leads to more misery; where growth and grief go hand in hand; where inequality nurtures the very qualities of the model? Are we stuck in a situation where the wealth-creating power of markets and the annihilation of poverty are mutually exclusive? Do markets dominate because of or despite dividing people, products and organizations into winners and losers?

> **To produce long lasting value, capitalism needs values.**

A fist full of dollars

We should all feel the heavy hand of history on our shoulders. Deregulation can result in degeneration. Capitalism without character is dangerous. In fact, not only from an ethical but also from an efficiency perspective, capitalism needs character. Without character people lose their confidence in capitalism. When they no longer trust the system and its leaders, they simply stop shopping and the entire machine begins to break down.[490] Also remember that over time societies that are incapable of combining efficiency, equal opportunity and empathy tend to erode – economically and emotionally. "A people that values its privileges above its principles soon loses both," contended Dwight D. Eisenhower. For once, we should not do as the ancient Greeks and Romans.

Neo-liberals often forget that Adam Smith's entire theory of the invisible hand that governs the liberalized economy is based on ideas introduced in his less well-known first book *The Theory of Moral Sentiments*.[491] He claimed that for the free-market system not to collapse and eventually result in anarchy, those at the helm had to see also to the public interest and not only their private benefits.

The behavior of the ruling class must conform to prevailing norms. Smith writes about sympathy. But what if our society is out of sympathy and solidarity? What happens when norms are no more and people are loyal only to themselves? "Communism toppled because of too little private interest; could capitalism be undermined by too much?" asked Henry Mintzberg and two of his colleagues in an article.[492]

Capitalism, like communism, comes at a cost. Without empathy to complement efficiency, the invisible hand quickly turns into a very visible fist coming down on those who lack capabilities and capital. Global market capitalism is not a political ideology – not right or wrong, good or evil as such. Market capitalism does not necessarily lead to exploitation of the environment or child labor, for instance. The market mechanism is just one way to determine the price of something. Also in planned economies, we did and still do see children being exploited and the environment polluted. The difference is just that a central committee rather than supply and demand determines the price – concentrated versus distributed idiocy.

The market mechanism is just one way to determine the price of something

Market capitalism is merely a machine – not perfect, but the least imperfect one that we have invented so far. This fact notwithstanding, a machine does not have a soul. Markets understand efficiency – nothing more and nothing less. We have to develop the character of capitalism as we go along. Otherwise, we may very well wake up one morning realizing that although we went to bed with a beauty, we woke up beside a beast.

The opportunities for leading a richer life, creating organizations that are inspiring to work for, and societies in which more people have a genuine chance of realizing their dreams, have probably never been greater. But in order to get rid of that human shadow called poverty – worldly and spiritual – we have to make up our minds as to the ancient question of what a good life really is – beyond drugs and docu-soaps, the modern equivalent to the bread and circuses of the Roman Empire. Technological progress without purposeful developments also in our institutions and values will not really produce that much long-lasting value.

"An old and continuing social problem is how to maintain mass control over elites," notes Yale's Charles E. Lindblom.[493] For some cosmocrats, it seems as if "we" has become a four letter word. It forces them to think about those left outside the karaoke club. Yet, if those in charge of the purse and the pen (or perhaps the keyboard is a more accurate metaphor for capturing the weapon of many contemporary competents), are not willing to include the others, there is a clear risk that the masses will eventually resolve to violence to remedy the situation. Some people would probably say that to a certain extent, this has already happened – in the streets of Seattle and Genoa, with the destruction of the Twin Towers, the tragedy in Bali and so on. And it is indeed hard to argue with a gun in your face no matter how much money or how high your IQ.

The invisible hand quickly turns into a very visible fist coming down on those who lack capabilities and capital.

"To save capitalism it needs to be inclusive and pay attention to people at all levels. The global economy needs to work locally," says Rosabeth Moss Kanter, professor at Harvard Business School.[494] A somewhat more rational or perhaps even cynical comment comes from marketing guru Philip Kotler: "Capitalism will leave the seeds of it's own destruction if it does not find new markets. The rich can only consume so much output."[495] This may or may not be true. There are certainly no masses of wealth at the bottom of the pyramid.[496] And one could definitely argue that a global upper class is potentially much more profitable for corporations to exploit than a local middle class.

Even so, the real threat to globalization and capitalism is from those who feel that they do not have a stake in it.

Human beings are one of only three species on this planet capable of self-awareness, the others being chimpanzees and orangutans. Now, we must prove that self-deception is not a more significant characteristic of our kind.[497] But elites, continues Professor Lindblom, "usually deny their hostility to popular control, and in fact they do not always recognize it themselves".[498] To build a sustainable society with opportunity for all, it is absolutely essential that man escapes the vision vacuum we see around us. The time has come to get rid of the *less* in meaningless. The absence of a shared idea and ideals means that the law of least resistance kicks in. Market capitalism, which as such is amoral, becomes the home of the new evangelists.

Mankind, is left with a choice between capitalism with a cause or a curse.

"When you elevate the invisible hand of the market to religious status... greed ceases to be a deadly sin and instead becomes a life-asserting virtue," notes professor Rakesh Khurana.[499] Instead of the glorification of greed, we need a new common ground.

Maybe the time has come to ask ourselves what price we are prepared to pay for prosperity. We are both creatures and creators of the world around us. Whether we like it or not, mankind is left with a choice between capitalism with a cause or a curse. Ironically, we may be moving closer and closer to a virtual reality while also moving further and further away from a virtuous world. Perhaps what we really need are markets with morality and meaning – an elite with ethics.

Let us revisit Paris à la 1792 the world of liberté egalité and fraternité. Since then we have tried to build societies based on freedom. And while the US dominates the world economy, far from all the people in that country are living on the sunny side of Market Street. Freedom comes with advantages and disadvantages. But studies also show that inequality has little effect on Americans' sense of well being. It does have a major impact on most Europeans, however. As noted by Robert Kagan, who has written the book *Of Paradise and Power*, "Americans are from Mars and Europeans are from Venus".[500]

So Europe sought to create equality. But while most people in Northern Europe, the prime example of this socio-economic experiment, were given more and more opportunities to develop themselves regardless of gender, social class, etc., the system also ran out of the steam so necessary for wealth-creation. Equality often came at the expense of quality. If one person wants to watch Channel One on TV and another Channel Two, the best solution to the dilemma is not to unplug the TV.[501] Equality, like freedom, comes with pros and cons. As Richard Sennett says: "Which evil you tolerate depends on what good you pursue."[502]

In an age of increasing individualization, the challenge is to develop a society with circular qualities where there is actual and authentic common ground. In the old and geographically structured world the lowest common denominator used to be the passport, but in a world without borders the real challenge is finding the new glue that unites us. What we are left with is brotherhood – or sisterhood for that matter. In the face of fragmentation and the death of distance, we need to figure out how to create the UI and UT rather than the UN – United Individuals and United Tribes rather than the United Nations.

Efficiency & empathy unite

Most people would probably argue that the world of karaoke capitalism is fairly efficient but also displays certain elements of inhumanity. More or less all of us agree on the overarching objective of trying to create a kind of system that is highly productive yet also humane – a global governance structure high on both efficiency and empathy. But we certainly differ on the means necessary to meet this objective.

Among the anti-globalists and anti-capitalists the only solution to this dilemma seems to be the one of regulating markets once again. However, if you take a look at the long-term consequences of such a way of trying to remedy the problem, you end up with a situation that can only be described as the tragedy of good intentions. The first thing that will happen when we start regulating these markets is that they will

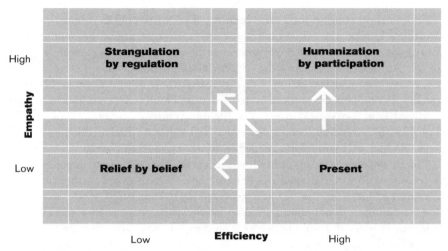

High	**Strangulation by regulation**		**Humanization by participation**
Empathy			
Low	**Relief by belief**		**Present**
	Low	**Efficiency**	High

become less efficient. As markets become less efficient, the pie to share will start shrinking. Those in charge, however, will still have the power in their hands – at least unless we start confiscating financial capital and lobotomizing competent individuals (and cutting off the feet of footballers Ronaldo and Raul). So the rulers of the egoconomy will demand as much out of a much smaller pie as they did before the regulations. In essence, we will end up in a situation in which the poor will become even poorer. This is just committing *strangulation by regulation.*

A second approach that we see a lot of these days is *relief by belief.* Life on planet earth sucks but if you put your trust in higher powers you'll get pie in the sky when you die. Or even better, sign up to become a martyr and kill innocent people. What a great way to build a better world. Any type of fanaticism, religious or other, has always been and will continue to be opium for the people – keeping them from focusing on the important issues and measures that need to be taken.

A third and more viable, yet very demanding, alternative it seems is *humanization by participation.* "Everyone thinks of changing the world, but no one thinks of changing himself," wrote Leo Tolstoy many years ago. Today, each and every one of us must realize that we have an individual responsibility for creating capitalism with a cause – the kind of capitalism that cares. Ask yourself three questions:[503]

1 Would you like a higher salary tomorrow than the one you have today?
2 Do you want lower rather than higher prices when you go shopping?
3 If you are fortunate enough to be able to save some money, would you like a high rather than low return on you investment?

The individual answers are self-evident, but so is the more general conclusion. We get the kind of capitalism that we deserve – the mirror, the mirror. If we all want higher salaries, lower prices and a better return on our investments, don't be surprised when the Dr. Jekyll becomes Mr. Hyde, when the beauty turns into a beast. Don't be surprised that a few companies are tempted to exploit child labor in the third world. Don't be surprised that some managers can't refuse the temptation to practice creative accounting. Character is not the logical consequence of competence nor capitalism. Can and should we really expect the leaders of the world to act any differently than we do? After all, they (or at least most of them California is now run by a T-800 cyborg) are human too.

We have an individual responsibility for creating capitalism with a cause.

Many of us now play more than one role. We need to accept responsibility as customers, as competent individuals, and as capitalists when we invest our savings (if we have any). And while equal opportunity should definitely not be mixed up with equal outcome, our vision of a sustainable society of the future is one based not only on the principle of nature. Nurture is and should be natural. "A regime which provides human beings no deep reason to care about one another cannot long preserve its legitimacy, "concludes Richard Sennett in his book *The Corrosion of Character.*[504]

Growing individual responsibility does not mean that companies can swear themselves free from what is happening. For a lot of prospective employees and customers, what a business stands for is as important as what it sells. But farsighted firms will become more socially responsible not only because this is a great way of differentiating the company in the face of a shrinking State, but also because they realize that with greater liberties come even greater duties. Otherwise, there is a great risk that eventually those freedoms will be revoked. In addition, nation states and supra-national bodies like the European Union need to accept responsibility. To begin with, they could stop making it so difficult for poor countries to sell their farm and textile products. Today, for example, rich countries' total farm subsidies are greater than Africa's GDP.[505]

Neither should individual responsibility exclude collective action – planned or emergent. But unless people stop blaming the current situation on the politicians, the business leaders, the religious leaders, the European Union, the WT0 and the IMF, we're afraid that nothing much will change. Perhaps instead we should all listen to the Beatles: "You tell me it is the institution, well, you had better free your mind instead." Those without guilt prepare to cast the first stone. Or as psychologist CG Jung put it, "If there is anything that we wish to change in the child, we should first examine it and see whether it is not something that could better be changed in ourselves."

Getting real

Oscar Wilde once noted that we are all lying in the gutter but only some of us are looking at the stars. The image is curiously apt for our times. The gutter is now a global autostrada, but the stars are as bright as ever – and new ones are being discovered all the time.

Accepting responsibility for the way the world works must start with personal accountability. Tourists and refugees inhabit our world, says Italian artist Francesco Clemente – either you embrace change or you try to escape from it.[506] Nelson Mandela embraced it, while Austrian nationalist/populist

The good news is that all of us are potential kings of the world.

There is a social storm, a political typhoon and a business hurricane blowing out there.

Jurg Haider tried and still tries to escape. But in Transparency Town where all the roads, doors and windows are wide-open there is nowhere to run and nowhere to hide.

The good news is that all of us are potential kings of this world. Mohammed Ali is not alone. You too happen to be the greatest. You are the best person in the world – at exactly one thing – being yourself. Every day you are competing with billions of other people. And we promise, you will wipe the floor with all of your competitors as long as you remain true to yourself. Because in a world of karaoke capitalism where pale copies of the real thing are plentiful there is but one way in which we can all succeed. In such a place you have to be 100% true to yourself.

Inside the chest of all human beings in the world – no matter how standardized we may be on the outside – sits a totally unique individual; as unique as your own fingerprints. There are no weak individuals, only weak societies and organizations depriving people of their right to develop the talents that we were all born with. The time has come to release those unique individuals – to break free from karaoke.

Listen to the wise words of the late philosopher Viktor Frankl, man who spent years of his life in a concentration camp. "Everything can be taken from a man but... the last of the human freedoms – to choose one's attitude in any given set of circumstances, to choose one's own way."[507] Economic freedom, or lack of such, does not necessarily translate to existential liberty (or restrictions). The mind can be free even if the body is stuck in a prison without (physical) walls.

There is a tsunami blowing out there – a social storm, a political typhoon and a business hurricane. Try to control the uncertainties of this world, and you're bound to go insane. Perhaps, instead, the best thing that we can hope for is some stability, security and certainty inside ourselves – inside our organizations. If we are indeed all condemned to existential freedom our only chance of surviving and thriving is to get real. To succeed, corporations and individuals must uncover their strengths and use them. Forget about your weaknesses for a while. Be the person that you were meant to be. Reveal that best kept secret of yours to the rest of the world. Otherwise there is a great risk that you will get lost.

"Ultimately, man should not ask what the meaning of his life is, but rather must recognize that it is he who is asked. In a word, each man is questioned by life; and he can only answer to life by *answering for* his own life; to life he can only respond by being responsible," writes Viktor Frankl.[508]

Living a meaningful life is dependent on creating meaning out of the moment and in every moment. Perhaps we should all ask not what our life can do for us, but what we can do for our life. Or as Abraham Lincoln put it: "It is not the years in your life which are important, but the life in your years." This is the moment of truth.

Remember the ultimate choice: either we (continue to) play the lottery or we arm ourselves with the knowledge and skills that enable us to be truly original. In any case, we're going to need luck. A well thought-through life strategy will only get you so far. Most people did not meet their partner because they had developed a superior competitive strategy. But luck is not random. There is a difference between luck and chance. As opposed to what most people think, you can actually manage luck.[509] In fact, we must learn to manage luck.

The seven habits of lucky people

These men and women have a positive outlook on life – a can-do attitude. Without aspiration and ambition, you will never experience success.

They position themselves to be exposed to luck. Such people are not afraid to move to a cluster of creativity. Just think about what gays and bohemians do to economic growth. Alternately, they roam the world to link problems at one location to solutions existing elsewhere.

These individuals have a different kind of perception of reality. They have an open mind, but are also in touch with themselves. Finding yourself requires that you are prepared to search. And this is a life-long journey, rather than a weekend trip to a sensory training program.

Lucky people are also pro-active. Like successful companies they change before they have to. They know that they can change the future, but not the past.

The final three principles? These individuals practice, practice and practice. Changing behavior requires that you rewire your brain for success and fortune. So, the only way in which you can assure change is by rehearsing.

To thrive we have to stop looking at others. We are competing with ourselves. Imitation will get you nowhere. Look inside. For all we know, the road to the future may still end up in Silicon Valley. But you can be absolutely certain of this; it must pass through your own soul and values on the way.

Success is based on leaving the copycats of karaoke capitalism behind. Stop singing the songs of the past and start writing the tunes of tomorrow. Innovate or deteriorate. Now, we need to decide if we are going to take part in writing the history of the future, or if we are satisfied being by-standers looking at the future of history?

* * * * *

Brothers and Sisters:

Don't tune in. Tune out or fade out. Accept no imitations – no limitations. You are here for a reason. You've got the power and the rights. It's your life – you decide. Stand up for your rights. You can take charge. Successful regions, corporations, men and women know that it is always better to be a first-rate version of themselves than a second-rate version of someone else. Free your mind – and the rest will follow.

Do you understand?

Notes

1   *Fortune*, August 11, 2003.
2   Swedish sports columnist Mats Olsson who writes for *Expressen* has used these examples.
3   *Aftombladet*, July 13, 2003.
4   Weber, M., *The Protestant Ethic and the Spirit of Capitalism*, London, Allen and Unwin, 1976, First published 1904–5.
5   The originator of Homo, Faber is Florentine Renaissance Philosopher Pico Della Mirandola. See Sennett, R., *The Corrosion of Character: The Personal Consequences of Work in the New Capitalism*, New York and London, WW Notion & Company, 1998.
6   *Expressen*, November 20, 2001.
7   Meyerson, M., "Human Genetic Variation and Disease", *The Lancet*, Vol. 362, July 26, 2003.
8   *Fortune*, January 20, 2003.
9   Enriquez, J., *As the Future Catches You: How Genomics & Other Forces are Changing Your Life, Work, Health & Wealth*, Crown Business, New York, NY, 2000.
10 For instance, the current trend for breast-implants is that they are getting bigger and bigger (*Expressen*, November 23, 2001).
11 The expression is borrowed from Taylor, J. and Wacker, W. (with Means, H.), *The 500 Year Delta: What Happens After What Comes next*, Harper Business, 1997.
12 Klaus Wowereit of Berlin and Bertrand Delanoe of Paris have both come out.
13 *Fortune*, December 24, 2001.
14 *Business Week*, August 28, 2000.
15 Means, H., *Money & Power.' The History of Business*, John Wiley & Sons, 2001.
16 Ibid.
17 Taylor and Wicker (1997).
18 For a deeper analysis see the Information Age trilogy: Castells, M., *The Information Age: Economy, Society and Culture*, Blackwell Publishers, Malden Mass and Oxford. Vol. I: *The Rise of the Network Society*, 1996; Vol. II, *The Power of Identity*, 1997; Vol. III, 1, 1998.
19 Micklethwait, J., and Wooldridge, A., *A Future Perfect: The Challenge and Hidden Promise of Globalisation*, William Heinemann, London, 2000.
20 www.di.se.
21 This is Chris' catalogue of what he auctioned: I have collected my personal information, as is my right under the Data Protection Act 1998, from my bank account, my supermarket reward card, my mobile phone service provider and a credit reference agency. The data is full and correct at the time of compilation (spanning 2000-2001). All privacy sensitive details have been removed (account numbers & passwords). Lloyds TSB: Approximately 500 pages of personal data including an analysis of banking products they believe I might be interested in. Also includes overdraft limit maintenance history (hand written), risk management history data (93 pages) and a full list of letters sent over the previous 5 years (completed by hand). All data and codes come with explanatory notes provided by Lloyds TSB. Original cost £10. Sainsbury's: Dated 12 July 2001, this data is split into five separate reports. *Report 1*. Operational report (name & address etc.) *Report 2*. Operational report again, with summarized details and the last 31 transactions on the card. *Report 3*. Drawn from the main data repository and includes the 'Acorn' standard marketing categorization. Includes the assumption that we are 'better-off inner-city executives living in a partially gentrified multi-ethnic area'. *Report 4*. Shows the transactions made using our reward card. *Report 5*. This is a list of EVERYTHING we bought from Sainsbury's over a 3 year period where we bought it and how much we paid. This data has been co-produced with my partner whose individual data has been removed. Orange: Somewhat inaccurate and measures just 40 pages. Shows payment history from 1996 and logs of detailed customer service interactions. Unfortunately does not include individual call details. These however are available on my monthly bills which will be available at auction in the coming months. Experian: A full copy of

my credit file, which contains ALL the information they hold about me. Just four pages long and three of those list the details of my Mum's, my Dad's and my Sister's credit card, mortgage and loan history details. Their individual data has been removed."

22   Thurow, L.C., Building Wealth: *The New Rules for Individuals, Companies, and nations in a Knowledge-Based Economy*, Harper Collins, Publishers, New York, NY, 1999.

23   Pfeffer, J., interviewed in *Business Minds*, Brown, T, Crainer, S., Dearlove, D. and Rodrigues, J.N., eds., Financial Times Prentice Hall, 2001.

24   When referring to the Man, we are thinking about the big guy in the sky rather than Van Morrison.

25   Enriquez (2000).

26   McKibben, Bill, *Enough: Genetic Engineering and the End of Human Nature*, Bloomsbury, 2003.

27   Patrick Dixon, *Speech in St Paul de Vence*, June 2, 2003.

28   Enriquez (2000).

29   Ibid.

30   Ibid.

31   Goleman, D., interviewed in Brown et al (2001),

32   Meyerson (2003).

33   In 1974, the cost of sequencing a gene was approximately $150 million. By 1998, costs were down to $150. Today, we are talking about $50 (Enriquez, 2000).

34   In 1995, 22,000 such patents were requested. One year later, the equivalent figure was 500,000 (Enriquez, 2000).

35   McKibben (2003).

36   Meyerson (2003).

37   McKibben (2003).

38   Cairncross, E, *The Company of the Future: How the Communications Revolution is Changing Management*, Harvard Business School Press, Boston, Mass, 2002.

39   Wolfe, M.J., *The Entertainment Economy: How Mega-media Forces are Transforming Our Lives*, Times Books Random House, 1999.

40   Handy, C., *The Elephant and the Flea: Looking Backwards to the Future*, Hutchinson, 2001a.

41   www.nua.ie.

42   *Dagens Nyheter*, August 28, 2003.

43   The IT revolution is here to stay but we also see clear differences between different countries. Even within the so called Western industrialized world we have differences. A few countries, such as Sweden and Finland, rank highly as regards to both Internet, PC, and cell phone penetration. By highly we are thinking about more than 50% of the population. But most countries have their weak spots. In the case of the United States cell phone penetration is still fairly low. Italy is high on cell phones but low on the Net, whereas countries such as France, Germany, and the UK are still low in both dimensions. Evidently, this will have a major impact on the growth of electronic commerce in these countries.

44   *Fortune*, June 12, 2000.

45   According to www.gcis.ca, citing a Chinese government official, by September 2002, China had 54.4 million Internet users.

46   *Time*, August 12, 2002.

47   The German example is from *The Economist The World* in 2000, arid the Japanese case is borrowed from Micklethwait and Wooldridge (2000).

48   Alexander Bard, speech in Lurid, February 16, 2000.

49   Bard, A. and Söderqvist, J., *Det Globala Imperiet Infomationsålderns Politska Filosofi*, Bonniers, 2002.

50   Citizens of the US, for instance, spend 58% of their waking time interacting with media (Wolfe, 1999).

51   Fortune, October 28, 2002.

52   Micklethwait and Wooldridge (2000).

53   Ibid.

54   The concept of a cathedral of modernity is borrowed from Zander U., "When Muhammed Goes to the Mountain: Globalization, Cathedrals of Modernity and a New World in Order", in eds. Havila, V, Forsgren, M., and Håkansson, H., *Critical Perspectives on Internationalisation, Pergamon Press*, 2002.

55   *The Economist*, 12 April 2003.

56   Enriquez (2000).

57   *Fortune*, July 9, 2001. In Western Europe the equivalent figure is only 50%.

58 *Business Week*, August 30,1999.
59 *Business 2.0*, June 13, 2000.
60 Micklethwait and Wooldridge (2000).
61 *Fortune*, June 11, 2001. But a shrinking state requires economic growth. And one can seriously doubt if we are going to see any significant cuts in the future. Micklethwait and Wooldridge (2000) put forth three arguments: 1) we have an aging population, 2) the middle class lives off the public sector, 3) people occupied in the public sector do vote.
62 *Financial Times*, September 15, 2003. This could also explain the so called stiff upper lip.
63 *Fortune*, March 3, 2003.
64 Charles Handy is quoted in Crainer, S., *A Freethinker's A-Z of the New World of Business*, Capstone, 2000.
65 Bard, A. and Söderqvist, J., *Netocracy: The New Power Elite and Life After Capitalism*, Reuters, Pearson Education, 2002. In addition, while 105,405,100 votes were cast in the 2000 US Presidential election, some 100,000,000 votes were cast in 2002 for Fox Television's American Idol competition (*Fast Company*, December, 2002).
66 The four countries being Denmark, The Netherlands, Norway, and Sweden. The US and Japan, for example, both give less than 0,1% of GDP In addition, foreign aid from the OECD countries decreased by some 20% in real terms between 1992 and 1997 (Micklethwait and Wooldridge, 2000).
67 Micklethwait and Wooldridge (2000).
68 *Financial Times*, September 13/14, 2003.
69 *Divorce Center*, Time, September 25, 2000. Sweden's 64% is topped only by Russia with 65%.
70 *Newsweek*, June 4, 2001.
71 Ibid.
72 Ibid.
73 Ibid.
74 *The Economist*, 3 May 2003.
75 Putnam, R.D., *Bowling Alone.. The Collapse and Revival of American Community*, Simon & Schuster, New York, NY, 2000.
76 Ibid.
77 www.un.org.
78 Wolfe (1999). The number of TV-sets increased from 83.3 million in 1983 to 99 million in 1998.

79 Florida, R., Cushing, R. and Gates, G., "When Social Capital Stifles Innovation", *Harvard Business Review*, Special Issue, August 2002. Areas with high levels of social capital include Bismarck, North Dakota; Birmingham, Alabama; and Cleveland.
80 Based on an example used by futurist Patrick Dixon.
81 Lifton, R.J., *The Protean Self: Human Resilience in an Age of Fragmentation*, Basic Books, New York, NY, 1993.
82 Rushdie, S., *Imaginary Homelands*, London, Granta Books, 1991.
83 Reich, R.B., *The Future of Success*, Alfred A. Knopf, New York, 2000.
84 *Fortune*, September 7, 1998.
85 *The Economist*, 3 May 2003.
86 *Newsweek*, December 23, 2002.
87 www.gucci.com.
88 *Financial Times*, July 12/July13, 2003.
89 *Fortune*, August 14, 2000.
90 Enriquez (2000)
91 *Dagens Industri*, September 8, 2003, referring to the book *The New Income Trap* by Elisabeth Warren.
92 We will pursue this argument at greater depth in Chapters 11, 13 and 14.
93 *Wall Street Journal*, August 24, 1998.
94 nationmastercom
95 *Wall Street Journal*, August 24, 1998.
96 www.iadb.org.
97 Ibid.
98 Micklethwait and Wooldridge (2000).
99 Ibid.
100 Don Tapscott, speech at the University of Alberta, June 4, 2001 (www.dontapscott.com).
101 In 1750, the difference between what one person produced in a rich and poor country, respectively, was a factor of 5 to 1, today it is a factor of 390 to 1 (Enriquez, 2000).
102 Ibid. Figures between 1970 and 1995.
103 Micklethwait and Wooldridge (2000).
104 *Fortune*, October 28, 2002.
105 Micklethwait and Wooldridge (2000).
106 Ibid.
107 *Science*, February 7, 2003.
108 *Fortune*, October 28, 2002.
109 *Business Week*, April 21, 2003.
110 Economist Xavier Sala-i-Martin of Columbia University has used official data

from the World Bank and the UN (Business Week, April 21, 2003). The only region with a growing number of people making less than $2 per day is Africa (Fortune, October 28, 2002)

111 For instance, almost all of the 116 countries on Amnesty's list accused of torture are poor. (Micklethwait and Wooldridge (2000).

112 For a deeper discussion see Enriquez (2000)

113 According to Enriquez (2000) in 1999, for example, 12 countries produced 95% of all patents handed out in the United States. A couple of years ago IBM developed more US patents than the combined efforts of 139 countries.

114 Ibid.

115 Ibid.

116 Ibid.

117 Economists usually measure inequality with the so called Gini Index. Rising inequality after 1980 is the rule in this data, with limited exceptions mainly in Scandinavia. See Galbraith J.K., "By the Numbers", Foreign Affairs, July/August, 2002.

118 Reich (2000).

119 Securitas is a leading player in the global security industry.

120 Reich (2000) talks about talent, education and network.

121 The Economist, August 8, 2002.

122 Thurow (1999).

123 Expressen, November 15, 2000.

124 Thurow (1999).

125 Expressen, November 15, 2000.

126 Enriquez (2000).

127 Fortune, June 24, 2002.

128 Micklethwait and Wooldridge (2000) as well a Reich (2000) claim that these CEOs made 419 times more than average workers.

129 Mentioned in Kets De Vries, M., The Leadership Mystique: A User's Manual For the Human Enterprise, Financial Times Prentice Hall, 2001.

130 Martin, R.L. and Moldoveanu, M.C., "Capital Versus Talent: The Battle That's Reshaping Business", Harvard Business Review, July 2003

131 Andersson, D. & Kainelainen, A. in Aftonbladet, October 23, 2002. For a deeper analysis see the LO-report, Näringslivet ökar takten. En studie av inkomstutvecklingen for makteliten perioden

1950-2000, LO 2002.04.

132 LO-report, 2002.04.

133 Fast Company, July, 2002.

134 Gates, J., Democracy at Risk.. Rescuing Main Street from Wall Street, Perseus Publishing, 2000.

135 Thurow (1999) makes the comparison to the least wealthy 110 million Americans. The rest of the figures come from Enriquez (2000),

136 Kets de Vries (2001).

137 Sennett (1998).

138 Wired, December, 1997.

139 Reich (2000).

140 Ibid.

141 Ibid.

142 Thurow (1999).

143 Fast Company, March, 2000.

144 Reich (2000).

145 Ibid.

146 Ibid.

147 Crainer, S. and Dearlove, D., Business, the Universe and Everything, Wiley, 2003.

148 Campbell Quick, J., Cooper, C.L., Quick, J.D. and Gavin, J.H., The Financial Times Guide to Executive Health.. Building Your Strengths, Managing Your Risks, FT Prentice Hall, 2002.

149 Address to the annual Gridiron dinner April 22, 1987 (Campbell Quick et al, 2002).

150 Newsweek, June 30, 2003.

151 Wolfe (1999).

152 Reich (2000).

153 The strange thing is that the Stress Society has also produced celebrity chefs such as Jamie Oliver and Nigella. Perhaps, when something becomes really scarce, we look for individuals capable of turning the essentials into experiences. Yesterday, we were forced to cook. Today, it functions as therapy and entertainment. Pressure requires pleasure.

154 Sennett (1998).

155 Fast Company, March, 2000.

156 Crainer and Dearlove (2003).

157 Fortune, December 11, 1995.

158 Sort of similar to what George and Tony did to Saddam.

159 Aftonbladet, September 5, 2002.

160 The exception to this rule is generally referred to as increasing returns. We will

touch upon this concept later. For a more thorough discussion consult Arthur, B.W, *Increasing Returns and Path Dependence in the Economy. Economics, Cognition, and Society*, University of Michigan Press, Arm Arbor, Ill, 1994.

161 Wicker, W and Taylor, J. (with Means, H.), *The Visionary's Handbook: Nine Paradoxes That Will Shape the Future of Your Business*, Capstone, 2000.

162 *Fast Company*, January-February, 2000.

163 Michaels, E., Handfield-Jones, H., and Axelrod, B., *The War for Talent*, Harvard Business School Press, Boston, Mass, 2001.

164 AC Economist Intelligence Unit (*Business Week*, October 4, 1999).

165 Dickson, T., "How Can Companies Weave a Web of Talent, *European Business Forum*, Issue 6, Summer 2001. Also note that in 2010, 43% (97 million) of Americans will be 50+ (*Fast Company*, August, 2000).

166 All three examples from Johnson, M., "The Global Search For Talent Gets Tougher", *Financial Executive*, June, 2002. In addition, by 2025 close to 26% of the Japanese population will be 65+ (*Fortune*, November 22, 1999).

167 *Fortune*, July 8, 2002.

168 *Fast Company*, May, 2001.

169 *Financial Times*, September 2, 2003.

170 *Business Week*, August 25, 2003.

171 Handy, C., "Why Companies May Be Held To Ransom By Their Employees", *European Business Forum.*, Issue 6, Summer, 2001b.

172 Ibid.

173 If we should learn anything from the last few years, though, it is that stupidity also makes capital dance from time to time. In fact, some might suggest that just about anything seems to have made capital dance at one time or another. But not everything. Research suggests that the chance of a business idea actually turning into a company that goes public is about 1 in 6 million. Only some 0.6% of all business plans we actually funded by VCs, and the percent of entrepreneurs who receive seed money from venture capitalists and eventually end up in bankruptcy is around 60% (Nesheim, J1., *High Tech Start Up: The Complete Handbook for Creating Successful New High Tech Companies*, Simon &

Schuster, 2000). Failure by trying is the engine of a marker economy.

174 *Financial Times*, July 12/13, 2003

175 Davies, S. and Meyer, C., *future WEALTH*, Harvard Business School Press, Boston, Mass, 2001.

176 For a similar argument, see Martin and Moldoveanu (2003).

177 Enriquez (2000).

178 *Dagens Industri* November 25, 2002. On the Internet, some 0.5 to 1% of the people with this kind of background leave Sweden every year – on par with the percentage of all Swedes that left the country from 1880–1914.

179 Enriquez (2000). One might also add that their companies generated 50% in sales as what India exports in a year.

180 Micklethwait and Wooldridge (2000).

181 University of Chicago Educational Studies.

182 Reich (2000).

183 Zander (2002).

184 Hirschman, A.O., *Exit, Voice, and Loyalty. Responses to Decline in Firms, Organizations, and States*, Harvard University Press, Cambridge, Mass, 1970.

185 Many French people would probably beg to differ about viewing the US an idea or a cultural expression – claiming that the only culture that exists over there grows in their yoghurt. Georges Clemenceau went as far as to argue that the US was the "only nation in history which miraculously has gone from barbarism to degeneration without the usual interval of civilization."

186 Reich (2000).

187 Mulgan, G., *Connexity: How to Live in a Connected World*, Harvard Business School Press, Boston, Mass, 1997.

188 *Time*, June 11, 2001.

189 For a more thorough discussion of these laws consult Downes, L. and Mui, C., *Unleashing the Killer App: Digital strategies for market dominance*, Harvard Business School Press, Boston, Mass, 1998.

190 Coase, R., *The Nature of the Firm*, Economica, 1937.

191 Transaction costs can take many different forms. Downes and Mui (1998) discuss six basic types of transaction costs; search costs; information costs; bargaining costs; decision costs; policing costs; and enforcement costs.

192   When information is abundant and
      asymmetrically distributed or
      symmetrically distributed but scarce, we
      get hybrid forms. Between markets and
      hierarchies we find networks.
193   Handy (2001a).
194   *Business Week*, April 3, 2000.
195   *The Economist. The World in 2000*.
196   Watson, R, *The Modem Mind: An
      Intellectual History of the 20th Century*,
      Harper Collins Publishers, 2001.
197   amazon.com.
198   Hamel, G., *Leading the Revolution*, Harvard
      Business School Press, Boston, Mass, 2000.
199   www.live365.com.
200   *Business Week*, August 28, 2000.
201   Drucker, P.F., *Management Challenges For
      the 21st Century*, Harper Business, 1999.
202   *Fast Company*, November 2002. Also note
      that while from 1990 to 1995 productivity
      grew by 1.5% per annum, growth then
      increased to an annual 3% between 1996
      and 2000 (Reich, 2000).
203   Hammer, M., *The Agenda: What Every
      Business Must Do to Dominate the Decade*,
      Crown Business, New York, NY, 2001.
204   Dolan, E.G., Economics, 4th Edition, The
      Dryden Press, New York, NY, 1986.
205   Residence, 4, 2003.
206   Seybold, P.B., *The Customer Revolution: How
      to Thrive When Customers Are in Control*,
      Crown Business, New York, NY, 2001.
207   Cairncross (2002).
208   Based on Seybold (2001)
209   *Fortune*, May 27, 2002.
210   *Fortune*, November 11, 2002.
211   *The Economist*: The World in 2000.
212   *Fast Company*, March 2000.
213   *Fortune*, January 21, 2002.
214   Research by Morgan Stanley Dean Witter
      also shows that of all the high-tech
      companies which have gone public since the
      arrival of the PC in 1980, just 5% have
      yielded 77% of all the shareholder value
      (Red Herring, August, 2000). The
      implications are clear. The winner takes all.
      The leader is bigger than all the rest. Back
      in 1920 there were 508 car manufacturers
      in the US. Now we are down to three,
      whereof one is more German than
      American. (Ibid.) We are seeing the same
      development on the Internet.

215   *Fast Company*, August, 2000.
216   www.www.di.se.
217   *The Economist*, January 29, 2000.
218   *Fast Company*, September, 1999.
219   Today, we see at least two very different
      types of firms. We are still surrounded by
      dynasty firms – eternal enterprises – but
      progressively we are also seeing the growth
      of more disposable firms – ephemeral
      enterprises. The latter type of firm is a
      much more elusive beast to capture. It
      profits from opportunity jumping.
      American academic and consultant Jim
      Collins claims that "at no time in history
      has it been easier to reallocate capital
      without creating lasting value" (*Fast
      Company*, March, 2000). His argument is
      that these days a lot of companies are built
      to flip rather than built to last. They are
      essentially set up by people who want to
      make a quick buck with an IPO rather than
      to build something much more ever-lasting.
      And while it is certainly true that a lot of
      companies have been built too fast rather
      than to last, there is basically nothing
      wrong with having a lot of disposable
      companies in a dynamic cluster. Stability
      shifts from the level of the firm to the level
      of the cluster. However, this development
      clearly has political implications, as well as
      financial implications, for those who invest
      traditional capital in these ephemeral
      enterprises.
220   Schwartz, E.I., *Digital Darwinism: 7
      Breakthrough Business Strategies For
      Surviving in the Cutthroat Web Economy*,
      Broadway Books, New York, NY, 1999.
221   *Business 2.0*, October, 2001.
222   Brown, J.S. mid Duguid, R, *The Social Life
      of Information*, Harvard Business School
      Press, Boston, Mass, 2000.
223   There are many reasons why it is very
      difficult for companies to make money on
      the Internet. Tom Phillips, former CEO of
      deja.com, points out that searching is the
      dominant mode of the Internet (*Fast
      Company*, August, 2001). The mentality of
      the information seeker is that I can find it if
      I keep looking. Then, why should I pay for
      anything? The average Internet download
      takes some 22 seconds – or in other words
      21 seconds longer than the typical

consumer wants to wait. And if we take a look at the Internet generation, while there is certainly a lot of internal variation, they all seem obstinate and impatient. Remember, the impatient young Internet users of today are also future employees and customers. Given all this and the question marks still surrounding security and privacy, no wonder that 65% of all online consumers bail out of the transaction before the final step (*Business 2.0*, August 8, 2000).

224 See, for instance, Brealey, R.A., Razavi, B. and Myers, S.C., *Principles of Corporate Finance*, 7th edition, McGraw Hill, 2002.

225 *Fortune*, March 5, 2001.

226 See Smith, A. *An Inquiry Into the Nature and Causes of the Wealth of Nations*, Oxford edition, 1776.

227 Exodus 18:25.

228 Chandler, A.D., *Strategy and Structure*, MIT Press, Cambridge, Mass, 1962.

229 Bartlett, C.A. and Ghoshal, S., *Managing Across Borders: The Transnational Solution*, Hutchinson Business Books, 1989.

230 Bartlett, C.A. and Ghoshal, S., Matrix *Management: Not a Structure, a Frame of Mind*, Harvard Business School Press, Boston, Mass, 1990/2003.

231 Kevin Kelly, speech in Stockholm, November 10,1999.

232 *The Industry Standard*, June 19, 2000.

233 Reich (2000).

234 *Fortune*, Much 20, 2000.

235 Evans, P. and Wurster, T.S., *Blown to Bits: How the New Economics of Information Transforms Strategy*, Harvard Business School Press, Boston, Mass, 2000.

236 Reich (2000).

237 Hedlund, G., "The Intensity and Extensity of Knowledge and the Multinational Corporation as a Nearly Recomposable System (NRS)", *Management International Review*, Vol.39, Special Issue 1, 1999.

238 Mintzberg and Waters refer to strategy as "a pattern with a stream of actions". See Mintzberg, H. and Waters, J., "Tracking Strategy in an Entrepreneurial Firm", *Academy of Management Journal*, Vol. 25, 1982.

239 Hedlund (1999). Also see Ridderstrile, J., *Global Innovation: Managing International*

Innovation Projects at ABB and Electrolux, Published Doctoral Dissertation, IIB, Stockholm, 1996.

240 We guess one could claim that the Cup was won by cash. The leader of the Swiss team, Ernesto Bertarelli, a 37-year-old biotech billionaire, essentially bought a team of great New Zealanders headed by skipper Russel Courts that won him and Switzerland the Cup. The Kiwis were branded as traitors back home, however.

241 *Business Week*, August 28, 2000.

242 *Fortune*, November 22, 1999.

243 Ibid.

244 Micklethwait and Wooldridge (2000).

245 Ibid.

246 *Business Week*, August 25, 2003.

247 Enriquez (2000).

248 *Business Week*, April 3, 2000.

249 *Fortune*, November 11, 2002.

250 See, for instance, Enrique (2000) for a discussion of industry convergence and blurring boundaries. Nokia's N-Gage game console, mobile phone, MP3-player, FM radio, PDA, is another interesting example of what kind of products and competitive landscape to expect in the years to come.

251 *Time*, August 12, 2002.

252 The seminal article is Takeuchi, H. and Nonaka, I, "The New New Product Development Game", *Harvard Business Review*, January – February, 1986.

253 Bennis, W and Ward Biederman, R, *Organizing Genius: The Secrets of Creative Collaboration*, Perseus, 1997.

254 Kets de Vries (2001).

255 *Business Week*, August 28, 2000. All in all, in 1985 a little more than 1 million patents were filed. Fifteen years later we were looking at more than 7 million patents (*The Economist*, June 23, 2001). At the same time the average cost to litigate a patent case is in the area of 2.5 million dollars, rising by 10-15% each year (Pearson, J., Nickson, N., and Marvel. S., "Court in session: Intellectual property at risk", *Risk Management*, New York, February, 2001).

256 Micklethwait, J. and Wooldridge, A., *The Witch Doctors: Making Sense of the Management Gurus*, Times Book Random House, 1996.

257 *Business Horizons*, December, 2002.

258 *Business Week*, October 4, 1999.

259 *Fast Company*, March 2002.

260 Harnel (2000).

261 Baumol, W.j., *The Free-Market Innovation Machine: Analyzing the Growth Miracle of Capitalism*, Princeton University Press, 2002.

262 *Fast Company*, June, 2000.

263 *Fast Company*, October, 1999.

264 *Fast Company*, August, 2000.

265 *Fast Company*, August, 2000.

266 The seminal reference on hierarchy is Simon, H.A., 'The Architecture of Complexity", *Proc. Amer. Phil. Soc.*, No. 106, 1962.

267 Rigby, D. and Zook, C., "Open Market Innovation", *Harvard Business Review*, October, 2002.

268 *The Economist*, February 9, 2002.

269 Hedlund (1999).

270 In fact, six eight-studded Lego bricks can be put together in 102,981,500 ways.

271 Ridderstråle, J. and Engström, R, *Toward a Knowledge-Based Theory of Organizational Design*, CASL, Research Paper Series, 2000.

272 Drucker (1999).

273 *Fast Company*, July-August, 1999.

274 Johnson (2002).

275 *Business 2.0*, August 8, 2000.

276 Handy (2001b).

277 "In Search of Global Leadership", *Harvard Business Review*, Special Issue, August, 2003.

278 Handy (2001b) makes a similar argument.

279 Michaels et al (2001).

280 Buckingham, M. and Clifton, D.O., *Now, Discover Your Strengths*, The Free press, New York, NY, 2001.

281 Ibid.

282 Buckingham, M. and Coffman, C. *First Break all the Rules: What the World's Greatest Managers do Differently*, Simon & Schuster, New York, NY, 1999.

283 Buckingham and Clifton (2001).

284 Moore, K. and Rugman, A., *US Multinationals Are Regional Not Global*, Business Strategy Review, Winter, 2003.

285 See, for instance, Trompenhaars, E, *Riding the Waves of Culture*, Nicolas Brealey, London, 1993.

286 Buckingham and Coffman (1999).

287 *Fortune*, Much 18, 2002.

288 *Fortune*, May 26, 2003.

289 www.manpowercom

290 *Fast Company*, August, 2001.

291 *Fortune*, February 18, 2002.

292 *Fast Company*, July, 2000. Likewise, in 1995 IBM had a mere 117 minority executives working in the US. Four years later the equivalent number was 270.

293 *Fast Company*, April, 2001.

294 See Orenstein, R, *Flux: Women on Sex, Work, Kids, Love and Life in a Half Changed World*, Doubleday, 2000. She shows that less than 40% of female senior executives are mothers, while 95% of their male peers have kids and about three quarters of them have a wife that stays home. Research also shows that gay men earn about 22% less than straight men, controlling for education, race, age, etc. Gay women, however, earn approximately 30% more than similarly qualified heterosexual women (*Business Week*, April 21, 2003).

295 *Fast Company*, November, 1999.

296 *Fast Company*, November, 2001.

297 *Fast Company*, September 1999.

298 Rosener, J., *America's Competitive Secret Women Managers*, Oxford University Press, 1995.

299 Ibid.

300 *The Times*, October 24, 2002.

301 *Fast Company,* August, 2000.

302 *Fast Company*, October, 2000.

303 *Fast Company*, June, 2003.

304 "Behind the Numbers", *Harvard Business Review*, Special Issue, August, 2003.

305 Coutu, D.L., "HBR Interview, Psychologist Karl E. Weick: Dense and Reliability", *Harvard Business Review*, April, 2003.

306 Quoted in Davenport, TH. and Prusak, L., *Working Knowledge: How Organizations Manage What They Know*, Harvard Business School Press, Boston, Mass, 1998.

307 Quoted in Edquist, K. and de Man Lapidoth, I., *Den nyttige egoisten: Det nya rörelsekapitalets manifest*, Bookhouse Publishing, 2003.

308 Fast Company, August, 2000.

309 "How Presidents Persuade", Harvard Business Review, January, 2003.

310 Reimer Thedens, OgilvyOne Worldwide, speech in Phuket, September 4, 2003.

311 *Business Week*, March 17, 2003.

312 Hofstede, G., *Culture's Consequences:*

International Differences in Work-related Values, Sage Publications, Beverly Hills, CA, 1980.

313 Hall, D.T. and Moss, J.E., "The New Protean Career Contract: Helping Organizations and Employees Adapt", Organizational Dynamics, Vol. 26, No. 3, 1998.

314 www.behavior.net/column/bennis. A conversation with Warren Bennis.

315 Fortune, May 26, 2003.

316 Fortune, January 20, 2003.

317 Ridderstråle (1996).

318 Reich (2000).

319 Morgan, G., Images of Organizations, Sage Publications, 1986.

320 Quoted in Kers de Vries (2001)

321 Coser, L., The Functions of Social Conflict, The Free Press, New York, NY, 1976.

322 Fortune, January 20, 2003.

323 Hedlund (1999)

324 Brown and Duguid (2000).

325 de Meyer, A., "Tech Talk: How Managers Are Stimulating Global R&D Communication", Sloan Management Review, Vol. 32, 1991.

326 Polanyi, M., The Tacit Dimension, Anchor Day Books, New York, NY, 1966.

327 See research by Wharton Professor Karen Shen in Leader to Leader, Fall, 2001.

328 See Hofstede (1980) and Trompenhaars (1993).

329 The seminal reference is March, J.G., "Exploration and Experimentation in Organizational Learning", Organization Science, Vol. 2, 1991. Also see Hedlund, G. and Rolander, D., "Action in Heterarchies: New Approaches to Managing the MNC", in eds. Bartlett, C.A., Doz, YL. and Hedlund, G., Managing the Global Firm, Routledge, London, 1990, as well as Hedlund, G. and Ridderstrale, J., "Toward a Theory of the Self-Renewing MNC", in eds. Toyne, B. and Nigh, D., International Business: An Emerging Vision, University of South Carolina Press, 1997.

330 March (1991).

331 The study is quoted in, Mello, A., "Creative Destruction or Concentrating on the Core: Which Is the Right Path to Growth", Harvard Management Update, Next Generation Growth, January 2003.

The two companies were General Electric and Eastman Kedak.

332 Levitt, B. and March, J.G. "Organizational Learning", Ann. Rev. Social., Vol. 14, 1988. Also see March, J.G., Decisions and Organizations, Blackwell, New York, NY, 1988.

333 Christensen, C.H., The Innovator's Dilemma: When New Technologies Cause Great Firms to Fail, Harvard Business School Press, Boston, Mass, 1997.

334 Thaler, R.H., The Winner's Curse: Paradoxes and Anomalies of Economic Life, Princeton University Press, 1994. Thaler challenges received economic wisdom by presenting examples of anomalies such as why the winners at auctions are often the real losers – they pay too much and suffer the "winner's curse" – and why gamblers bet on long shots at the end of a losing day. He also demonstrates that markets do not always operate as efficiently as we would like to think.

335 Hammer (2001).

336 Ibid.

337 Hamel (2000).

338 Wacker et al (2000),

339 Davenport and Prusak (1998).

340 Amabile, T.M., Hadley, C.N. and Kramer, S.K., "Creativity Under The Gun", Harvard Business Review, Special Issue, August 2002.

341 Business Week, August 28, 2000.

342 Ladislaus Horatsius, speech in Stockholm, May 12,2000.

343 Lufthansa Magazine, 5, 2003.

344 Hammer (2001).

345 Fast Company, June, 2000.

346 Fortune, January 8, 2001.

347 Fortune, May 26, 2003.

348 Farson, R. and Keyes, R., "The Failure Tolerant Leader", Harvard Business Review, Special Issue, August, 2002.

349 For the cooperation argument see Blau, PM., Exchange and Power in Social Life, John Whiley & Sons, 1964, and as for contract and monitoring costs consult Powell, W.W, "Neither Market Nor Hierarchy: Network Forms of Organization", Research in Organizational Behavior, Vol. 12., 1990.

350 See Mayer, R.C. & Davis, J. H., "The Effect

of the Performance Appraisal System on Trust For Management: A Field Quasi-experiment", *Journal of Applied Psychology*, Vol. 84., 1999.

351 Kets de Vries (2001).

352 Schumpeter, J.A., *The Theory of Economic Development*, Harvard University Press, Cambridge, Mass, 1911/1934.

353 Ibid.

354 Foster, R. and Kaplan, S., *Creative Destruction; Why Companies That Are Built to Last Underperform the Market – and How to Successfully Transform Them*, Doubleday, 2001.

355 We would not go as far as Nicholas G. Carr who in a recent *Harvard Business Review* article (May, 2003) claimed that IT does not matter. Of course IT matters as an enabler but stand alone technology will not provide companies with sustainable competitive advantages.

356 *Business Week*, August 28, 2000.

357 *Fast Company*, March 2002.

358 Global study carried out by Advanced Micro Devices. *International Herald Tribune*, July 14, 2003.

359 Ibid.

360 *Fortune*, July 21, 2003.

361 Teece, D., "Capturing Value from Knowledge Assets: The New Economy, Markets for Know-How, and Intangible Assets", *California Management Review*, Vol. 40., Spring, 1998.

362 *Fortune*, March 3, 2003.

363 Ibid.

364 *Fast Company*, May, 2003. Nokia has a 38% global market-share.

365 See Micklethwait and Wooldridge (2000). In addition, Nokia accounts for 25% of Finland's exports and 49 out of 50 Finns making more than one million Finn Marks per year work for the company (*Fortune*, February 4, 2002).

366 Darwin, C., *On the Origin of Species by Means of Natural Selection*, John Murray, London, 1859 (Harvard University Press, 1964). The book ends as follows: "Thus, from the war of nature, from famine and death, the most exalted object which we we capable of conceiving, namely, the production of the higher animals, directly follows. There is grandeur in this view of life, with its several powers, having been originally breathed into a few forms or into one; and that, whilst this planet has gone cycling on according to the fixed law of gravity, from so simple a beginning endless forms most beautiful and most wonderful have been, and are being, evolved."

367 www.serpentfd.org.

368 Darwin, C, *The Descent of Man, and Selection in Relation to Sex*, John Murray, London, 1871 (Princeton University Press, 1981).

369 Later, Darwin added the dynamics of pangenesis – a theory of heredity, which says that each body cell produces hereditary particles that circulate in the blood before collecting in the reproductive cells (wordreference.com).

370 See Wright, R., *The Moral Animal: Why We Are the Way We Are: The New Science of Evolutionary Psychology*, Pantheon Books, New York, NY, 1994; and Miller, G., *The Mating Mind: How Sexual Choice Shaped the Nature of Human Evolution*, Vintage, 2001.

371 While we see many companies breaking up for reasons of efficiency – by actively using out sourcing to focus on the core competences of the corporation – we also see a number of firms coming together in terms of mergers and acquisitions. This latter logic is mainly driven by power – power of the customers. One reason why customers are becoming more powerful relates to over-capacity and fragmentation, i.e. the large number of sellers. To remedy the situation corporations seek to decrease capacity by initiating activities aimed at consolidating the industry. Typically, this strategy is implemented by acquiring one or several competitors (or by mergers). So, we should not be surprised that in industries from pulp and paper to banking, and automotive to Internet consulting, we have seen firms following aggressive M&A strategies. Despite all the talk about synergies and critical mass, as well as less 'rational' arguments about senior executives boosting the value of their stock-option plans, it should be absolutely clear that these moves have also been triggered by a genuine desire to reduce the power of increasingly demanding customers.

However, for such strategies to be truly successful, there must be genuine underlying reasons why big is not only more powerful, but also better. If the firm cannot restructure its assets, create economics of scale and travel further down the experience curve, alternately use its new-won power to standardize diverse market needs, from a long-term, perspective growth by acquisition may be counter-productive. This point is especially valid since digitization and the consequent 'marketification' has decreased the minimum efficient scale in many industries. More networked constellations of firms may be able to attain the same advantages without ownership and sunk costs that limit flexibility. There is also the question of whether or not this new and larger entity is fit to survive in a fundamentally new competitive environment with an emphasis on agility and the continuous recreation of competitive advantages The outsourcing logic is also questionable. Outsourcing, downsizing, breaking up is primarily explained by a wish to minimize transaction costs. Yet, this entire perspective is focused on exactly one thing – costs. It does not tell us much about how to boost revenues. In addition, it focuses on the present and does not take the future into account. It is a question of minimizing existing transaction costs, not a question of increasing future value. Lastly, but not the least important, it neglects the fact that a lot of relationships are characterized by tacit knowledge flowing back and forth.

372 *Business Week*, October 4, 1999.
373 Hamel (2000).
374 *Fortune*, December 24, 2001.
375 Hamel (2000).
376 Quoted in Joan Magretta, "Why Business Models Matter", *Harvard Business Review*, May 2002 (Original quote in "Wal-Mart Stores, Inc.," HBS case no. 9-794-024).
377 Ibid,
378 Hamel, G. and Prahalad, C.K, "The Core Competence of the Corporation", *Harvard Business Review*, May-June, 1990.
379 *Business Week*, August 25, 2003.
380 Magretta (2002).
381 *Fortune*, July 7, 2003.
382 *Business Week 50*, Special Issue, Spring 2003.
383 Downes and Mui (1998).
384 *Fast Company*, November 2002.
385 Cairncross (2002).
386 *Fortune*, November 11, 2002.
387 *Business Week*, September 26, 1994.
388 www.nokia.com
389 Magretta (2002).
390 *Fortune*, April 14, 2003. 392 Fast Company, November 2002.
391 *Fast Company*, November 2002.
392 At least theoretically companies will profit from dynamic rather than fixed pricing. Some customers will of course enter lower bids, but a number of them will also enter higher ones. More importantly however, is the fact that some customers, who would not have bought at all, will now enter bids that will enable the company to operate at a level where marginal income is higher than marginal cost. On the other hand, experience also shows that people mainly shop online for information rich products. For a deeper discussion see Schwartz (1999).
393 *Fortune*, March 17, 2003.
394 Magretta (2002).
395 Wacker et al (2000).
396 Hamel (2000).
397 *Fortune*, March 13, 2003.
398 *Fast Company*, November 2002.
399 See Lovallo, D., and Kahneman, D., "Delusions of Success: How Optimism Undermines Executives' Decisions", *Harvard Business Review*, July, 2003, (also see the editorial by Thomas Stewart for the example).
400 *Fast Company*, June, 1999.
401 Weick, K., *Sensemaking in Organizations*, Sage Publications, 1995.
402 Kets de Vries (2(01).
403 Ibid.
404 Quoted in Steen Jensen, I, *Ona fyr För dig som vill lyckas tillsammans med andra*, Bookhouse Publishing, 2003.
405 *Fortune*, January 24, 2000.
406 *Fast Company*, November, 1999. Independent studies suggest that it was 1/6 rather than 1/3 of the iMac customers.
407 Enriquez (2000),
408 Wright (1994).
409 See for example www.deadlysins.com

410 Savage, D., *Skipping Toward Gomorrah: The Seven Deadly Sins and the Pursuit of Happiness in America*, E P Dutton, 2002.

411 *Sydsvenskan*, August 2, 2003.

412 Ibid.

413 *Science*, 7 February, 2003.

414 Tedlow, R.S., 'What Titans Can Teach Us", *Harvard Business Review*, Special Issue, December, 2001.

415 Lipitor.com

416 Micklethwait and Wooldridge (2000). The authors also point out that the LA/Silicon Valley porn cluster employs 20,000 people. At one paint in time in 1999, 20% of all films in production in LA were porn films.

417 *Marketing Week*, 27 May, 1999, quoted in Hamel (2000).

418 *eCompany*, August, 2000.

419 *Dagens Industri*, 3 March, 2000

420 Ibid.

421 Ibid.

422 Hamel (2000).

423 *Science*, 7 February, 2003. 4

424 McKenna, R., "Real-Time Marketing", in ed. Tapscott, D., *Creating value in the Network Economy*, Harvard Business School Press, Boston, Mass, 1999.

425 *Fast Company*, November, 2000.

426 We have later been told by people that the girls were likely Chinese and hired to bring the special bag back home in order to copy it. Other individuals have told us that the girls belonged to the Japanese mafia who uses the receipt/bag combo for money laundering purposes (re-selling the bags in Asia while keeping the receipt). No matter what, the story still illustrates the power of brands.

427 Miller (2001).

428 *Financial Times*, April 24, 2001.

429 *Wall Street Journal*, December 14, 1998.

430 www.home.uestra de/uestra/busstop/morrison.html,

431 *Fast Company*, September, 2002.

432 *Time*, March 20, 2000.

433 *Time*, July 31, 2(00.

434 Forbes ASAP, *Be a Design Freak. It's the Best Path to Exceptional Growth*, Peters, Tom, April 6, 1998.

435 www.tompeters.com.

436 Hamel (2000).

437 Tedlow (2001).

438 Professor C.K. Prahalad uses a similar framework.

439 Quoted in Ulrich, D., Zenger, J. and Smallwood, N., *Results-Based Leadership: How Leaders Build the Business And Improve the Bottom Line*, Harvard Business School Press, Boston, Mass, 1999.

440 *Fast Company*, April, 2000.

441 Wheatley, M., interviewed in *Business Minds*, Brown, T, Crainer, S., Dearlove, D. and Rodrigues, J.N., eds., Financial Times Prentice Hall, 2001.

442 *Fortune*, July 10, 2000.

443 Bennis, W and O'Toole J., "Don't Hire the Wrong CEO, *Harvard Business Review*, May-June, 2000, quote a study by MIT's Rakesh Khurana.

444 "Leading in Unnerving Times", *Sloan Management Review*, Vol. 42, No. 2, Winter, 2001. Panel discussion facilitated by Warren Bennis.

445 Kotter, J.P., "What leaders Really DO', *Harvard Business Review*, Special issue, December, 2001, reprint, originally occurred in 1990.

446 Michaels et al (2001).

447 Bennis and Ward Biederman (1997).

448 Hill, L., "Leadership as Collective Gemus", in ed. Chowdury, S., *Management 21C: Someday We"ll All Manage This Way*, Financial Times, Prentice Hall, 2000.

449 *Fast Company*, June, 1999.

450 *Fast Company*, November, 2001.

451 "All in a Day's Work, *Harvard Business Review*, Special Issue, December, 2001.

452 Coleman, D., Boyatzis, R. and McKee, A., "Primal Leadership: The Hidden Driver of Great Performance", *Harvard Business Review*, Special Issue, December, 2001.

453 Ibid. Also see Kellaway, L., "Winning Smiles", *Financial Times*, September 14, 2003, for some interesting behavioral research coming out of Chicago.

454 Crainer and Dearlove (2003).

455 *International Herald Tribune*, July 14th, 2003.

456 *Fortune*, December 6, 1999.

457 Ibid.

458 Interview with Stuart Crainer, Summer 2003.

459 Kunde, J., *Corporate Religion*, Financial Times Prentice Hall, 2000.

460 Crainer, S., "Ten secrets of success", *The Times*, November 17, 2002.

461 Crainer, S. and Dearlove, D. (eds.), The *Financial Times Handbook of Management*, FT Prentice Hall, 2004.

462 Ibid.

463 Ibid.

464 Bossidy, L., "The Discipline of Getting Things Done", *Leader to Leader*, Summer, 2002.

465 Interview with Randall Tobias, *Business Strategy Review*, Winter, 2003.

466 Interview with Michael Critelli, *Business Strategy Review*, Spring, 2004.

467 *Business Week*, August 26, 2002.

468 For more info check out Viagra.com on the web.

469 *Fortune*, Much 20, 2000.

470 As far we know, the expression "condemned to freedom" was first coined by Søren Kierkegaard.

471 Ginsberg, A., *Howl.*

472 Heilbroner, R., *Teachings From The Worldly Philosophers*, WW Norton & Company, New York, NY, 1996.

473 www.www.di.se.

474 Reich (2000).

475 Ibid.

476 *Dagens Nyheter*, November 3, 2002.

477 *Fast Company*, October, 2003.

478 Weber, M., *Economy and Society*, University of California Press, Berkley, CA, 1978.

479 According to the leader of the free world, George W Bush, "the role of government is to create an environment in which change occurs, the market place adjusts, entrepreneurialism is strong, and people are willing to take risks" (*Fast Company*, October, 2000).

480 Current US dominance is primarily economical and political, rather than cultural. Quite often in Europe we hear a lot of talk about US cultural imperialism. And while people may certainly love to watch *Sex & the City or The Sopranos*, this is not at the heart of Europe's problems. In fact, all the talk about US cultural imperialism may be exaggerated. For instance, in 1998 none of the main Western European markets had any American series among the top ten programs. The counter-argument is of course that many of the so called European TV-shows use American programming formats (Micklethwait and Wooldridge, 2000).

481 *Business Week*, October 4, 1999. In addition, between 1990 and 1997 11 million new jobs were created in the US. The equivalent number for the European Union countries was around 71,000 jobs, whereof none in the private sector (Thurow, 1999).

482 Wolfe (1999).

483 Thurow (1999).

484 *Fortune*, September 16, 2002.

485 In 1990, none of the top ten richest individuals in the world were Americans. In the year 2000 six out of these top ten richest individuals were Americans (Enriques, 2000).

486 If genetics have anything to do with future of economic growth, the United States certainly seems to have the upper hand (Enriques, 2000). First, there is a strong anti-genetic lobbying going on in Europe, so there is a clear risk that the minds will move to the US. Second, to do qualified research you need super large computers. Out of the world's 500 largest computers 217 can right now be found in the US, Germany has 63, Japan 56, France 26, and the UK 24. To stand a chance Europeans need to. cooperate.

487 "Increasingly we see that states need markers, but markets also need states," says Nicholas van Prug, a spokesman for the World Bank.

488 Thurow (1999).

489 Heilbroner (1996).

490 Traditionally, recessions are triggered by companies cutting back on investments and capacity. As supply is more limited, prices increase causing inflation. In addition to political uncertainties caused by recent terrorist attacks, the recession of the early 21st century seems set off more by lacking consumer rather than corporate confidence in the system and situation. This causes people to stop shopping. In effect, demand decreases and causes deflation or at least very limited inflation.

491 Smith, A., *The Theory of Moral Sentiments*, eds. Raphael, D.D. and MacFie, A.L.,

Clarendon Press, Oxford edition,
1759/1976.

492 Simons, R., Mintzberg, H. and Basu, K.,
"Memo To: CEOs – Re: Five Half-Truths of
Business", *Fast Company*, June, 2002.

493 Lindblom, C.E., *The Market System: What it
is, How it Works, and What To Make of It*,
Yale Nota Bene, Yale University Press,
2001.

494 Moss Kanter, R., interviewed in *Business
Minds*, Brown, T, Crainer, S., Dearlove, D.
and Rodrigues, J.N., eds., Financial Times
Prentice Hall, 2001.

495 Kotler, P, interviewed in *Business Minds*,
Brown, T, Crainer, S., Dearlove, D. and
Rodrigues, J.N., eds., Financial Times
Prentice Hall, 2001.

496 The World Bank estimates that people in
low income nations account for less than 4%
of global private consumption. (*Fortune*,
October 28, 2002).

497 Crichton, M., *Prey*, Harper Collins
Publishers, 2002.

498 Lindblom (2001).

499 Khurma, R., *Searching for a Corporate
Savior. The Irrational Quest for Charismatic
CEOS*, Princeton University Press, 2002.

500 Kagan, R., *Of Paradise And Power: America
and Europe in the New World Order*, Knopf,
2003.

501 For an interesting discussion of conflict
resolution by integration of interest see
Graham, R, *Mary Parker Follet: Prophet of
Management*, Harvard Business School
Press, Boston, Mass, 1995.

502 Sennett (1998).

503 Reich (2000).

504 Sennert (1998).

505 *Financial Times*, September 8, 2003. In
1999, for instance, the EU citizens spent 7%
of EU's CDP, that is $600 billion, for the
privilege of keeping cheaper products out
(The *Economist*, 22 May, 1999).

506 *Scanorama*, November, 2000.

507 Frankl, VE., *Man's Search for Meaning*,
Washington Square Press, Simon and
Schuster, New York, NY, 1963.

508 Ibid.

509 Loosely based on an interview with
psychologist Richard Wiseman in *Fast
Company*, July, 2003, and our own
experiences.

Photo credits

p.2	Scanpix	p.158	Getty Images, Corbis
p.4	Getty Images, Corbis	p.163	Corbis
p.5	Getty images, Corbis	p.167	Corbis
p.8	Corbis	p.170	Corbis
p.9	Katarina Lapidoth	p.172	Getty Images
p.11	Katarina Lapidoth	p.175	Corbis
p.12	Scanpix	p.178	Corbis
p.15	Getty Images	p,181	Corbis
p.21	Getty Images	p.184	Corbis
p.23	Getty Images	p.188	Scanpix
p.26	Getty Images	p.191	Corbis
p.30	Corbis	p.193	Corbis
p.35	Corbis	p.194	AsQer Visual Communication
p.37	Pressens Bild	p.197	Christer Jansson
p.39	Ikea	p.204	Getty Images
p.40	Getty Images, Corbis	p.206	AsQer Visual Communication
p.43	Corbis	p.212	Ikea
p.50	Getty Images	p.213	eBay Inc.
p.52	Corbis	p.220	Getty Images
p.53	Corbis	p.226	Corbis
p.56	Corbis	p.233	Corbis
p.62	Corbis	p.235	Scanpix
p.72	The Scream by Edvard Munch/Corbis	p.237	www.elizabeth-carson.com
p.76	Corbis	p.242	Getty Images
p.80	Corbis, Scanpix	p.243	Corbis
p.83	(c) Danjaq Produktions	p.246	DNA/Claesson Koivisto Rune Arkitektkontor
p.85	Getty Images		
p.87	Corbis	p.249	Corbis
p.88	Liberty Leading the People by Eugene Delacroix/Corbis	p.252	Corbis
		p.255	Corbis
p.95	Pressens Bild	p.259	AsQer Visual Communication
p.101	Getty Images	p.272	Corbis
p.102	Corbis	p.274	Corbis
p.105	Pressens Bild	p.275	AsQer Visual Communication
p.106	Corbis	p.276	AsQer Visual Communication
p.114	Corbis	p.280	Getty Images. Corbis
p.118	Getty Images	p.285	Corbis
p.120	Getty Images	p.291	Corbis
p.125	Corbis		
p.126	Corbis		
p.129	Getty Images		
p.132	Pressens Bild		
p.134	Ericsson		
p.137	Scanpix		
p.141	Corbis		
p.146	Corbis		
p.149	Corbis		
p.152	Corbis		

Christer Jansson grew up in Helsingborg in southern Sweden, but lives in voluntary exile in Stockholm. For nearly 20 years he has been a professional photographer, working for advertising agencies and magazines. Christer is currently working as photo editor at *Spoon Publishing*, where he provides picture material to a handful of magazines. christer@spoon.se

Katarina Lapidoth graduated from The Art Institute in Houston, Texas and has been a professional graphic designer since 1992. She now runs her own company in Stockholm – *Lapidoth Design*. She has a distinct passion for book and magazine design. In addition she has created several appreciated graphical profiles. katti@lapidoth.com

Jonas Ålkerlund is one of the most successful music video and commercials directors/editor today, with more than 250 projects under his belt. Jonas has worked with artists such as Madonna, Christina Aguilera, Paul McCartney, Lenny Kravitz, Ozzy Osbourne, Blondie, U2, Metallica and others. He works within a variety of different media: commercials, music video, still photography, short films, documentary films, circus shows, art projects and most recently of course his feature film *Spun*.